FROM MAO TO MARKET

ROBIN PORTER

From Mao to Market

China Reconfigured

HURST & COMPANY, LONDON

First published in the United Kingdom in 2011 by
C. Hurst & Co. (Publishers) Ltd.,
41 Great Russell Street, London, WC1B 3PL
© Robin Porter, 2011
All rights reserved.
Printed in India by Imprint Digital

The right of Robin Porter to be identified as the author
of this publication is asserted by him in accordance with
the Copyright, Designs and Patents Act, 1988.

A Cataloguing-in-Publication data record for this book
is available from the British Library.

ISBN: 978-1-84904-084-6 *hardback*
      978-1-84904-083-9 *paperback*

This book is printed using paper from registered sustainable
and managed sources.

www.hurstpub.co.uk

For Katie, to tell her something more of her 'other country'

CONTENTS

ACKNOWLEDGEMENTS

A professional lifetime of involvement with China has been enriched by contact with many people whose assistance and support have been invaluable, and whose insights have helped to inform my own perceptions. Among them in particular are Paul Lin, Louis Veilleux, Mike Mason, Charles Curwen, Jerome Ch'en and Jack Gray. Colleagues at Concordia University, Montreal, the University of Melbourne, La Trobe University, Keele University and the University of Bristol have facilitated my teaching, or have been kind enough to receive me in a visiting capacity during periods of research.

In China, work colleagues at Xinhua News Agency, colleagues and contacts made during nearly four years as Science Counsellor at the British Embassy, and Chinese and foreign friends from all walks of life made since my first visit in 1972 have all contributed very significantly to my understanding of China. Among them have been Rewi Alley, Ma Haide (George Hatem), Dr. Wang Tianbao, Professor Chen Zhicheng, Ruth Coe, Eleanor Bidian, Du Ying, and Helena Ou Huiqing.

I of course owe much to the many scholars who have worked on China over the decades, especially from the early 1960s to the present day, and also to those in academia and in the Foreign Office who taught me Chinese.

Finally, I owe a tremendous debt to my wife Jan and daughter Katie, who both have lived and worked professionally in China, and have their own well-founded views.

To all I express my gratitude and appreciation.

PREFACE

In recent years, China has embarked upon a major programme of rapid and far-reaching change, the latest phase in what, conventionally, we call its modernization.[1] Leaving aside for the moment the more subtle arguments about the nuances of this development, or even its desirability in environmental terms, there can be no denying the extraordinary significance of the process that is under way. The world's most populous and most ancient state is responding as never before to the demands of the modern age.

Much has been written on both the micro and the macro level about the changes under way. Since the command and co-operative economies of the first three decades of the People's Republic have appeared to be set aside, many observers have sought and found evidence of the growth of free enterprise and a new entrepreneurial spirit at all levels of the Chinese economy, and even in the largest bureaucratic organizations. These observers find that a significant and perhaps critical process of transition has recently been occurring, as it were, "from Mao to market."[2] Borne along by figures showing a consistent above-average growth in GDP, and a dramatic expansion and diversification of China's foreign trade, many see China, having followed in the footsteps of Japan and the newly-industrialized countries of the region but on a much larger scale, constituting the major economic and political force in the world in the new century.

It is the contention of this book, however, that this most recent evidence of change must be seen in the context of China's overall struggle for modernization if it is to be more fully understood.

The issues faced by China that are explored in this book all have a long pedigree; they did not simply appear when China began to open up in 1979. Central to this process of modernization, for example, is the acquisition of modern technology. There can be little doubt about the commitment of most of China's leaders in recent years to the acquisition of new technology from abroad, though there is much less agreement on the implications of this, or what to do about them. The transition from the policy of self-reliance in development, pursued in one form or another for much of the period since the founding of the People's Republic in 1949, to reliance on Western and Japanese technology, and most recently to a new emphasis on home-grown research and development, has been a consequence of evolving economic, domestic, political and foreign policy considerations.

The ten years of the Cultural Revolution, with its disruptions and ideological imperatives, left the Chinese economy stagnating, even in terms of the policy of self-reliant development. Politically, the moral capital of the Party with the population at large was exhausted by recurrent campaigns and officially tolerated outbreaks of violence; exhortations to China's people to work harder for the common good were not enough any more to motivate them to do so. Nor were appeals to heed the lessons of the pre-revolutionary past. Young people wanted tangible evidence of technical progress, and a short cut to a better standard of living. On the diplomatic front, following the death of Mao there was a pressing need to mend fences with the West, not only for conventional strategic reasons, given greater impetus at the time by the continued hostility of the Soviet Union and the growing animosity of Vietnam, but also precisely because better relations with the West would make possible import of the new technology that China so desperately needed.

For their part, foreign companies, encouraged by their governments, were eager to explore the commercial opportunities that were believed to exist in China. Japan, from the mid-70s, and most Western companies from the early 80s sent mission after mission to China to try to sell products, capital equipment, technology or services. In many cases expectations were unrealistic, but in some successful business was done, and key items in the programme for modernization were filled in. For a time at least, and especially during the stages which preceded implementation, both sides were happy.

The thirty years of communist rule, and in particular the ten years of the Cultural Revolution, therefore, meant that the Party in 1979 had little alternative but to initiate a process of technical "borrowing" from the West and from Japan. It found foreign companies, banks and governments more than ready to assist in the process. This "borrowing" laid the foundation for the emerging domestic effort in research and development of recent years.

Yet leading up to the new century and throughout its first decade, tensions have persisted at all levels in Chinese society. Most obviously, continued political deprivation resulted in the tragic events of mid-1989 around Tiananmen Square. Beneath this, however, is a whole range of tensions and conflicts which have arisen as a consequence of the process of modernization itself, and which feed into and reinforce political discontent. Some of these, it will be argued, are cultural in origin, and have to do with the impact of the demands of modernization on traditional cultural attitudes and usages, and of those practices on the modernization effort. Other tensions are the consequence of the structures and demands of the Leninist state, imposed like a veneer on the more traditional political heritage in 1949. Many of these may prove antithetical to the successful implementation of modernization. Still others may be the result of conflict between political and cultural factors. Politics and culture, and their interaction, will be recurring themes in this book.[3]

The manner and rate of progress from Mao to market, therefore, could be said to be influenced by factors dating from much earlier in the twentieth century, or in the nineteenth century, or even 2,500 years ago. The tapestry of Chinese history is a close weave, and no part of it can be properly appreciated in isolation from the rest, even in the newly globalized circumstances of the present day when many other influences are brought to bear.

It is appropriate finally to say a few words about the purpose and structure of this book. First, the purpose. Over many years of engagement with China as an academic, adviser to industry, and diplomat, the author was often asked to recommend a single book that people who were interested could read to introduce them to the country's complexities — its achievements and its problems, its habits of mind, its social and political structures, and its aspirations. While much has been written and published on China in recent years, the range of material available that was neither "too scholarly" or narrow for the general reader, nor "too popular" and sometimes lacking in rigour, was somewhat limited. It seemed worthwhile therefore to try to make a modest contribution to the band of literature that lay in between, in the hope that it would both appeal to the general reader and be suited to the needs of undergraduates as a supporting text.

As to structure, the book opens with a chapter in which the process of modernization is discussed in general terms. There then follow three broadly "narrative" chapters: in the first of these, essential features of "traditional" Chinese society are brought out, and the main points of China's modern history up to the revolution in 1949 are recalled; in Chapters 3 and 4, the important developments in China from the founding of the People's Republic up to the present day are traced in two parts — 1949 to 1979, and 1979 to 2009. In the remaining two thirds of the book, individual chapters are devoted to an analysis in some detail of a number of broad themes considered to be important in contemporary China: the impact of the Confucian heritage; the relationship between orthodoxy, ideology and law; contemporary China's record on science and technology; the way command structures work; the "enterprise culture" of post-Mao China; the conflict between public policies and the goals of the individual; and the issue of democracy, the "fifth modernization."

SIGNIFICANT EVENTS IN CHINA'S RECENT PAST

1839–1899

1839–1842:	First Opium War, beginning of unequal treaties
1856–1860:	Second Opium War
1862–mid 1870s:	Self-strengthening Movement
1895:	Defeat by Japan
1897–1898:	Scramble for foreign "spheres of influence"
1898:	Guang Xu's "100 days" of reform
1899:	Beginning of the Boxer uprising

1900–1949

1911:	Collapse of the Qing Dynasty
1919:	May 4th movement
1920:	Communist Party founded
1927:	Civil war begins
1937–1945:	Anti-Japanese war
1949:	Communist Party takes power

1950–1979

1951–1958:	Co-operatives and communes established
1953–1957:	First Five Year Plan
1958:	Great Leap Forward
1966–1976:	Cultural Revolution
1976:	Chairman Mao Zedong dies
1977:	Deng Xiaoping reinstated, becomes Vice-Premier
1979:	Modernization and reform begin
1979:	Posters appear on "Democracy Wall"

1980–2009

1980 onward:	Technology transfer from the West and Japan
1980:	Reform of the legal system begins; First "special economic zones" established
1982:	Communes disestablished, agricultural free markets appear
1986:	Initial demonstrations in favour of greater democracy
1987:	Party Secretary General Hu Yaobang forced to resign
1989:	Mass protests, Tiananmen incident occurs on 3 June
1989–1991:	Foreign loans and assistance drastically curtailed
1992:	Foreign loans and assistance fully restored
2002:	China joins the World Trade Organization
2007:	The environment becomes one of the Party's top priorities
2009:	China about to become world's second largest economy
2009:	China about to become world's largest exporter
1980–2009:	Growth in GDP on average exceeds 8 per cent per annum

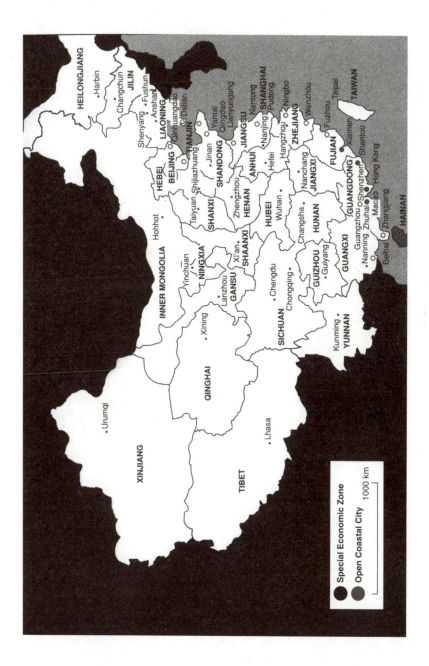

NOTE ON LANGUAGE

The romanization of Chinese names in this book is based on the Pinyin system used in mainland China. However some names may occasionally appear in the earlier Wade-Giles version when this seems appropriate. Thus, for example, Beijing may appear as Peking in the context of a discussion of China's nineteenth-century history.

MODERNIZATION, DEVELOPMENT AND CHANGE

The task of modernization

If we are to understand the thirty-year period which is the principal focus of this book as the most recent phase in China's modernization, it will be necessary first to try to define the term modernization. Although the ensuing discussion may cover ground that has been well traversed, the way in which we see modernization is so important to what follows in this book that it is best to return to first principles. This is the more necessary because in China, the debate over strategy for development and modernization has, since 1949, encompassed policies and possibilities which have not been contemplated elsewhere.

Most obviously, modernization is what it means to the great majority of people. Generalization at this level is based on the simple observation that some countries are more "advanced" than others, by which is usually meant that their economies are more advanced, or specifically that the technology used in processes of production, communication, transport of goods and people, and other forms of activity are more highly developed and sophisticated. Sometimes the definition may be extended to people and culture. Thus a population may be described as being quite modern or advanced, which often means that it exhibits a mentality that is flexible and open to change. A culture may sometimes be described as advanced if its achievements in terms of the complexity and spread of its language, literature, art and architecture, music, codes of behaviour, social relations and other features are notable in comparison with those of other cultures.

However, this brief preliminary observation shows that the further away from level of technology the argument proceeds, the more relative and the more culturally-biased, or value-laden, the generalizations become. While it is recognized therefore that political, intellectual and social trends are very important components of the modernization process, which will be dealt with in other chapters, the discussion that immediately follows will focus on technology as a main driver of change.[1]

In this sense, the use of the term modern — and broad acceptance of the term as having meaning — must be inextricably linked with the Industrial Revolution in Europe and North America, beginning in England around 1780.[2] The convergence of the spirit of inquiry, which encouraged the inventive genius that produced the steam engine, investment capital derived from 200 years of profitable merchant activity, abundant supplies of coal, and the reorganization of agriculture, giving rise to growing numbers of dislocated people, ready and willing to work in factories, created the necessary conditions for major change. By this definition, what comes before the introduction of industrial technology into a society is pre-modern. As the factory system and the use of modern technology in transport, communications, defence and other areas spread, a society is said to become more and more "modern."

In production, the central feature of this new activity is the widespread use of power-driven machinery to automate and speed up processes, and therefore the decreased use of manpower and time per unit of output. This is balanced however by the tendency to produce more and more of the item, the "mass production" that automation makes possible. In due course, local and even national markets for the item in question may become insufficient to take everything that is produced. If profits are to continue to grow, both to benefit owners and shareholders and to enable further investment in technology, markets must be sought outside national boundaries. This need, coupled with a desire to locate and secure further suitable raw materials for industrial processing, contributed substantially to the new evangelical fervour with which European merchants and millowners approached the pacification of overseas territories in the nineteenth century.

In social terms, the propensity to ever greater production draws many more people than before into the non-agricultural productive process. Whether voluntary or not, there is a significant movement of population away from the land and into towns and cities, where they are absorbed into larger and larger factories. While mass production in due course makes possible economies of scale, reducing the prices of many items, many more people are now incapable of satisfying their needs except within the cash economy. In many cases, therefore, they may become more dependent, and much worse off than in pre-industrial times.

The concentration of people in and around factories, themselves increasingly in major centres, significantly changed the landscape of countries where industrialization occurred. People needed housing, even if only of a cramped and primitive kind. They needed shops, public houses, places of worship and places of entertainment. Ultimately it was even conceded they would require hospitals and schools. Thus was created in the cities of Europe and North America the model of the great conurbation, with manufacturing, commercial, financial, governmental and other types of activity, all the many facets of a "modernizing" economy, represented. These "centres of industry," in the broadest sense, became both the subjects and objects of all policy.

If the central feature of the modern age has been industrial production, there have also been important ancillary developments without which it could not have taken place. Most significantly, the new intensity of production has required new means of transport, especially of goods. The "de-localization" of production has meant that raw materials in great quantity, and supplies of coal for energy, have had to be moved considerable distances and concentrated adjacent to the places of production. Similarly, much of the final product has also had to be moved hundreds if not thousands of miles from its place of manufacture.

This movement of goods was made possible in England from the late eighteenth century by the rapid growth of canals. As the scope of activity increased in the early nineteenth century, the canals were initially augmented, and then almost supplanted by the railways. In the twentieth century, road transport supplemented rail. In each case technology, in the form of power machinery driven by steam, and more recently the internal combustion engine, has made possible the solution of logistical problems that would otherwise have severely impeded industrial development. In recent decades, the establishment of viable transport networks has often been seen as a prerequisite for industrial investment.

Improved means of communication have also played an important part in the modernization process overall, becoming more essential as development gathered pace. A regular and secure postal service within and between countries began to complement individual couriers in the early nineteenth century. This in turn was followed by the telegraph from around mid-century, the telephone in the late nineteenth century, and radio, television, telex, fax and electronic mail and other systems in the twentieth century. All these methods of transmitting information were critical both in managing modernization from a technical and commercial point of view and in implementing domestic and foreign policy in support of development objectives.

For the past 200 years, the degree of "modernity" achieved by different countries or societies has largely determined the balance of power in the world, and particularly between the traditional societies of Asia and Africa and the West. Led initially by Britain, and sustained by an ideology of progress derived from the extraordinary technological lead they had achieved in the Industrial Revolution, the Western powers were determined to conquer, or at least master, as much of the rest of the world as possible. To argue, as many Marxists have done, that Western conquest was immoral, seems almost beside the point; the gap in technology that had developed made it the only likely outcome at the time.

For the most part, influenced by the passion of the Victorian age for "progress" and domination over nature and over other states, historians until the late twentieth century accepted this view, that "modernization" was a great leap forward, facilitated by technology, that all societies would experience in time.

Modernization and development

It may be useful at this point to explore briefly the nature of the relationship between modernization and development.

It is not possible to engage here in a comprehensive discussion of development theory as it has evolved over the past fifty years; it would be inappropriate within the confines of the present study to attempt to do so.[3] However, it is important to notice in passing the multi-disciplinarity of the debate that has taken place, the link to the geopolitical imperatives of the post-Second World War situation, and the more recent disillusionment that has set in among analysts of development trends, even as practitioners continue in many parts of the globe to pursue the objectives first set forth half a century ago. Moreover, it has been felt necessary to review the origins of development briefly, to place the body of development theory in context, before offering some provisional conclusions on its applicability to the Chinese case.

Development literature has seen contributions from history, economics, politics, sociology, cultural studies, and area studies, and peripherally from other areas of the humanities and social sciences. There has been a proliferation of both micro and macro approaches to the delineation of development requirements and experience, initially prescribing — and more recently, as Passe-Smith has observed, accounting for the failure of — the various stages of development.[4] As analysts grapple with widening gaps between rich and poor nations, and widening gaps between rich and poor within poor nations, they turn to cultural explanations, systemic factors in the world economy, or the failure to implement privatization or other policy prescriptions, to account for the success of a few, but the failure of most to meet expectations.

And yet, it is contended here, it may be that the premises on which "development" is based are themselves to blame. If this is true, development may be an unsuitable lens through which to view and judge China's experience.

The origins of the concept of "development" in international affairs, as distinct from the process of modernization referred to above, may be said to lie in the political imperatives of the post World War II world. The United States in particular was committed to decolonization, to a policy of trying to persuade the European powers to bring their colonies to independence. In Europe itself through the Marshall Aid plan, and to a degree elsewhere through UNRRA, the US began to contribute substantial amounts of money to reconstruction and projects to update infrastructure. At the same time, relations with the former Soviet ally took on the character of the Cold War, as much of Eastern Europe came under increasing political control from Moscow. In Asia pro-Communist forces began a long struggle for independence in Indo-China, the Communist Party won the civil war in China in 1949, and US and allied forces confronted pro-Communist North Korean and Chinese troops from 1950 to 1953 in Korea.

The development imperative and its supporting scholarly literature, therefore, may be said essentially to have grown out of the need to bring as much of the world as possible into the Western "camp"; as such, it was principally an American phenomenon at first. The European powers that still possessed colonies — Britain, France, the Netherlands,

Belgium, Spain and Portugal, but principally Britain and France — showed at first no enthusiasm for the devolution of Empire, or for the cessation of an economic relationship with their colonies in which those dependent territories offered captive markets for European manufactured goods while at the same time providing an assured supply of often vital raw materials. In the first place, and indeed perhaps later as well, it was usually the inability of the metropolitan power to keep control of the colony that determined the decision to let it go. This was certainly the case with Britain in India in 1947, with the Netherlands in Indonesia in 1949, and with France following defeat in a bloody war in Indo-China in 1954.

Yet the process of decolonization gathered momentum. Britain's acceptance of the inevitable made a virtue out of necessity with the withdrawal from territories right across Africa, beginning in the late 1950s and heralded by Prime Minister Harold Macmillan's "Winds of Change" speech. The logic of this decision later carried over to British territories in other parts of the world. France's change of heart over Algeria, leadng to its independence in 1962, was part of a process of withdrawal from the whole of Africa as a colonial power, though not total political and economic disengagement. Belgium, and later Portugal, were effectively driven out by circumstances beyond their control.

In the meantime, the Western world at least accustomed itself to thinking of the process of "catching up" faced by the newly independent territories as one of "development." These countries, riven by tribal or factional strife, and more a product of nineteenth-century administrative decisions than of geopolitical logic, were commonly perceived to be "underdeveloped."

Certainly they shared a need for infrastructure, for educational and health facilities, for stable political and judicial institutions, and for economic reform — a need that could be addressed by the growing number of specialist functional bodies under the United Nations, and the proliferating community of international non-government organizations. Yet the application of the underdevelopment label to these states tends to obscure the very important differences among them, especially with respect to their local conditions and the circumstances that may constrain their ability to act. These differences must also call into question the whole notion of underdevelopment, and the development theory that underpins it.

Moreover, if attention is paid to the world beyond Africa, the political nature of development soon becomes more apparent. In Asia, the political decision of Indonesia, India, and China, three of the world's largest countries, to identify themselves as part of the "Non-Aligned" movement in 1955, placing themselves between "the West" and the bloc led by the Soviet Union, at the same time seemed to compromise their eligibility for development assistance. Elsewhere in Asia, the "four tigers" — Hong Kong, Singapore, South Korea and Taiwan — from the 1960s onwards followed their own distinct path to rapid economic improvement. In Latin America, where great wealth and great poverty stood in stark conflict, "development" was seen as less of an issue because throughout the 1950s and 1960s the United States could be confident of almost total support from these countries in the international arena, as is evident from voting patterns at the UN.

The point about development must surely be that for a variety of reasons it is of only limited use as a conceptual tool. Countries begin the process of modernization from widely differing starting points. The objective geographical, demographic and economic situations with which they must contend may have very little in common. Their political and cultural circumstances may be to a large degree unique, as will be contended about China in this book. For historical reasons, their tolerance of outside interference with the parameters for economic growth, with the objectives and methods of growth, and ultimately with their system of government, may be very low indeed.

In this sense, a mode of analysis born out of the geopolitical imperatives of the Cold War may be entirely unsuited to the circumstances of China. With a very long history as a state (one whose borders are largely co-terminous with the spread of its dominant ethnic group), a common written language, a very large population which its agriculture was able to sustain in good times, a tradition of scientific experiment going back many centuries, and a highly sophisticated and all-embracing culture, China hardly matched the stereotype of candidate states for development in the post-colonial world. When, added to this, it is borne in mind that the same Western states that now espoused development had constrained China for a century through the "unequal treaties," and that many of them under US leadership later isolated China for twenty years following the founding of the People's Republic, it is scarcely surprising that the conceptual parameters of "development" do not seem to fit the Chinese case, and are not accepted by the Chinese people themselves. It is no accident that the Chinese government speaks in terms of "modernization" rather than "development," seeing this objective as achievable largely through the introduction of advanced equipment and methods, rather than through the sort of institutional change that might be advocated by development theorists or by the World Bank.

The management of change in differing social systems

Underlying both modernization and development is a process of change. It may be appropriate here to reflect on how change itself is seen and managed differently in differing social systems. Three different views are considered briefly below — a "traditional" view, exemplified by but not necessarily typified by China up to the twentieth century, a "Western" view that has become prevalent over the past 200 years, and a Marxist view, of which China over the past half century and more has been one exemplar.

In many of what are commonly thought of today as "traditional" societies, those "ripe for change," change has been seen as inherently threatening, disturbing to the social order, at best requiring the acquisition of new skills to survive and prosper, and at worst bringing annihilation. This certainly was the attitude in traditional China, where reverence for the past and hostility to disruptive forces of any kind was elevated to a virtue. As will be seen in later chapters, Confucius, who himself is held to have lived around 500 BC, posited a much earlier mythical golden age as the cornerstone of his philosophy, and Confucian orthodoxy, which conditioned China's political life down to the twentieth century, exhorted rulers to refer and return to the values of that golden age as the way of achieving peace and harmony within society. Even when China was confronted by the aggression and military might of the Western powers in the nineteenth century, the initial response to defeat was to try to separate what the Chinese call the "*ti*" and the "*yong*," preserving the "essence" of the old Chinese way of life and accepting only so much of the Western technology as would help, it was thought, to keep the West at a distance.

In the development of Western civilization, by contrast change has featured much more prominently, from the rise and fall of Greece and Rome to the rise over the past 500 years of the European nation-states and their offshoots, and the industrial and other revolutions of the past 200 years, as noted above. The Industrial Revolution and its consequences, and to a lesser degree perhaps the political revolutions of the past two centuries, gave rise to a belief in progress which for many has cast change in a new and positive light. People have come to expect that new technology will enable them to have more and better things, a better standard of living, and a greater measure of control through political change over decisions affecting their lives. In a word, change has been seen as "good" by large numbers of people in the most economically and politically active parts of the world — Western Europe, and its settled territories, including most notably the United States.

The purpose of change in this view, therefore, is always to improve; the new is always better than the old. The objects of change are the products of all kinds that enable us to live our lives — food, fuel, manufactured goods, equipment and services — the technology required to produce them, and ultimately people themselves, their attitudes and outlook. The instruments of change may conveniently be characterized here as organizations — governments, corporations, research institutions, social and political movements, for example — and ideologies: the prevailing ethos of progress and democracy in present-day capitalist societies, the radical egalitarianism of revolutionary France, or, outside Western Europe, the revolutionary historical materialism of the Soviet Union.

The Soviet example raises unequivocally the main alternative approach to change of the twentieth century, that of the movement for revolutionary change inspired primarily by the nineteenth-century writings of Marx and Engels, and the twentieth-century writings of Lenin, Mao, Ho Chi Minh and others.

While the particular cultural circumstances of Russia, China, Vietnam, North Korea, Cuba and other countries destined to experience a Marxist revolution varied widely, a common strand was the revolutionary elite's belief in the need for radical change, and in practice the decision when political power had been achieved to implement that change from above. Here the twin features of ideology and organization in achieving this objective are more obvious than may be the case in Western capitalist societies, as their deployment is systematic and the result of a conscious policy decision. In the particular case of China, the innate conservatism of much of the population, influenced by Confucian values as noted above, had also to be overcome.

In China and other Marxist societies the raison d'être of the ruling party, in China the Communist Party, was to implement revolutionary change. This meant placing some of those who had been at the bottom of society at the top, and reducing many of those who had enjoyed power and privilege to a level of bare subsistence. Change would also mean death for many. As Mao memorably observed, revolution was not a dinner party.

The methods that would be employed by the Party are discussed later in this book. The organizational mechanisms would include the Party itself, organs of the State structure, the judiciary, the police, the army, the militias, the so-called mass organizations, and at different times various semi-official revolutionary groups and organizations. The ideological mechanisms would include education and re-education, political campaigns, the study of Marxism-Leninism-Mao Zedong Thought, propaganda and the manipulation of news, the use of socialist-realist themes in literature, art and the performing arts, and other means of getting the message across. Similar mechanisms would be used in other Marxist societies.

Thus, in those countries that have experienced a Marxist government in the twentieth century, change was quite literally the order of the day. While there was a desire shared with Western societies for a better material standard of life, and perhaps an even greater belief in the ability of technology to bring this about, ideology and organization were both used extensively to elicit support for the policies by which the ruling party intended to achieve this change. Change for most people was not something that "just happened," but rather a main goal to which they were required to dedicate their lives.

A close knowledge of policies that directly related to a citizen's particular area of work was also required. Change for the better in the workplace was a constant obligation of all staff, whether Party members or not. The results, it was believed, would be reflected in better methods of work, improved quality, increased output and by implication a better standard of living for all. Examples of positive change in the workplace could in theory be used to motivate others, with, in the case of China, the Commune at Da Zhai and the chemical works at Da Qing particularly held out and publicized to stimulate emulation by other production units.

Finally, it should be noted, in Marxist societies the presumption of a capacity for positive change underlay the whole central planning process, which when political power had been achieved was the most important remaining raison d'être for the continued existence of the

Communist Party. In China, in this sense the future and its possibilities were as important to China's new political elite as the past was to the traditional elite. In the last half of the twentieth century therefore China unequivocally embraced change, though for most of that fifty year period it chose to manage that change through the blunt instruments of the Leninist state.

By contrast, in Western market economies economic change, along with the other dimensions of change that have followed economic change, has tended to be determined by the competition of companies looking for better and more profitable goods and services to make and market, with varying degrees of intervention by government. As modern companies "manage" change, they generally require of their employees a belief in the product and commitment to strategies to improve it through new structures, new processes and the introduction of new technology. Yet in most Western countries, apart from an urge to conformity which may be greater in some places than others, there is no requirement for the individual *as citizen* to support the notion of constant and positive change; neither government nor workplace expect this, and citizens are free to make up their own minds about the value of change in the course of history.[5]

2

HISTORICAL FACTORS AND
OBJECTIVE CONSTRAINTS

Salient aspects of China's tradition

It can be strongly argued that the preparation China has had for modernization, in terms of both its remote and its more recent historical development, is unique. If this is so, it may go some way to explaining the particular difficulties China has faced in meeting the challenges of the technological age.

Much Western historiography of China has emphasized the common features of the impact of imperialism on the different parts of Asia.[1] This view holds that the rise of nationalism in the various colonies and semi-colonies of the region in the twentieth century was an inevitable consequence of the aggression of the nineteenth. To a degree, this view is shared by Marxist historians in the newly independent states of the region and elsewhere, and by liberal historians in the West, moved by concern for the complicity of their own societies in the aggression.

And yet, as has been shown since the countries of the region have attained independence, nationalism can be a cloak for a wide variety of domestic social policies and attitudes. Moreover traditional culture and political usage from before contact with the West have often been more potent in determining the nature of post-colonial society than the colonial or semi-colonial experience itself, especially where there is an overwhelmingly dominant ethnic group whose distribution is coterminous with the boundaries of the post-colonial state.

A view conditioned by a reading of history that stresses the common experience of colonial subjection, the rise of nationalism and the

13

achievement of independence will tend to lead to an expectation that the modernization process, which to one extent or another has followed independence in the countries of the region, also contains much that can be generalized about. Indeed, most of the theory of development economics over the past forty years has been based on this assumption, whether the recipient country is in Asia, Africa or Latin America. Only recently has development theory started to come to terms with the diversity of traditional experience and practice in developing countries — in large part, ironically, because of the failure of development strategies in so much of the world, stuck fast in the sands of corruption and customary usage. Some Western observers have even lost interest in development altogether, taking the view that if the countries receiving development aid cannot respond rationally to this rational liberal initiative, Western donor nations should not bother with them.[2]

For its part, China presents to the development lobby both problems and opportunities in its traditional society as a starting point for modernization. It has an immensely long history as a state, some 2,200 years if the founding of the first of the great dynasties, the Han, is taken as the starting point; its written history and ethnic identity go back even further. From time to time broken up by marauding foreigners, or by domestic rebellion, the Chinese Empire was nonetheless re-established as a matter of course, its people held together by a common written language and a common sense of being Chinese, in opposition to the alien world outside.

In this will to unity and survival China has no parallel elsewhere. The people of the Roman Empire, having only an imposed common identity and language, made no effort to unite once Rome itself had fallen. The Moghals could only rule their Empire so long as they had the strength to do so. The British, having imparted language and law to their former colonies, lacked the will or the resources to continue to rule them. In the case of China, therefore, the longevity and cohesion of the state cum empire, despite periodic episodes of upheaval, place it in a category of its own among the modern states of the world, developing or otherwise. Beside China, the nation-states of the developed world are at the infant stage.

The longevity of the state has also contained the substance of a lesson that has been drawn by the Chinese people about the relationship between chaos, "*luan*," and social change. This, in its simplest form, is that through much of China's past change has brought negative consequences, and often chaos. As will be noted below, in the absence of evolution driven by technology, essentially the Western European experience, change came to be associated above all with challenges to the social order. Whether these challenges came as a result of invasion or domestic rebellion, they invariably brought a decline or collapse of the fabric of normal life, disrupting agricultural production, destroying law and order, and leaving people at the mercy of vagabond armies.

For many in China in traditional times, therefore, change was anathema. People looked to the legendary golden age of Emperors Yao and Shun, alleged to have lived some 2,000 years BC, when wise men ruled and harmony and prosperity prevailed. Throughout the long life of the Chinese Empire up to the twentieth century, restoration of sound government was the antidote to all social ills. People looked back, rather than forward to a new and different future. This, it was believed, was why the Chinese Empire had lasted so long.

What, then, was the nature of traditional Chinese society? While no brief summary can possibly do justice to the complexity of traditional China, it is nonetheless appropriate to sketch some of the more important features of life in this sophisticated pre-modern state. Five characteristics stand out as the main determinants of the parameters of life in China before the modern age.

Above all, China was an agricultural society. The practise of agriculture had begun millennia before the creation of the first Chinese Empire in the second century BC, and was attributed to the work of deities who had come to earth to teach the skills of cultivation to the Chinese people. The soil in East China[3] was relatively fertile, and laced with a patchwork of natural waterways. With care, and attention to irrigation, sufficient crops could be produced to sustain a growing population, which even by the Han Dynasty was almost certainly the largest of any Empire or state of the day.

Thus population, and territory under cultivation, grew together in a symbiotic relationship. Yet not all land could be cultivated with the same measure of effort. Some in particular required the artificial regulation of water if it was to yield anything at all. This meant the development of an irrigation technology in traditional China which far surpassed any other in the world at the time. Networks of canals and irrigation channels were constructed, which could render fertile land that in its natural state would be useless for cultivation. Similarly dykes and dams on the major waterways helped to prevent the loss of crops and lives through flooding.

Public works on this scale required co-ordination and supervision. Under the Han Dynasty this task became, as never before, the responsibility of central government, which entrusted it to a centrally appointed bureaucracy. In this way, civil servants ensured that the peasants and local gentry co-operated in funding and carrying out projects of construction which would, hypothetically at least, benefit everyone by creating the necessary conditions for successful agriculture. Among the other important tasks of the bureaucrats were the collection and storage of grain against the possibility of drought or famine, the collection of taxes for the central government, and the maintenance of order.

Thus the nature of China's topography did much to determine administrative arrangements in pre-modern times. It also meant that, with some human modification of natural conditions, China's agriculture could be among the most efficient in the pre-modern world, and capable of sustaining large numbers of people. This in turn may have discouraged the exploitation of other technology, in which China had an early lead, which could have brought major changes to the nature of China's economy and society.

A second feature of importance from the Han Dynasty onwards was the pre-eminent position of Confucianism as the official orthodoxy of the state. From the second century BC down to the twentieth century, with only relatively short breaks[4] the teachings of Confucius and his disciples provided the essential prescription for the behaviour of the state towards the individual, and the obligations of the individual, both within the family, and towards the state.

Confucius himself is said to have lived from 551 to 479 BC, during the "Spring and Autumn" period of China's classical antiquity. At this time, China had not yet been unified, and was a political jumble of independent states owing nominal allegiance to a feudal king. Confucius was an itinerant scholar and teacher, who was moved by the growing rivalry between the states, and an increasing propensity to tyranny within them, to try to set forth a code of practice for harmony and good government.

Confucius' objective was the achievement of harmony in society through the ethical behaviour of individuals to one another. He likened the family to the state; just as the father governed the family, so should the head of state govern the population, applying wisdom and intelligence, and a concern for the welfare of everyone within it. The individual in turn owed allegiance to his ruler. If everyone carried out his duty to the best of his ability, there would be peace and prosperity.

Mencius and Hsun Tzu, disciples of Confucius who lived after his death, added to his teachings. Undoubtedly influenced by the descent of China into internecine strife during the "Warring States" period, Mencius (372–289 BC) modified Confucius' idea that the ruler ruled by virtue of having the "mandate of Heaven." According to Mencius, if any monarch descended into tyranny, and a successful rebellion were mounted against him resulting in his being overthrown, he was held to have lost the mandate of Heaven. In this case, the mandate immediately passed to the leader of the successful rebellion, who would instantly acquire legitimacy as the kingdom's next ruler. In this way, after unification China passed from dynasty to dynasty without ever having to abandon its traditional government structures and orthodoxy. Hsun Tzu (300–237 BC approximately) emphasized the need for education to promote moral rectitude, and the value of etiquette and decorum.

The impact of Confucius on China's traditional culture and political arrangements will be considered more fully below (see Chapters 5 and 6).

Another feature of China's pre-modern society, certainly for much of the thousand years preceding the Western impact, was the measure of fluidity among different classes, and the degree of social mobility both upward and downward. From Han times, the principal social groups in Chinese society were the peasantry, who tilled the soil, and the so-called scholar gentry,[5] who did not carry out any manual labour, and who constituted the elite. There were of course other groups — merchants large and small, workers in traditional and handicraft industry, soldiers, vagabonds and rebels, and notably the royal court and extended imperial family around the Emperor. In reality, though, the pattern of daily life in China was described by the activity and interactions of those two principal groups.

The peasantry by and large lived a life of bare sufficiency, if they achieved even that. Most rented small plots of land from landlords whose ties to the official class reinforced their status in the village. Many peasants were landless labourers, hiring out their labour. A few owned the titles to their own plots, and might in good times be able to afford to hire help. All were affected by the vagaries of agricultural life, periodic droughts and floods, famine, lawlessness and rebellion.

Scholar-gentry is the term often used to describe the overlapping class of bureaucrat/administrators and landed gentry. The landed gentry, a broadly-defined group which might encompass any family from the richest peasant in the village up to families owning vast tracts of land and many houses, had as a rule the financial resources to be able to educate their male children, and it was from among these educated young men that China's administrators were chosen. These officials, once in office, were able both to enrich themselves and their families through sanctioned graft, and quite frequently were able to advance in more subtle ways the interests of the family or clan, despite mechanisms employed by the state to try to discourage this.[6]

By the Tang Dynasty, the principle of determining admission to the bureaucracy through competitive examination was gaining growing acceptance at court, and in ensuing years a system of centrally administered examinations was set up leading to three levels of degree, which have been likened to the modern bachelors, masters, and doctorate degrees. Holders of the doctorate, the "*chin-shih*," could expect in due course to occupy positions of importance in the bureaucracy, and some would occupy the highest administrative posts in the land.

What is startling by comparison with Western experience of the time is the in-built emphasis on merit, albeit of a certain kind, in the choice of a civil service to run the Empire. Examinations emphasized a knowledge of the Confucian classics, as well as setting practical problems of statecraft to which candidates were expected to respond with imagination and foresight. The other critical point about the examinations is that they were open to anyone with the ability to take them. This meant that education, and not birth, was the ultimate determinant of access to power.

Of course, to some degree wealth and power were still linked, as most peasant families would expect both their male and female children to work alongside adults from an early age. But where a male child was obviously bright, a family might explore all avenues to provide him with an education, calling if necessary on the extended family or on kin to put forward the money to pay for a tutor. In this way, it was possible for some male peasant children to become literate and acquire an education, and ultimately to pass the examinations for admission to the bureaucracy.

The social mobility that this afforded in traditional Chinese society was considerable, and the myth of mobility even greater. It has been shown that, from 1368, during the Ming and Qing Dynasties, up to the end of the examination system in 1906, of the *chin-shih* degree holders who held high office some 30 per cent had come from families that within the three previous generations had been among the poorest peasantry. Some had achieved elevation from great poverty within their own lifetime. As the size of the bureaucracy overall remained relatively constant, there must also have been a comparable rate of downward mobility of families who, having had a son who was a member of the bureaucracy, could not in subsequent generations produce a male heir capable of sustaining an education, or achieving success in the examinations. With no official connection, the wealth of such families would tend to dissipate over time, and some would fall back to the level of the peasantry.[7]

A fourth characteristic of traditional Chinese society was its ethnocentrism. From the earliest times, China felt itself to be under threat from outside its borders. Nomadic tribes from the north-west, the Xiong Nu, and later the Mongols and even the Manchus all invaded China proper at one time or another, occupying Chinese territory with varying degrees of success. One of the earliest tasks of the Han Dynasty was the construction of the Great Wall, militarily of limited efficacy, but a clear statement of purpose. China formed the view very early on that most foreigners were hostile, and of inferior culture to Chinese, excelling only in the military arts. They were to be both feared and despised. This was a perception shared by everyone from the Emperor down to the poorest peasant.

There was little in China's experience over the years to modify this point of view, based either on contact with the northern tribes, or on its limited exposure through early sea trade to other civilizations. As Chinese society became ever more sophisticated, with its complex administrative structure, its written language and literature, art and music, the cultural gap with its immediate neighbours widened. In its foreign relations, China developed a network of suzerain ties with neighbouring kingdoms. In this way, in due course Tibet to the west, Annam to the south, Korea and for a time Manchuria to the north east all accepted the primary role of China in the region, recognizing China as the source of the civilizing arts, and sending tribute missions periodically to China in return for the gifts and benevolence of the Chinese Empire. Even Japan, during China's Tang dynasty, repeatedly sent missions to China, bringing back the Chinese system of writing, literary forms, ideas on government and religion, art and architecture, all of which were subsequently moulded to Japanese requirements.

Nor did the earliest contacts between China and the West leave much impression. Marco Polo's two trips to China in the thirteenth century resulted only in his being absorbed for a time into the Chinese bureaucracy, and carrying back to the West with him the first direct account of Chinese civilization. The Jesuits, for their part, in the late sixteenth century were able to gain admission to China, and for 150 years acted as advisers to the Chinese government. Yet the subjects of their advice were astronomy, mathematics, and military technology. They found scant interest in other aspects of Western culture. Their own objectives of conversion to Christianity of the court and high officials were almost wholly unmet. In the mid-seventeenth century they were expelled for activity deemed to be a threat to the integrity of the state.

Thus, by the time of the major impact of the West on China, in the early nineteenth century, the Chinese government and people subscribed monolithically to the view that all foreigners were hostile, or inferior, or irrelevant to China's needs. The known world revolved around China, and the Chinese words "*zhong guo*," middle kingdom, were an apt and literal summation of a universal truth.

A final notable attribute of traditional Chinese society was its failure to fully exploit its own technology. By the beginning of the Tang Dynasty, in 618 AD, China's technological lead over the rest of the world was indisputable. China's capacity for invention in early times was prolific,[8] and among the most outstanding achievements were gunpowder and rockets for warfare, glass, glazed porcelain, paper, the printing press, the astrolabe, the compass, the stern-post rudder which enabled ships to navigate accurately, and a host of other items.

When, eventually, this Chinese technology filtered through to Western Europe, some of it was instrumental in transforming the face of Europe, and fundamentally altering its relationship with the rest of the world. The printing press in particular, in due course would serve to spread ideas and knowledge among ordinary people as never before, to their inestimable benefit. The aids to navigation were put to use in Europe's exploration, and ultimate conquest, of much of the rest of the globe.

Yet China itself failed to build on this early technological lead. Although it developed a substantial export trade in porcelain, silk and furniture with territories bordering the Indian Ocean during the Tang dynasty — a trade in which Arab vessels also participated — and sent out massive fleets on seven extraordinary voyages to assert Chinese influence under Admiral Zheng He during the Ming, in the context of what might have been achieved it made little further use of its navigational aids. During the Qing dynasty, the last before the Western impact, Chinese vessels rarely ventured farther than destinations in Far Eastern waters. There was no attempt to send ships to "discover" Europe, as Europe would shortly send ships to open up its own trade with China.

Nor did Chinese merchants, many of whom profited by the Indian Ocean trade, seek to invest money in promoting invention, in the hope that new technology in manufacture might bring them untold wealth. The pattern of the Industrial Revolution in Europe and America was not to be followed in China. For reasons that come more sharply into focus in the late nineteenth century, technology did not develop in a way which might challenge the social order, as happened in the West with mechanized mass production ultimately bringing a new class into being.

The significance of this failure to generate indigenous industrial change, with its attendant military ascendancy, cannot be exaggerated. It meant that China in the nineteenth century was still a wholly agricultural and handicraft economy, even though some handicrafts, such as the manufacture of porcelain, were carried out on a massive scale. China still lacked not only any methods of machine-based mass production, but also any modern means of defence, transport or communication. It had been left behind by the West technologically, and was completely vulnerable.

The explanation for this state of affairs has been the subject of much speculation. In part, it may have been due to the status accorded to merchants and entrepreneurs in the Confucian state. The man who was interested only in what was profitable could not aspire to be a gentleman (although this did not stop scholar-officials from amassing wealth). Thus in status terms, there was little point in a successful merchant investing in new ventures, and the ostentatious use of wealth to promote schemes of dubious merit would have been wholly counterproductive in status terms. Such schemes in any case challenged the view that change, unless it was a return to better traditional practice, was undesirable. Far better for the merchant to put his money into land, and try to buy respectability for himself and his family. Then he

could legitimately hope that his male heirs, having had the best education that money could buy, might gain admission to the bureaucracy.

In addition, there was no perceived market for mass produced consumer goods like textiles, the staple of industrial production during the
early years of the Industrial Revolution in the West. Within China,
many of the needs of the peasantry were met outside the cash economy,
through handicraft sidelines carried on at home. What could not be
made probably could not be reasonably aspired to. Nor did any equivalent of enclosure on the land offer any likelihood of large numbers of
people being impelled into the cities and forced into the cash economy,
made dependent on the very products of the Industrial Revolution they
were helping to create. Outside China, markets for such products
might potentially exist, but for reasons noted there was little knowledge of or interest in these.

Another possible explanation has to do with the efficiency of the
Chinese economy at doing what it did at an adequate and acceptable
level. This is the theory of the "high-level equilibrium trap."[9] According to this view, the practice of agriculture in China had by the Qing
dynasty reached such a high level of sophistication and productivity
that, in peacetime and in the absence of civil strife at least, it was able
to satisfy the need for food of a very large population. There was no
logical reason to develop agricultural technology further because
employment needs and work that needed to be done were broadly in
balance, and the automation of processes, if it had been contemplated,
would only have destroyed this equilibrium.

This view is not incompatible with the widely held belief in China at
the time that, more generally, China was already able to generate internally everything that its people could possibly want, and needed nothing from the outside world. The Emperor Qian Long expressed
precisely these sentiments to the first official British envoy to China,
Lord MacCartney, in 1793. Indeed, in the eighteenth century much
Western opinion, influenced by over a century of Jesuit writing, was
inclined to accept the perception of China as a kind of self-sufficient
utopia. The critical change in the West came with the imperatives generated by the Industrial Revolution, to find both markets and sources
of raw material overseas. However self-sufficient China might be, it
could not be allowed to continue going its own way. The projection of
market opportunities, and the heightened rivalries of the Western powers in all parts of the world, determined otherwise.

China's early modernization

China in the early nineteenth century, therefore, faced the Western powers in their most dynamic and expansive phase. The trade that had developed with Britain was by the 1830s, not inconsiderable, but traditional in nature, with tea exported to Britain in return for quantities of opium imported, illegally, from British India. The election of a Whig government in Britain in 1830, sympathetic to laissez-faire notions of world trade, gave encouragement to those merchants and manufacturing interests who wanted to see what they believed to be the "vast" China market opened up. The British East India Company's monopoly on British trade with China was removed in 1834, and within five years the pressure became irresistible. The pretext of a Chinese attempt in 1839 to stop the illegal opium trade was taken to go to war with China, and from this first Opium War is generally dated China's opening up to the West.

Although the war lasted technically until 1842, there was no doubt from the beginning who would win it. The critical factor was the level of military technology on each side. The British navy's steam driven vessels completely out-manoeuvred China's war junks, just as British cannon and rifles were much more accurate and potent than anything China had available. It soon became clear that sheer numbers were no military advantage in a contest between traditional and modern weaponry. This was China's earliest lesson in the ways of the modern world, and because of it the acquisition of military technology became the first focus of China's response to the West.

Both the evolving relationship between China and the Western powers, and the successive stages of China's attempt to come to terms with the modern world in the hundred years that followed, have been dealt with in great detail in the literature on China's recent past.[10] Here it is possible to draw only the outlines of what happened, in particular as it pertains to China's current task of modernization.

Diplomatically, China's defeat in the Opium War, and in a subsequent war with Britain and France from 1856 to 1860, challenged as never before China's traditional ideas on the way in which foreign countries should relate to the Chinese Empire. For the first time China was obliged to concede, though recognition came only slowly, that it was a nation-state in a world which contained other sovereign nation-states, most of which were not prepared in any way to show deference to the

Chinese Emperor. Diplomatic relations were to be on the basis of equality. Representation and the right of residence had to be granted in Peking. Foreigners had to be permitted to live and work in the many "Treaty Ports" which were opened up to trade, and ultimately anywhere in the Chinese Empire.[11]

China's status in the Western powers' eyes was closely linked to their perception of its ability to defend itself, govern itself, and to adapt successfully to the demands of the modern age. None of these things, in the late nineteenth century, was China able to do. In consequence demands were made of China to which it was compelled to submit, and which by the turn of the century included not only the granting of "concession areas" of substantial size, amounting to occupied territory, in many of the country's major cities, but also the ceding of "spheres of influence" to the major foreign powers, in which they would have the prior right to exploit mineral resources, build railways, and generally profit from any investment opportunities as they saw fit. By the turn of the century such a sphere was granted to Russia in Manchuria, to France in south China, to Germany in Shantung, and to Britain in central China and along the Yangtze.

In this way China became what Marxist historians called a "semi-colony," exploited by the Western powers, and latterly by Japan, while retaining its own government and sovereignty. The tension to which this state of affairs gave rise, allied to Peking's progressive inability to guarantee good government, produced periodic eruptions of popular discontent. The most spectacular of these, from the foreigners' point of view, was the Boxer Uprising of 1899–1900. This secret society rebellion, directed initially against the dynasty and subsequently turned against the foreign community, resulted in the siege of the foreign legations in Peking and Tientsin in the summer of 1900. After this, though China was obliged to make reparation to the Western powers, Western pressure on China reached a plateau, and subsequently declined, extraterritorial privilege coming to an end in 1943. In the twentieth century it was Japan that China had most to fear.

China's response to the technological challenge represented by the Western impact was equally unsteady, and marked by distinct stages. The earliest of these was the stage in which China sought only to acquire Western technology for military defence, or "self-strengthening" as it was termed. Leaders of the self-strengthening movement, which began in the 1860s, but reached its high point in the 1870s and

1880s, were military men or high officials who campaigned to have the Court accept the need for China to import the latest military hardware, and to acquire the technology to make it itself. Some of these campaigners took it upon themselves to start arsenals or shipyards to show what could be done. In this way, China was able to achieve some capacity, albeit limited, to build modern weaponry and warships, while at the same time collecting tax on its expanded international trade through the newly-established Maritime Customs.

The theory behind these developments was that of "*ti-yong*," articulated most succinctly by one of the conservative reformers, Zhang Zhidong, in the 1890s. This was that Chinese learning should be the "*ti*," the essence or foundation, of Chinese society, but Western learning could be the "*yong*," the practical application, or could in other words provide the tools, or the technology, to deal with specific threats and problems in such a way as to preserve the Chinese essence. This formulation was rooted in neo-Confucian ideas of the relationship between the inner substance and outer function of anything. Critics proclaimed that new techniques were ultimately bound to affect values, and that the two could not be separated in this way. A similar critique could be applied to the much more recent belief that the Communist Party in the 1980s could import new technology without it having any substantial effect on the nature of Chinese society or the Party's hold on power.

Yet the conservative reformers' entreaties fell on deaf ears at Court, where the ultra-conservative Empress Dowager conspired with her chief eunuch adviser to defeat innovation at every turn. When Japan went to war with China over who should control Korea in 1894, China was defeated as easily as in the Opium War, fifty years earlier.

After this, proponents of modernization extended the scope of their proposals to include manufacturing industry that was not military in nature, as well as modern means of transport and communications, commerce, and even political institutions and ideas. The young Emperor Guang Xu in 1898 gave the reformer KangYouwei the opportunity to draw up and implement a comprehensive set of proposals embodying all these elements to transform China into a modern state. A hundred days later both Kang and the Emperor were seized and imprisoned, the Emperor dying mysteriously one day before the Empress Dowager herself in 1908. Again, the prospect of change had been too threatening; the dynasty, though it could not foretell future events, opted for oblivion rather than transform itself.

The minor changes carried out in the first decade of the twentieth century could not long postpone the collapse of the dynasty. With a child on the throne, and no agreed policies for the restoration of good government, the Qing Dynasty succumbed in 1911 to a rebel alliance of revolutionaries, disaffected military men and Han chauvinists. What followed was not, and could not have been, a progression to constitutional government as some had hoped; it was rather a decline into warlordism and the fragmentation of political power.

The May 4th Movement of 1919 heralded a new phase. The Movement was a direct reaction to the failure of the Versailles Peace Conference to restore the province of Shandong to China following its occupation by Japan during the First World War; China's first major student-led protest marked this event, and was followed by strikes and demonstrations throughout China's principal cities in ensuing months. However, the long-term significance of May 4th is that it represented an almost total rejection of Confucian orthodoxy, and spurred on a discussion by intellectuals of the policy alternatives for China that had begun around 1915, and would continue throughout the twentieth century. The debate over the respective roles of science and democracy in the new China which it was hoped to create is dealt with more fully in Chapter 11 below.

In the ferment following May 4th, two new political forces were born, the Nationalist Party, restructured along Leninist lines in the early 1920s, and the Chinese Communist Party, whose First Congress was held in Shanghai in 1921. These two parties would form the main protagonists in the struggle to determine the nature of Chinese society up to the victory of the Communists in 1949. Japan, which encroached steadily on Chinese territory before declaring all-out war in 1937, constituted the third point in the triangle.

Both the Nationalists and the Communists offered ideological prescriptions for China's ills. For Sun Yat-sen and the Nationalists, the programme was "nationalism, democracy, and the people's livelihood" — or freedom from foreign interference, progress to constitutional government, and an ill-defined socialism to meet the crisis of distribution. Chiang Kai-shek, who ultimately inherited the mantle of power following Sun's death in 1925, in fact paid scant attention to the latter two.

For the Communists, the programme was Marxism, Leninism and, as time passed, Mao Zedong Thought — offering an explanation of why things were the way they were, how to achieve power, and the way in which social revolution could be managed in the particular circumstances of China. With the Communists forced into the hinterland by the Nationalists in 1927, and ultimately establishing a base area in remote Yenan, much of their programme had to be postponed until after 1949.

Both prescriptions were presumed to embrace the ways and means of achieving modernization, yet neither in fact did so. It will be argued later in this book that the very notion of all-embracing orthodoxy itself served to stifle the spirit of enquiry necessary to successful development.

So what had been achieved in the way of technological change in the period up to 1949? Limited initiatives by Chinese entrepreneurs in the late nineteenth century to introduce foreign production technology into small factories and workshops had little real impact.[12] An important change came in 1895 when, as a consequence of the treaty that ended the Sino-Japanese War it became legal for the first time for foreigners to build and operate factories in China. After that date both foreign-owned and Chinese-owned factories began to appear, producing consumer goods, and located for the most part in the Treaty Ports along China's coast, where foreign owners could enjoy extraterritorial protection from Chinese law. By the 1920s there were estimated to be several thousand factories in China, of which only a few hundred had one hundred workers or more. Most of China's several hundred thousand workers worked in factories with only a few dozen employees.[13] This remained true right up to 1949.

Complementing this limited industrial development was the construction in the late nineteenth and early twentieth century of a network of railways, corresponding in coverage to the strategic and commercial interests of the foreign powers that put up the capital for them, and only incidentally enhancing China's national unity or promoting its national interest. In a similar way, foreign investment in Treaty Port harbour facilities primarily served the needs of foreigners and China's comprador class. Even the postal service and the Maritime Customs were run by foreigners on behalf of the Chinese government, a legacy of the time when the Qing dynasty had sought assistance in securing an important source of tax revenue.

Despite recent work purporting to show a very substantial rise in economic growth throughout the first half of the twentieth century, and a widespread attendant improvement in the standard of living, given impetus by the strength of industrial production,[14] it is still possible to conclude that the type of industrial development that occurred in this period did little to promote China's modernization. Indeed, a case can be made that even by 1949 China was stuck in a time warp of primitive mass production of the kind that characterized the factory system in England or America in the early nineteenth century.

Most critically, production was confined very largely to textiles, tobacco and other consumer products, to the exclusion of machine industry, which would be capable of producing equipment able to make China industrially self-sufficient. All such equipment, even in 1949, had to be imported. Furthermore, much of China's industry, up until the Communist takeover or just before, was Western or Japanese owned, and there was scant evidence of any tendency for Chinese-owned industry to supplant that in foreign ownership;[15] the Communist Party even had to rely on foreign managers for a time to keep some of the plants going after 1949.

Most of the larger industries were located in a few of the bigger Treaty Ports, and especially Shanghai, which were chosen primarily because they offered security and a lifestyle which was congenial for foreign managers. China's hinterland was almost completely untouched by modern industry, and retained a wholly traditional life and vision, except for the occasional visitations of soldiers with modern weapons, or pedlars with the ubiquitous packets of British American Tobacco cigarettes. In no sense could the strength or modernity of the country as a whole be said to have been advanced by the industrial enclaves in the Treaty Port cities; to the contrary, under the Nationalists the government of China was increasingly run for the military, who wished to preserve the rural status quo, and for the Chinese commercial interests in the cities,[16] who were to fund the repeated campaigns in the 1930s against the Communist Party in Yenan.

The degree to which China had become modern by 1949, therefore, was very limited. On the basis of the country's experience thus far, many Chinese were prepared to accept Mao's insistence in 1949 that social revolution, and transformation of the economy, could only be achieved after national liberation, and the expulsion of the Western powers from China. It is ironic that, three decades later, the Western powers would be invited back to China, and that foreign technology and capital investment would once again be made welcome.

Objective Constraints

On 1 October 1949, the day when the People's Republic of China was formally proclaimed amid much fanfare in Beijing, the scale of the task of nation-building facing the Communist Party was without precedent, and almost unimaginable.

To begin with, the military victory was still not yet complete. Pockets of resistance by the Nationalist forces continued to exist, notably in the northeast and west of the country, which would take many months of further fighting to subdue. The process of pacifying and disarming former Nationalist troops, attempting to re-educate them politically, and deciding which could be incorporated into the Communist forces and which could not, was lengthy and fraught with complications. The transition to a peacetime role for the Red Army, now to be renamed the People's Liberation Army, would also need to be carefully monitored, given the propensity for armed men to become undisciplined where an immediate common threat had receded.

Politically, the Chinese Communist Party, since the late 1930s essentially under Mao's leadership, faced the problem of transition to peacetime rule, and the need to establish not just its control but also its legitimacy throughout China. The model on which it was based — that of a Leninist style hierarchically structured party characterised by democratic centralism, cellular in its organization, and clandestine in operation — may have been suited to the task of taking power when the Party was in opposition; in peacetime, when power had been achieved, the appropriateness of this model remained to be seen. Nonetheless, the "vanguard" role of the Party was to be preserved, and Party organs would be established to supervise the organs of government and to monitor and influence decision-making at every level. As in the Soviet Union, the Party structure was to parallel that of the state, with the Party to be the final arbiter in every case.

If the revolution was about the taking of power to effect a fairer and more generous distribution of benefits to China's people, then concern for the state of the economy would be paramount. As has been noted, almost a century of intercourse with the modern world had still left China only marginally touched by industrialization and the infrastructure that goes with it. In 1949, such infrastructure as China had was partially or wholly in ruins in consequence of thirty years of intermittent civil war and war with Japan. Roads, railways, factories, power stations, dams, canals and communication links all needed to be rebuilt if the country was to begin to function again.

Beyond this, the new government would have to address the longer-term need for more focused economic activity, and the decision was taken to try to manage this through central planning and collective organization. However, if the Party was to achieve something more in this respect than mere equality in poverty, the economy would need to be modernized, more specifically China would have to import or construct within its borders the kind of equipment that would facilitate widespread introduction of modern industry, enabling it ultimately to become self-sufficient in the modern world of increasingly complex demands, different altogether from the old China's self-sufficiency in agriculture. This in turn would require investment on a massive scale, which would have to be generated. With much of China's business community having so recently fled from Shanghai to Hong Kong with its capital, plant and equipment, this must have seemed a millennial hope at the time.

China's people needed to be won over. Weary of warfare, China's peasantry and the several million Communist fighters drawn from their ranks looked forward to peace and prosperity under the new regime. Yet their very expectations posed a potential threat to a new government acutely aware that, in the Chinese idiom, they were the fish who must swim in the people's sea. With the immediate threat from the Nationalists over, old resentments could and would return. The issue of land distribution would come quickly to the fore. Land-lords and their families would have to be dealt with. The bourgeoisie, some of whose skills the Party would need for a time, would have to be assessed and re-educated. Intellectuals, the wellspring of the Party's founding ideology but by some regarded as notoriously unreliable, would need to be watched and trained and brought securely into the fold.

The decision to promote a Chinese version of Marxism based on Mao's own adaptation of Marxism to Chinese circumstances was a foregone conclusion. As is discussed more fully in Chapter 6 below, Marxism-Leninism-Mao Zedong Thought was seen both as a means of motivating people and as the best explanation of China's particular objective circumstances. The fighting had not yet stopped when political teams began to disperse all over China, spreading the new ideology which would set the political parameters for the next thirty years.

On the diplomatic front, as was noted in Chapter 1, the transition from the World War Two alliance between the USA and the USSR to a situation of hostility and Cold War between the two had a profound impact on international politics. Although only two or three years earlier the US had shown every sign of staying neutral in the imminent struggle between the Chinese Nationalists and the CCP, events in Europe progressively caused America to realign itself in China with Chiang Kai-shek as the only apparent bulwark against the further spread of communism. The "fall" of China to the CCP in 1949, taken in conjunction with events in Korea, Vietnam and Eastern Europe, precipitated the rise of McCarthyism in the United States and the decision to ostracize China.

The American refusal to recognize diplomatically the new Chinese government, and the policy of "isolating and containing" China, presented the Party with a conundrum. How could China in its existing state of development and skills stand alone in the modern world? Only Britain among Western powers recognized the new People's Republic, reaching a unique agreement with the new regime which enabled Britain to maintain a Chargé d'Affaires in both Beijing and Taibei. Yet even Britain remained cautious. Other countries that were potential sources of trade and, more important, industrial technology, were put under pressure not to develop any relationship with the new state. This left China with only the USSR and its new satellites in Eastern Europe as potential sources of technology and assistance.

So as the People's Republic embarked on its first decade, it would be the Soviet model that would have the greatest influence, and Russian technology that would equip its earliest heavy industries, at last giving it the machines that would make machines — and ultimately the capacity to be self-sufficient. It need not have been so, and would almost certainly not have been the Party's, or even Mao's, first choice. It would have been impossible at the time to predict that this might delay China's integration into the modern world by three decades.

3

CHINA UNDER THE PEOPLE'S REPUBLIC

The broad outlines of China's development over the past fifty years are well known. In this and the following chapter it will be possible only to remind the reader of certain key features which have marked China's progress under the People's Republic, and its ultimate integration into the global economy.[1]

The 'golden years'

With the benefit of hindsight, or the historical distance of more than half a century, it is possible to conclude that the balance sheet of the Party's achievements during the first decade of the People's Republic was broadly positive. This much is claimed by many of China's older citizens when they consider the Party's record in the 1950s, though of course it would very much depend on who you were, and what was to be your prescribed role in society. The rulers of the new China would demonize and pillory their enemies as never before, but their enemies were now in the minority, and for the most part the Chinese people were prepared to give the Party a chance to show what it could do. For many, the years from 1949 to 1958 were the "golden years" of Party rule.

Consolidation

Military consolidation was the first task, as has been noted above, closely followed by the establishment of political and administrative control. The flight of Chiang Kai-shek to Taiwan in late 1948, and the progressive isolation and surrender of many of his remaining troops enabled the People's Republic to be declared in Beijing by the victorious Communists on 1 October 1949. Nevertheless it would be mid-1950 before the last pockets of resistance on the mainland were cleared away, leaving an unresolved civil war, and diplomatic headaches that would persist for China into the twenty-first century.

In the early years of Communist rule, the Red Army, now the People's Liberation Army, would be both the first and the last line of defence against insurrection, a role for which it was prepared by its strict code of discipline developed during the many years of opposition, when the quality of its relationship with the peasantry had been crucial to its survival. In the turbulence of the early 1950s, when major changes were taking place in society in consequence of the Communist victory, the PLA could be and was used as a model for citizens to emulate, and sometimes as an arbiter to settle disputes in the implementation of new policies. In due course new administrative structures would evolve which would secure for the PLA a significant place in the hierarchy of organizations alongside the Party and the structures of the state. The Central Military Commission would be the symbol of this special status, which would endure largely unchallenged throughout the first three decades of Communist rule.

Ostensibly complementing the PLA in the task of keeping public order were the people's militias, whose origins could be traced back to the use of peasants as auxiliary forces from the early 1930s. These bodies survived into the new era, although they did not necessarily possess the neutral character and good reputation of the army. The militias were often used in the first few years of the People's Republic to promote land reform activity, which by its nature was acrimonious and often violent. The militias, with their strong local ties, not infrequently became involved in factional disputes, and this augured ill for their behaviour much later during the Cultural Revolution.

In due course, though at a different pace in different parts of China, police forces were reconstituted, sometimes using re-educated officers from the old Guomindang police, and sometimes not. A new Public Security Bureau was established to take responsibility for all normal policing duties, including the investigation of criminal activity, throughout China, and for maintaining surveillance of all citizens. From its formation, it had the power to determine guilt or innocence of an alleged offender, and for much of the first three decades it was able to pass sentence as well, by-passing the courts in some cases. A Supreme People's Court and a Procurator-General's Office existed from 1949, but were effectively subordinate to the Party and the executive arm of government. Martial law remained in force until September 1954, when new civil and criminal codes began to be introduced.

It had long been Mao's contention that power grows out of the barrel of a gun. Thus the purpose of the military consolidation, and of the subsequent establishment of police enforcement mechanisms in the 1950s, was to support and enable control by the Communist Party. In the immediate years after 1949, the Party's main purpose was to strengthen its hold on power. In terms of political institutions, this meant a refining and adaptation to peacetime purposes of the Party structure that had evolved during the civil war and the making of revolution. It also meant replacing the Nationalist government's institutions of state with other institutions of state better suited to the Party's objectives.

For the first five years, up to September 1954, the Chinese People's Political Consultative Conference was the main legitimizing body of the State structure. The CPPCC was established in 1949 as a "united front" assembly to represent peasants and workers, and elements of the "petty" and "national" bourgeoisie who had supported the Communist Party against the Guomindang. Initially with 622 delegates drawn from these groups, but excluding any landlord participation, this body met at regular intervals to give its approval to laws and policy formulated by the Communist Party. In 1954 it was succeeded in this role by the new National People's Congress, and receded in importance, meeting only occasionally to offer advice to policymakers.

The National People's Congress was made up initially of 1,226 members chosen by lower level congresses which had been set up for the purpose. Delegates to these lower bodies were ultimately chosen by the people in unopposed elections following their nomination by the Communist Party. The NPC was now the highest organ of State authority in China, and had the power to make laws, and to enforce and amend the new Constitution, also just introduced. Its role, and its relationship with the Communist Party, will be discussed in more detail in Chapter 8 below. The NPC was not of course a parliament in the conventional sense, a fact underlined by the requirement for it to meet in plenary session only once every five years, which it has done on average since its formation. In the intervening periods its powers were to be exercised by a Standing Committee, initially of fifty members, who might meet twice a month.

In 1954 also the State Council was established as the highest executive organ of government, with the power to oversee day-to-day administration through the various functional Ministries and Commissions which were responsible to it. The State Council comprised the Premier, usually several Vice Premiers, Ministers, and Heads of Commissions. In addition to supervising administration at the central government level, the State Council has from the beginning had responsibility for giving direction to bodies charged with the task of implementing government programmes at the provincial and local level.

Simply in order to run the country, and carry out the Party's policies, it was necessary for China to have a full range of Ministries and offices dealing with every aspect of activity that concerned the state, and some that would not have concerned the State in other countries. Those Ministries dealing with production under the new First Five Year Plan (1952–57) were particularly important, and were formed broadly on the model of their counterparts in the Soviet Union, from which the whole planning system would draw much inspiration.

Government organs were additionally set up at the provincial, county, district and village level, and in China's cities. In most cases these were based on, and used some personnel from, institutions inherited from the Guomindang. In most cases these bodies continued to function after a fashion during the early years of the People's Republic, with only their status clarified by the Constitutional reforms of 1954. We shall return to their role in a later chapter.

Over all of this the Communist Party exercised control. The fount of authority within the Party has always been the Central Committee, established in 1921 soon after the Party was created. By 1949, the Central Committee had forty-four members, but it developed the practice of meeting only annually in plenary session to approve and endorse policies and programmes. To carry on the business of running China in the meantime, a Politburo of eleven members, later expanded, was chosen in 1949, and a Standing Committee of the Politburo was instituted in 1956, comprising at various times between five and nine members. The Politburo met frequently, but not daily. The Standing Committee from 1956 was intended to meet, and usually did meet, on a daily basis often to initiate and always to decide on the most important aspects of policy, and to hand down orders for implementation by lower levels of the Party and by the state. The Standing Committee has been likened by some to an "inner cabinet" in a Western government. Without a doubt it has, since its inception, been the institutional locus of absolute power in China, except for a brief time during the Cultural Revolution.

Also at the centre, since 1949 there has been a series of National Party Congresses held by the Chinese Communist Party following on from the first Congress in Shanghai in 1921. The seventh such Congress was held before the Communist victory, in 1945, and the eighth only in 1956; generally since that time a Congress has been held every five years on average. In essence, the Congress has heard reports, and given formal sanction to the Party's line and policy. Its agenda has normally been prepared by the Politburo.

The Party has also had since 1949, under various names, a Military Affairs Committee to supervise the armed forces and make policy on defence, and a Central Control Commission to maintain morale and discipline within the Party.

Finally, note should be taken of the Party's Central Secretariat, first established in 1956, comprising between six and twelve members whose task was to control and supervise the work of the various functional departments of the central Party organization, which with their equivalent Party organs at the provincial, district, municipal and other levels shadow and oversee the activity of the corresponding organs of the state. It is through these functional departments that the Party has, since 1949, directed and controlled the implementation of its policies by the organs of the state, achieving the duality of Party and State that is the hallmark of a socialist system.

These, then, are the political institutions put in place in the early months and years of the People's Republic, whose operation will be referred to again later in this book. Over these institutions prevailed one dominant individual. Mao Zedong, in 1949 at the height of his power and popularity, would stamp his authority on the revolution he had fought to create. To do this he would not only use the organizational structures of the Party and state, but would also seek to engage the hearts and minds of those in whose name victory had been achieved. To do this he would use ideology to engage with the population in pursuit of the daunting economic and social goals of the revolution. It is to the economic and social arena that we must now turn to consider how, and with what degree of success, those goals were achieved.

Economic progress, social reform

On 1 January 1953, China put into effect its First Five Year Plan.[2] Influenced very substantially by advice from Moscow, with which it had been in negotiation intermittently since the formation of the People's Republic in October 1949, the Party had chosen to focus initially on the development of heavy industry. This would be introduced with Soviet technical assistance, and through the medium of credit extended by the Soviet Union, which would ultimately have to be repaid by shipments of surplus grain. Thus, over the next five years it is claimed that some 211 industrial plants of all kinds were set up in China with Soviet help, an aid and technical assistance package worth US$625 million, an enormous sum in the currency of those days.[3]

The decision to focus on heavy industry, the wisdom of which Mao Zedong himself later claimed to have doubted, was nonetheless intended to address an evident and urgent need. As we have seen in an earlier chapter, China before 1949 had almost no heavy industry, its largest factories being cotton and silk mills, and cigarette factories, located in a very few of the old "Treaty Ports." China's planners at the time felt that "machines to build machines" would be a pre-requisite not only to raising the overall level of prosperity, but also to securing the country's long-term independence. In retrospect this judgement appears to have been correct, and the achievements of the First Five Year Plan at least gave China the basis for a modicum of industrial self-sufficiency when Soviet assistance came to an end in 1960.

Thus all over China, but especially in large cities, factories were built, and Russian and Eastern European equipment was installed, enabling China over the course of the Plan for the first time to produce industrial chemicals, construction materials, steel, trucks, tractors, railway rolling stock, modern ships, power generation equipment, machine tools and a range of other items which would be essential to the country's further development. In the space of just over five years, through the mechanisms of a command economy, infrastructure was laid down that had still been lacking after 100 years of contact with the market-based economies of the industrial West. The industrial component of China's GNP grew over the period of the Plan by an average of 13 to 14 per cent per annum.[4]

In agriculture the rate of growth was only 2.6 per cent per annum[5] over the same period, barely enough to keep pace with what was believed at the time to be a population growth of 2 per cent per annum. In fact, population figures for this period have subsequently been shown to have been an underestimate. What was happening in agriculture, though, was a revolution in the way in which production was organized, and in the whole social structure of the countryside. The revolution in agriculture was at the heart of Mao's vision for the new China.

At first, immediately after 1949, land was taken from landlords throughout China, from state and religious organizations, and re-distributed in the form of private plots to individual peasants. This process was accompanied by an often violent political campaign to pillory the landlords and eliminate them as a class, simultaneously consolidating the popularity of the Communist Party in the countryside. However Mao wanted to raise the communal awareness of the peasants. In 1950 "mutual aid" teams were formed in some areas — combinations for mutual assistance in the busy seasons. In a further development, as early as 1951 the first of the "Agricultural Producers Co-operatives" were formed, retrospectively referred to as the "lower-stage" or "primary" co-operatives. In these, farmers pooled their resources, land and labour on a year-round basis, but still had the right to withdraw, and were paid both wages for their labour and a dividend based on land contributed.

In 1955 higher stage Agricultural Producers Co-operatives began to be introduced, in which property was held in common, and there were no dividends or right of withdrawal. In a report entitled "The High Tide of Socialism in the Chinese Countryside,"[6] Mao set forth his reasons for taking the co-operatives to the next stage. Essentially these were that larger co-operative units could better mobilize production to satisfy local needs, including not only agricultural but also consumer needs and some industrial needs, and would gradually accumulate capital to invest, facilitating both mechanization and increased prosperity. The whole process would also be an exercise in consciousness-raising. It was planned to have all of China's peasants working for a co-operative by 1958.

The transformation of society was achieved hand in hand with the restructuring of the economy, and through an overarching programme of political measures and campaigns derived from Mao Zedong's adaptation of Marxist ideology to China. Among the most significant early measures were several new laws promulgated in 1950: the Land Reform Law gave legal sanction to the redistribution of land; the new

Marriage Law provided, *inter alia*, for an end to arranged marriages and the guaranteed right to divorce; the Trade Union Law permitted once again the existence of trade unions, which were now, however, to function as mass organizations in support of Party objectives. Of these, perhaps the most significant was the Marriage Law which, while imperfect, was a first step towards rectifying the subservient position of women in the old society.

Political campaigns addressed the urgent need of the Party to achieve its policy objectives and to win over hearts and minds. The campaign against counter-revolutionaries, in the Spring of 1951, targeted landlords and unsurprisingly, given the passions aroused, deteriorated rapidly into violence. The Three Anti Movement at the end of the same year was aimed at eliminating graft, waste and bureaucracy within the Party. In the spring of 1952 the Five Anti Movement was launched, directed at remaining "capitalists" — usually small businesses — and sought to uncover cases of bribery, tax evasion, theft of state property, corruption related to government contracts, and theft of state economic secrets; in this way many employees of small firms were obliged to or agreed to report their employers. In 1953 a further campaign within the Party aimed to combat bureaucracy, commandism and violations of law and discipline. The major Hundred Flowers Campaign, foreshadowed by a speech by Mao in 1956, and implemented in May and early June 1957, invited intellectuals to express their views more openly, and to criticize the Party; it was immediately followed by an anti-rightist campaign to crack down on dissenters. A more detailed discussion of the role and nature of political campaigns appears in Chapters 6 and 10 below.

Finally, substantial change took place in the fields of education and public health. In the early years of the People's Republic, primary schooling was still neither universal nor compulsory. Nonetheless, and despite the fact that in rural areas half-work/half-study was the general rule, the number of children enrolled in primary school increased from twenty-four million in 1949 to eighty-six million in 1958.[7] In addition, part time education was made available to older people. Literacy was deemed of great importance, and much progress was made in this respect. It is estimated that by 1959 only 10 per cent of the Chinese population had no literacy at all, an achievement which was complemented by the publication of newspapers based on a restricted vocabulary, and using a progressively wider range of simplified characters.[8]

Secondary and tertiary education was geared much more to technical subjects than hitherto, and many new technical institutions were founded, while existing colleges were required to focus on subjects that would have a practical application. Throughout China's educational system political study was of great importance, and schools and colleges bore the responsibility for producing new generations of socialist men and women. Ideology was mixed with the subject matter of all courses.

In the area of public health, substantial numbers of doctors, nurses and ancillary workers were trained, hospitals were opened or expanded in large towns all over China, and rural clinics were built where previously there had been none. The scale of the public health problem was very great, however, and the investment was still inadequate to meet China's needs; moreover there was still much emphasis at this time on the training of specialists, and general practitioners on the Western model, which required time and resources. Only much later, during the Cultural Revolution, would "barefoot doctors" be introduced, to try to meet the need for basic medical care in China's hinterland.

By 1957 the Communist Party had been in power for almost eight years. Substantial progress had been achieved in the development of the economy and the transformation of society, facilitated and augmented by measures to establish the Party's political control and to inculcate its ideology. Now, in the Great Leap Forward and the implementation of the Communes in 1958, all these strands would come together in one great movement whose negative dimensions have been memorably, and perhaps somewhat controversially, captured in Jasper Becker's book *Hungry Ghosts*.

The immediate cause of this new activity was the realization among China's leaders in the autumn of 1957 that their prospective Second Five Year Plan, due to start in 1958, could not rely on continued massive inputs of aid from the Soviet Union. Partly in consequence of the extensive reorganization it had undergone, China's agriculture had simply failed to produce the large quantities of surplus grain which it had been intended to export to the Soviet Union to pay for the earlier assistance, and that debt was still outstanding. The decision was then taken to try to dramatically increase output in order to facilitate further expansion under the new Five Year Plan. In February of 1958, the nation was told to prepare itself for a "great leap forward."

The movement is remembered for its extraordinary attempt to encourage the human spirit to triumph over material limitations, and

41

in that sense it presaged the Cultural Revolution. It was also known for its excesses. Production quotas in both agriculture and industry were in many cases almost doubled. Twelve to sixteen hour shifts became common. Peasants and workers became exhausted, illness increased and accident rates soared.

The Great Leap exposed for the first time the naivety of some in the Party who believed that every obstacle could be overcome through political struggle. Some 600,000 "backyard furnaces" were set up in the countryside to smelt down and turn into steel any scrap pieces of iron that could be found; the resultant steel, 3 million tons of it, was of such poor quality that it was effectively worthless. Frenzied ploughing below the level of fertile topsoil, and close planting of seed, contributed to crop yields well below normal. A campaign to liquidate the sparrows held responsible for damaging the crops was so successful that the crops then fell prey to insects in vast numbers. These measures were soon abandoned.

In August 1958 the Party announced that with immediate effect China's 740,000 Agricultural Producers' Co-operatives would be turned into some 25,000 Communes, a further restructuring in pursuit of Mao's objective of self-sufficient economic units in the countryside. The land and implements of the old Co-operatives would become the property of the "whole people." Initially, peasant families were split up and segregated on the basis of sex, required to sleep in Commune dormitories and eat at Commune canteens. Family life was completely disrupted, and this in combination with very long hours of work caused morale to plummet.

By the end of 1958 most of these policies were recognized as having been mistaken. Hours were reduced, vegetable patches returned, and families went back to living at home. The Great Leap Forward was over. Despite these many errors, the Communes themselves remained as the units of organization in the countryside, with some changes in size, right down to 1982, and were among the Communist Party's most substantial and lasting achievements in their transformation of rural life. Moreover, the principles that Mao had sought to realize during the Great Leap, of self-sufficiency and capital accumulation in the countryside, rooted as they were in the Party's experience of rural industrial co-operatives before its assumption of national power, would re-emerge during the debates over economic policy in the early 1960s, and again during the Cultural Revolution (see below).

China in the world

Taking the decade up to 1960 as a whole, China's political options were limited not only by domestic circumstances, but also by international events and the diplomacy of the Great Powers.

It should be recalled that from 1842 to 1943 China's relations with those Powers had been governed by a network of treaties setting out conditions of trade, residence and other activity by foreigners, which were universally referred to by all parties in China as the "unequal treaties." The People's Republic was founded only six years after the final abrogation of those treaties. Moreover politics in Europe and elsewhere in Asia after the end of World War Two led the United States at least to see the Communist victory in China as just another extension of the Soviet Empire. The US, by now gripped with fear of communism, set out to "isolate and contain" China, in the hope that the new regime, deprived of diplomatic and commercial relations with the outside world, would wither and die.

In the event, the Treaty of Friendship, Alliance and Mutual Assistance signed between China and the Soviet Union in February 1950 not only paved the way for a decade of diplomatic support and protection by the Soviet Union (though that support wavered over certain issues),[9] but also gave China access to Soviet industrial technology and technical assistance, and that of Russia's East European allies. This link therefore provided a way out of the isolation that the US had sought to impose on China; in due course some other countries also made tentative contact with China to establish commercial ties. The first British trade mission to China was the so-called "Icebreaker Mission" of 1953.

Over this period of a decade, the diplomatic dimension could be summed up as having three elements. First, there were unresolved civil wars in neighbouring states. In Korea, where the pro-Communist Workers' Party was fighting from a base in the North for control of the whole peninsula, United States involvement on the side of the Southern forces led to a commitment of large numbers of Chinese troops to support the North, whose government had mounted a major attack on the South in June 1950. This war, which ended in a stalemate with a treaty in 1953, was a drain on China's resources which it could ill afford, and had the effect of confirming a bitter hostility in the US towards the People's Republic which would last for twenty years.

In Vietnam, where France had become trapped in a war of independence, China was not at this stage involved, though after the French defeat it sought to help broker an agreement at Geneva in 1954 which was intended to provide for a peaceful resolution of the continuing dispute between the two domestic factions.

Second, there were what might be described as issues arising from *irridenta*, territories that China claimed but did not control. These were, notably, Taiwan, where the Guomindang presence was seen straightforwardly as a consequence of the unresolved Chinese civil war; Hong Kong and Macao, which, with nuances of difference, were regarded as temporarily in foreign hands because of the unequal treaties (though this was not really the case with Macao); and finally Tibet, on China's inner-Asian frontier, which had traditionally paid tribute to the Chinese imperial court.

In the case of Taiwan, domestic preoccupations on the Chinese mainland, and the commitment of US forces and the US Seventh Fleet to the island's defence, made formal by a treaty in December 1954, deterred any immediate action. Nonetheless Taiwan was, and remains, a major cause of bitterness between the US and China. Two crises occurred over the island, the first in 1955 when China landed troops on a small uninhabited islet claimed by Taiwan, and the second in 1958 when China shelled the Taiwan-controlled offshore islands of Quemoy and Matsu. In neither case did the exchanges lead to war, thanks in part to China's forbearance, probably under the influence of its temperate Foreign Minister, Zhou Enlai.

Tibet was another matter. With no direct US interest involved, the British having recently withdrawn from India, and the Soviet Union distracted by troubles at home, in May 1951 China was able to impose an agreement on the Tibetan authorities which stated that Tibet was an "autonomous" part of China, sending in troops to take up residence there in September. Eight years of uneasy coexistence led to rebellion in Tibet in March 1959, the flight of the Dalai Lama, and the full-scale occupation of Tibet by Chinese forces since that time.

Finally, the third element in Chinese diplomacy in this period was its attempt to position itself as a leader of the non-aligned world. Related to this indirectly was China's belief in the inevitability of war with the capitalist West. Mao had by now come to see the underdeveloped world as analogous to the Chinese peasantry in the Chinese revolution — ultimately, he believed, the massive numbers of poor in the underdeveloped world would overwhelm the states of the capitalist West, just as the countryside had overwhelmed the cities in the struggle for China's liberation. Accordingly, China with its own recent experience of national liberation and social revolution could play a prominent role of leadership in this struggle. It could also, perhaps, win friends diplomatically by playing such a role.

Accordingly, at the Bandung Conference of non-aligned nations held in Bandung in Indonesia in April 1955, China committed itself to the emerging doctrine of neutrality in the bi-polar confrontation between the United States and the Soviet Union, joining the other participating states in a call for peace, mutual respect for national sovereignty, and economic co-operation on the basis of common interest. Non-alignment, Mao felt, could be a positive force in the struggle against imperialism. A programme of trade and aid followed with poorer countries in Asia being the principal recipients between 1955 and 1957. When the domestic economic problems of the Great Leap period intervened, however, the programme came to an end, and China was accused of dumping light manufactured goods in Asia, undermining local manufacture.

Throughout this period, and indeed up to 1971, China remained unrepresented at the United Nations, with Taiwan retaining China's seat both in the General Assembly and on the Security Council.

Decline and disequilibrium

Following the extraordinary and controversial effort of the Great Leap Forward in 1958, China entered on a period of greater uncertainty. The upheaval caused by the restructuring of administration in the countryside into Communes was exhausting, and even though the most unpopular aspects had soon been repealed, only the most ardent enthusiasts could have been entirely free of doubt over how this new experiment would turn out.

It is now clear that very substantial suffering occurred during the years immediately following the Great Leap Forward. There has been much debate about the numbers who died of starvation in this period. Estimates vary from perhaps twenty million (a Chinese official figure, cited by Gray) to as many as fifty or sixty million (Becker), though at this distance it is hard to know for sure. All Chinese alive at the time remember it as a period of great bitterness, though not all believe that the Party was principally to blame. The weather also played a major part. In 1959 and again in 1960 China was hit by extreme weather conditions, giving rise in different parts of China to both severe drought and flooding, and consequent poor harvests. The crop in 1961 was little better.

Moreover, in the early part of the Great Leap local cadres had reported much increased yields in grain, but then when the initial surge of activity died down were often afraid to report drastically reduced yields. When the problem could no longer be ignored, local Commune authorities with a surplus were often loath to give it up to feed other parts of the country where the yield had been very poor. These were patterns of behaviour not new to China in times of famine, but were exacerbated by the reaction to some of the radical early measures of the Great Leap. Only by 1962 did a much better harvest finally resolve the food crisis.

In 1960, the issue of the relationship with its major neighbour and only real source of industrial technology came to a head, when the Soviet Union suddenly and without warning finally terminated its programme of technical assistance, withdrew all its experts, and distanced itself from China diplomatically. Eight years of foreign aid and practical involvement with the development of China's industry had, from the Soviet point of view, produced almost no reciprocal benefit for the USSR. China had been largely unable to generate sufficient surplus in grain production to keep to the promised schedule of shipments to the Soviet Union. Moreover, after the USSR had committed itself in 1956 to a policy of peaceful coexistence with the capitalist West, relations with China, which still believed in the inevitability of war, had deteriorated substantially.

The withdrawal of Soviet expertise led to the decision to pursue a policy of "re-adjustment" and consolidation in both agriculture and industry, and this policy remained in force up to and including 1965, on the eve of the Cultural Revolution. Reflecting the new circumstances, the scale of new capital investment in industry was reduced, and agriculture (and especially grain production) became the priority, the "basis of the economy." In 1964 the existing Communes were subdivided, producing 74,000 Communes in place of the 26,000 of 1958, and reducing their average size to around one-third of the original.

Light industry would be promoted on the Communes, but regard was paid to the need to avoid the kind of shoddy production that characterized the back yard furnaces during the Great Leap Forward. In heavy industry, plants previously set up with Soviet assistance would continue to function, with a particular investment focus on the production of agricultural machinery, chemical fertilizers, and other goods that would be of use to agriculture.

In a departure from the trend thus far under the People's Republic, material incentives were re-introduced for harder or better work, while once again private plots were now allocated to individual peasants, and small markets appeared to facilitate the exchange of produce among the peasants. In 1963, there were small but significant increases in wages and salaries paid throughout China.

In the early 1960s, it was necessary for China to import grain from Canada and Australia in order to satisfy domestic demand. It is estimated, however, that by 1964, grain output had achieved once again the level reached in 1957, while by 1965 industrial output too had recovered, attaining the previous high registered in 1958.[10]

Overall this period, especially following the Soviet withdrawal in 1960, highlighted the need for self-sufficiency; over the next twenty years China received almost no technical input from outside the country. The debate over how self-sufficiency should be achieved was complicated by personal ambitions, the intrusion of political and ideological imperatives, and genuine differences of view over what would work.

By late 1965 the debate over economic policy was raging furiously at the highest levels of the Communist Party. In one view, most of the Party hierarchy, apart from Mao and his closest supporters, wanted to see a further relaxation of central control, with industrialization by "economic means," more material incentives, the introduction of profit and loss accounting, and expertise favoured ahead of ideological purity and mass participation. Mao on the other hand, who had been primarily responsible for the Great Leap, emphasized the importance of moral over material incentives, and looked to economic growth through the application of manpower to overcome a lack of capital and the low level of technology.[11] Mao's view of the centralization issue is, however, disputed.[12]

It became apparent that two distinct lines in the approach to economic policy were emerging, and the struggle between them, increasingly acrimonious as it was, fed into the Cultural Revolution. The economic historian Jack Gray was among the first to draw attention to the coherent nature of the development alternative offered by Mao's approach, which he saw as having also been behind Mao's thinking during the Great Leap Forward.[13] Mao was influenced by the Communist Party's successful participation in the Industrial Co-operative Movement during the Anti-Japanese War, in the course of which co-operatively run, small-scale rural industries had been set up to satisfy China's industrial needs during the wartime emergency.

Mao wanted to replicate these principles by emphasizing investment in the economic improvement of rural communities, decentralizing economic decision-making, and encouraging the initiative of rural communities in setting up small-scale industries. His theory was that these rural industries, using simple technology, locally-available materials, and small capital investment, could while producing goods that people needed achieve a high turnover of capital, and sufficient profit to invest in new and more modern equipment year by year.

Moreover, according to Mao, there would be a "dialectic" between politics and economics. People's socialist consciousness would be raised in the course of this process, and "a great spiritual force would become a great material force," further contributing to output. It will be apparent that this approach stood in complete contradiction to that of the Soviet-style "big industrial push," which Mao had first criticized in his essay "On the Ten Great Relationships" back in 1956. In his view the application of modified traditional skills to intermediate technology could produce a spiral of increasing technological modernization, increased incomes and investment, increased knowledge and confidence, and ultimately a greater readiness to accept higher levels of collective organization.[14]

In this way, the stage became set for a showdown in China just over fifteen years after the Communist Party had come to power. By 1965, the clarity of vision and singularity of purpose shown by the leadership of the revolution in its early days had been lost. As with so many other revolutions, conflict of interest and of purpose would eventually take hold.

The Cultural Revolution

The Great Proletarian Cultural Revolution, or simply Cultural Revolution as it came to be known, was by any standard one of the most remarkable social and political movements of modern times. It has also been subject to both partial representation and misrepresentation of the factual record, and also widely differing interpretations of that record. Many of those caught up in the movement suffered severely, and many died of this persecution as "class enemies" and "counter-revolutionaries" were identified and dispatched without even the formality of a trial. For these reasons, and because feeling ran high among those who participated in it, some of whom are still alive, it may be many years if ever before we arrive at a more objective understanding of its true dynamics. Nonetheless, it is still possible to form an interim judgement as to what this movement was about, and indeed this will be necessary if we are to understand how China ultimately moved from the equality in poverty of the 1950s to become a rising force in the global economy in more recent times; the Cultural Revolution was the catharsis which resolved a number of pressing issues, prompting China to move on.

The political scientist James Wang has offered a succinct summary of prevailing explanations for the Cultural Revolution: that it was an ideological crusade; a campaign against bureaucracy; a reflection of policy differences; a power struggle; and a response to events outside China.[15] How plausible is each of these interpretations?

First and foremost, the Cultural Revolution was an ideological crusade. Mao Zedong was unwavering in his commitment to the cause that had brought the Communist Party to power in 1949; by the mid-1960s he felt that many Party members of his own generation were losing their enthusiasm for this cause, while the rising generation no longer had any direct experience of revolutionary struggle. He wanted to unleash a movement which would foster revolutionary spirit among the young, "courting struggle to see what came out of it," as one commentator has observed.[16] A revival of class struggle, and a succession of intense political campaigns, were certainly an integral part of this process.

The Cultural Revolution was also in its early phase a campaign to counter bureaucratization. Given China's tradition of Confucian bureaucracy going back more than 2,000 years, it is scarcely surprising that organs of government under the People's Republic, and even the Party itself, should have become progressively more bureaucratic and less responsive to people's needs. Here a notable target identified by Mao was the Confucian presumption that "those who labour with their minds rule, and those who labour with their hands are ruled." This attitude, Mao felt, was completely unacceptable in People's China. To address this problem, the practice was introduced of forcing administrators (and other professionals) to move to the countryside, often to spend years performing *"laodong"* — manual labour. In this way they could, he felt, learn from the peasants, and gain a better understanding of their way of life.

A third dimension of the Cultural Revolution was that it was a reflection of genuine policy differences among the leadership of the Party. These were especially focused in the case of economic policy. As noted above, in the early to mid-1960s, many in the Party felt that the focus should still be on capital intensive heavy industry, that material incentives should be introduced, markets and private plots should become a permanent feature of the economy, profit and loss accounting should be introduced, and that the formation of a materially-privileged elite was acceptable. This approach was anathema to Mao and his supporters, who believed that such policies would constitute a complete betrayal of the revolution. On the issue of economic policy some of the most heated debate took place, and it was already clear by 1965 that neither side was ready to compromise.

Another way of understanding the Cultural Revolution is to see it as a power struggle. This explanation, favoured by some professional observers and the popular Western media of the time, tended to place emphasis on personal rivalry above all else. The belief was that Mao and his fellow revolutionaries, united by the struggle to achieve victory in 1949, had simply fallen out when the common threat of the Guomindang had been removed and the first flush of revolutionary success had faded. Party discipline, and the doctrine of criticism and self-criticism applied to various senior revolutionaries at different times, had undoubtedly compounded the jealousies which had grown up among the rather introverted clique of most senior leaders. Yet on its own this does not seem an adequate way of summing up this extraordinary mass movement.

Finally, in no small measure, the Cultural Revolution was a response to events outside China, and in particular the Vietnam War. The decision of the United States from 1964 onward to dramatically increase its direct involvement in the civil war in Vietnam raised the stakes very substantially for Vietnam's immediate neighbour, China. With progressively greater numbers of American troops, ships and planes within easy striking distance of China, the possibility that the US would attack China if, as was expected at the time, it scored a quick and easy victory over North Vietnam loomed very large in the minds of Chinese planners. For Mao and his group, essential to China having any prospect of fighting off this new potential enemy would be the thorough radicalization of her people, and their wholesale dedication through a series of political campaigns to the defence of the motherland. Thus not only would China supply and support North Vietnam throughout the period of the Cultural Revolution, but also the intense political activity within China at this time was deemed by some to be a tactic for the country's survival.

Each of these explanations, therefore, may be considered to be valid to describe and account in part for the Cultural Revolution. In reality, they must be taken together if we are to come anywhere near a holistic understanding of this event.

The principal incidents of the Cultural Revolution may be recalled here in outline; for those with a particular interest, further reading is recommended. In the event, the trigger for the Cultural Revolution was a fierce debate beginning in November 1965 over the meaning of a play entitled *Hai Rui Dismissed from Office*, written by Wu Han, the Deputy Mayor of Beijing. Apparently about the dismissal of a Ming Dynasty official for criticizing the Emperor, the play was taken by Mao and his supporters as a criticism of Mao. The two sides joined in literary and verbal conflict, with Marshal Lin Biao leading Mao's supporters on one side, and President Liu Shaoqi and the Beijing Mayor Peng Zhen his opponents on the other. "Big character posters," as they were called, putting one or other side of the argument began to appear on walls all over China. Mass criticism and purges of some of the anti-Mao faction followed in the spring of 1966. The debate spread to China's universities, initially Beijing and Tsinghua, where groups of so-called Red Guards were formed to defend Mao and protect the revolution.

On 8 August 1966, at the Eleventh Plenum of the Eighth Central Committee of the Communist Party, the defining document of the Cultural Revolution was published; this was the "Decision of the Central Committee of the Chinese Communist Party Concerning the Great Proletarian Cultural Revolution," or more briefly, the "Sixteen Points." The document urged China's people to:

...struggle against and overthrow those persons in authority who are taking the capitalist road, to criticize and repudiate the reactionary bourgeois academic "authorities" and the ideology of the bourgeoisie and all other exploiting classes, and to transform education, literature and art and all other parts of the superstructure not in correspondence with the socialist economic base, so as to facilitate the consolidation and development of the socialist system.[17]

The "Decision" went on, *inter alia*, to make clear that the masses of workers, peasants, soldiers, revolutionary intellectuals and revolutionary cadres would be the backbone of the Cultural Revolution, that the Party must "trust the masses," and that new "revolutionary groups, committees and congresses" would be significant organs of power during the Cultural Revolution. In September *Quotations from Chairman Mao Tse-tung* — the famous "little red book" — was published, providing an essential summary of Mao's ideology which could, and would, be studied assiduously by all Chinese over the next ten years.

The promulgation of this programme represented a clear victory in the short term for Mao and his supporters, and unleashed a wave of intense political activity. Throughout China, schools and universities closed as students were encouraged to form themselves into Red Guard contingents, and travel about the country criticizing teachers, professors, party cadres, factory administrators and experts everywhere for their allegedly bourgeois thinking and style of life. Only a year later did the Party Central Committee order the re-opening of educational institutions. However, some universities had still not reopened their doors four years later, while all suffered from a dramatic lowering of academic standards throughout the period of the Cultural Revolution.

Violent clashes took place with increasing frequency, between pro- and anti-Mao groups and even among groups claiming to be on the same side. Production was all too often disrupted. Revolutionary Committees were set up to displace Party organs in many areas, and on 7 May 1968 the first of many "May 7th Schools" was opened to indoctrinate and re-train supposedly wayward Party cadres. As early as January 1967 it was becoming apparent to Mao that the internal disorder he had helped to create was getting out of hand, and the People's Liberation Army was ordered to take action to restore the peace. This proved to be much harder than expected, however, involving as it did the effective countermanding of instructions given to China's young people only a few months before. Violence would continue to rise to a peak in the spring of 1968 before the PLA finally gained control of the situation, backed by unequivocal instructions from the top that the "creative anarchy" of the previous two years was to end. By 1969 China had regained some level of normality.

Yet the Cultural Revolution was not over, and many observers would take the view that in terms of a continuity of ideological values and objectives it ended only with the death of Mao in 1976. Constant political study in the fields and in the factories became the order of the day. Political campaigns succeeded one another, highlighting the need to learn from the masses, to criticize Lin Biao and Confucius, to root out liberalism and bourgeois rights, to focus on the dictatorship of the proletariat, to take class struggle as the key. Revolutionary Committees became in their turn ossified, or at the other extreme fraught with power politics and used as the means to settle personal scores. Mao's perceived opponents from among the original generation of revolutionaries were isolated and discarded, or disappeared under mysterious circumstances: Peng Zhen, Mayor of Beijing, and Luo Ruiqing, Chief of Staff of the PLA, among others, purged in 1966; Deng Xiaoping, forced to write a self-criticism and sidelined the same year; Liu Shaoqi, who was arrested in 1968 and expelled from the Party, and subsequently died; Lin Biao, who after allegedly trying to assassinate Mao, died in a plane crash in Mongolia in 1971. Of the inner circle only Zhou Enlai, Mao's circumspect Foreign Minister, survived unscathed throughout this period, only to die of cancer in 1976.

From around 1973, as Mao became less active both physically and mentally, a small group of his close advisers increasingly spoke on his behalf. Led by his third wife Jiang Qing, this group, which also included Zhang Qunqiao, Yao Wenyuan and Wang Hongwen, would be referred to retrospectively as the "Gang of Four." Indeed, Mao was said himself to have coined this phrase in a warning to them as late as May 1975. The accusation levelled at them after Mao's death would be that they had effectively usurped power from Mao as his faculties failed him, pursuing policies that were both muddled and reckless. However, that they could do this was in large part a consequence of Mao's own determination to undermine the institutions of Party and state which, by 1976, had left China exhausted, confused, and rudderless.

So what in the end was the outcome of the Cultural Revolution? Again, James Wang offers a succinct summary: the provinces gained in power at the expense of the centre; the military gained in influence; educational opportunities for rural areas had increased; bureaucratization was highlighted as a problem. All this was true, in the short term at least, though it could be pointed out that the military's influence did not last long, and that the positive climate for rural education was also short-lived. To these could be added major achievements in the provision of health care to rural communities through the "barefoot doctor" programme and in the widespread use of acupuncture and other forms of traditional Chinese medicine, as well as the emphasis placed on the role and potential of women in all walks of life and at all levels, an emphasis that has since been partially lost.

However, it could be contended that the most significant achievement of the Cultural Revolution was to exhaust the Chinese people's interest in and capacity for development driven by radical ideology. Mao had sought to implement political struggle as a way of life for China's people, most of whom in the event saw it only as a means to an end. The trauma of the Cultural Revolution left most people yearning for peace, and for prosperity to be achieved by almost any other means.

4

FROM MARXISM TO MARKETISM

The 'four modernizations'

The end of an era

In 1976, more than a quarter of a century after the founding of the People's Republic, China was ripe for change. Among the last of those remaining from the first generation of revolutionaries died that year — Premier Zhou Enlai in January, Marshal Zhu De in June, and Chairman Mao Zedong himself in September. Moreover, in July China experienced the tumultuous Tangshan earthquake, in which the final death toll was put at 242,000.[1]

Traditionally, a major natural disaster was seen as a harbinger of political change. In the end it was Mao's death on 9 September that triggered that change. For almost four weeks uncertainty prevailed, then the decision was taken to arrest the Gang of Four. With this step, the Cultural Revolution was unequivocally over.

With no clear procedure in place for political succession, it was some time before the matter of who was now to lead China was resolved. Deng Xiaoping was an obvious contender. Forced to make a self-criticism in 1966 in the early stages of the Cultural Revolution and subsequently demoted, Deng had become a Vice Premier once again by 1973. The Gang of Four believed him to be hostile to its goals, however, and as Mao was growing weaker, there was a determined effort to block him from power. In Beijing in early April 1976, at the time of the Qing Ming festival when the dead are honoured, a major expression of popular feeling had occurred when thousands of people attempted to lay flowers on Zhou Enlai's grave. Demonstrations in sympathy took place in cities across China, and were marked by anti-government feeling, resulting in many arrests. Deng was blamed, and once more dismissed. Hua Guofeng, who had been Acting Premier since February, was now confirmed as Premier.

Thus it was Hua and not Deng who appeared immediately to inherit the mantle of power, and claims were circulated that Hua had been Mao's own chosen successor. Yet Hua was inexperienced, and lacked any real power base of his own — his support came largely from those who wished to see Mao's policies continued. Early in 1977 a poster campaign began calling for the restoration of Deng Xiaoping. Such was the desire to see Mao's policies and those who still believed in them blocked once and for all that in July 1977 Deng was restored to the Politburo and its Standing Committee, and became once more a Vice Premier, Chief of Staff of the PLA, and a Deputy Chairman of the Military Affairs Commission. From this platform he would serve as the power behind the throne in China right up almost until his death in 1997.

Although there were occasional references still to Mao's contribution and to aspects of his ideology, the writing was increasingly on the wall (sometimes literally) for those who favoured radical political solutions. In February 1978 a new National People's Congress was convened (the Fifth), the revolutionary committees of the Cultural Revolution were finally abolished, and a new Ten Year Plan was announced which called for industry to increase by 10 per cent per annum, and agriculture by 4 to 5 per cent per annum. In April the *People's Daily* carried for the first time an editorial urging the integration of "moral encouragement with material rewards." A National Conference on Education Work in April called for higher academic standards and respect for teachers. In June, Deng Xiaoping in a speech to the PLA urged people for the first time to "Seek truth from facts!" (*shi shi qiu shi*), implying that ideological solutions which disregarded reality had for too long dominated the Party's work.

In December 1978 the Party committed itself to carrying out a programme of modernization throughout China, of industry, agriculture, science and technology and national defence — the so-called "four modernizations." Just before this China had signed two agreements for business co-operation with the United States, one for Coca Cola to be bottled and sold in China, the other for the purchase by China of three

Boeing jumbo jets. The beginning of co-operation with these companies, both icons of capitalism, was a symbolic and defining moment. A few days after the Party meeting, Deng Xiaoping embarked on his ground-breaking trip to the United States, the first by any leader of the People's Republic. By now, the die was cast.

The imperatives of modernization

In 1979, thirty years after the founding of the People's Republic, China was taking stock of itself. Up until the Communist takeover, 100 years of contact with the West, conditioned by the Unequal Treaties, had brought little in the way of modernity to China or economic benefit to the great bulk of its population. Ten years of hard slog after 1949 had, ironically with Soviet help, brought a degree of industrialization and a measure of self-sufficiency. Much had been achieved too in the broader sharing of the burden of China's continuing relative poverty, but the political means to achieve this had in time become an end in itself, and dragged the country down into the Cultural Revolution. If there was one thing on which almost all of China's people agreed at the end of the 1970s it was that the cost in emotional, psychological and even physical distress of the methods used during the Cultural Revolution was too great to be sustained or repeated.

Deng Xiaoping was therefore not alone in believing that another way must be found to take China forward. It could be argued that, as with some other Chinese leaders, underlying Deng's life-long commitment to Marxism was a strong vein of nationalism. Accepting in the 1920s that China was one nation among others, and no longer a universal Empire, Deng had always wanted to see China become strong and prosperous. By 1979 he had concluded that self-sufficiency and reliance on ideological exhortation would not achieve this, and that another way must be found.

Moreover the need for a new approach was urgent. The industrial technology that China had acquired from the Soviet Union in the 1950s was even then far from being the latest available — the Liberation truck for example, produced in China from 1955 to 1990, was originally a 1938 Dodge design acquired by the Soviet Union from the US under the "lend-lease" arrangement during World War Two. This was not only a matter of prestige, but also of practicality; old equipment broke down frequently and wasn't up to the job. China needed a very broad range of industrial equipment in great quantity to facilitate the upgrading of its infrastructure and the rapid development of its economy.

The essence of the problem was that as things stood China had no means of paying for this new technology. A return to the credit arrangements of the 1950s was not possible. Relations with most of the Communist world were very strained, while Western countries were generally unwilling to trade on that basis. Nor did China have the surplus grain to underwrite such an approach.

Clearly, the West and Japan would be the best sources of technology, and China would have to gear up to export to those countries to generate the foreign exchange to pay for the technology and equipment it needed. Indeed, it would have somehow to find the capital to buy the equipment to manufacture export goods to pay for more imports of equipment. The only course appeared to be to invite foreign companies to invest in China, initially through joint ventures with state-owned enterprises, and this was what was done.

To say that this was to turn Mao on his head would be to understate the case. A prime tenet of Marxism, and especially the Marxism of Mao Zedong, was the inevitable collapse of capitalism. For this reason, China under Mao had been careful never to involve itself to any great extent with the international economy, buying in small quantities from capitalist powers only those things that it really needed, and then usually for cash. Its exports to the West and Japan up until 1979 had been almost insignificant, consisting largely of handicrafts and specialist food items.

For China, therefore, the decision to "open up" to the global economy was of critical importance. Taking a path already followed by the East Asian tiger economies, but going well beyond what they had achieved, China would over the next few years become a major supplier of all kinds of manufactured goods to Western countries and Japan, through a variety of mechanisms which included subcontracted manufacture, foreign investment in joint ventures, and ultimately the acceptance of wholly foreign-owned subsidiaries. From the early 1980s onward, despite occasional uncertainties over policy, new technology poured into China at a rapid rate. This generated in time a self-sustaining momentum and an apparently unstoppable process of economic development, which was nonetheless not without its contradictions (see Chapter 10).

Ultimately, not only technical capacity was acquired, but a whole new view of the world consequent on China's engagement with the international economy just at the point when the communications revolution was reaching its take-off stage. Contact with foreigners grew exponentially, and it was not only the techniques of international business that were imbibed. Attitudes changed, tastes changed, and with them the expectations of young people who soon would have only the dimmest memory, if any, not only of the struggle for liberation but even of the Cultural Revolution.

Deng Xiaoping memorably summed up the spirit of the times with his comment that "...it doesn't matter if the cat is black or white, as long as it catches mice!,"[2] supposed to have been uttered in justification of adopting some of the approaches of capitalism in pursuit of what was still said to be the goal of socialism. In due course the phrase "socialist market economy" began to be used to describe the current transitional phase of the Chinese economic situation. In parallel with the campaign to encourage foreign investors to come to China, significant changes were taking place in the way the domestic economy was ordered and run.

The first of these affected the agricultural economy. From 1979, beginning in Sichuan, the so-called "contract system in agriculture" was introduced, under which an individual or a group could contract with a local government authority to cultivate privately tracts of land, paying a fee in cash or kind, and selling the rest of their produce in new small local markets. This change in policy, which was extremely popular because it effectively made the family once again the main unit of production in agriculture, soon spread throughout China. In 1982 the Communes were abolished as the main administrative bodies in the countryside, and land was no longer regarded as state-owned (though the precise locus of ownership in law remained for some time unclear). In some instances co-operatives were formed on a voluntary basis for the provision of services before and after production. The new system was characterized by flourishing free markets in produce, diversification of production, and in many but not all parts of China a new rural prosperity. On the negative side, there was a loss of unprofitable grain production, the cultivation of much unsuitable grazing land, the erosion of topsoil, and the neglect of public works.

In industry, in part to try to attract foreign investment, regulations governing the administration of factories were progressively and substantially revised. All state-owned enterprises were made responsible for their own profits and losses. Responsibility for the operation of individual enterprises was devolved downward onto their management from higher-level bureaux and Ministries, and the factory director was now supposed to have final control over planning, purchasing of supplies, production, marketing the product, hiring and firing staff, incentive systems, and other essential matters, changes introduced from the mid-1980s with effect at different times in different parts of China.

These new requirements were embodied in the Contract Responsibility System legislation of 1987. In fact there were many problems in the implementation of these regulations, and many supposedly independent factory directors complained bitterly about the continuing influence of the local Party Secretary over what they could and could not do (see Chapter 9). Further efforts would be made to refine enterprise management in the 1990s.

Accompanying these developments was a series of measures designed directly to facilitate trade. They included a progressively more comprehensive body of commercial law to regulate international transactions and the activities of foreign corporate entities in China; financial measures to attract foreign investment in joint ventures in China; the publication of information about key Chinese requirements for foreign technology; and the designation of four (later five) Special Economic Zones in Shenzhen, Shantou and Zhuhai in Guangdong Province, Xiamen in Fuzhou, and later of Hainan Island. In these latter areas especially favourable terms were available to foreign investors with respect to matters such as customs procedures, taxes, employment legislation and building regulations.

Here, mention should also be made of the dramatic growth in the number of township and village enterprises in China from the mid-1980s. A precondition for this was the dissolution of the Communes as administrative entities, beginning in 1982, opening the way for greater initiative at the local level in the manufacturing of goods and the provision of services. In some instances, these ventures drew in the early years on capital from agriculture, derived from the successful cultivation and sale through the new free markets of new crops that were profitable and in demand. In other cases, initial capital came from local authorities. Either way, the "TVEs" contributed very substantially to the rise in prosperity at the local level in much (though not all) of China. Such enterprises were believed to number twenty-two million by 1995 (Chen Hongyi).

They did, however, suffer from certain drawbacks. The TVEs could perhaps be seen as following a precedent established in China by the pre-war and wartime co-operatives, and echoed to a degree by local industrial ventures under the post-1949 Co-op and Commune systems; just as with the pre-1949 experiments with small-scale industry, many manufacturing TVEs lacked both capital and scale, and were unstable in consequence, remaining both local and low-tech operations. Their contribution to the upgrading of China's *strategic* industrial and technological capacity has therefore been limited. The TVEs' greatest success has perhaps been in the provision of local services, such as hotels, restaurants, and other tourist facilities.

There were two other areas in which developments beginning at the end of the 1970s should be noted. In foreign policy, China benefited from a thaw in relations with the United States. The superpower that had been the architect of the policy of isolation and containment in the early 1950s had already made a move to disengage from that policy with Richard Nixon's visit to China in 1972. It had not been possible to do much more while the Cultural Revolution persisted, but the US withdrawal from Vietnam in 1975, and Mao's death in 1976, removed two obstacles to further progress towards normalization of relations; indeed, by 1980 China was fighting its own brief war with Vietnam. On 1 January 1979 full diplomatic relations were established between the US and China, and on 1 July the US upgraded its representation in Beijing from Chargé d'Affaires, which had been the level since the office first opened in 1972, to Ambassador. The first diplomat to fill the new post was George Bush Senior. Now China would have unprecedented access to the modern technology and expert assistance that it would increasingly desire.

The other development was the first real attempt to push at the bounds of political freedom since the Party had come to power in 1949 — indeed, it could be said, since the May 4th Movement of 1919. In October 1978 young people in Beijing began to put up posters on a wall beside the Xi Dan bus station bearing essays and poems calling for measures to implement socialist democracy in China. All over the country their actions were replicated by other young people, hoping to influence the imminent meeting of the Party Central Committee. Unauthorized magazines began to appear carrying titles like *China's Human Rights*, *Enlightenment* and *Exploration*. The atmosphere of expectancy was heightened by the return to Beijing and other cities of people exiled to the countryside during the Cultural Revolution, as well as large numbers of unemployed, and many who had been victims of abuse and injustice during the ten years of upheaval. Collectively they were known as the "petitioners."

It was in this context that Wei Jingsheng, a cadre's son, electrician and former PLA man, in December 1978 put up his poster calling for democracy as the "Fifth Modernization." He followed this with two longer pieces in December and January in *Exploration (Tansuo)*, the journal which he edited. Wei argued that socialist democracy was the pre-condition for the release of the productive forces, and China's modernization, and should not be put off as something to be achieved in time. He criticized the Party's record in achieving progress for ordinary people, deploring the continuing poverty, abuse and corruption of everyday life.

As the arguments of Wei and others began to circulate more widely, demonstrations occurred in Beijing and other cities with some people beginning to call for "human rights and democracy." By mid-January the authorities had had enough. A series of arrests followed, culminating most notably in Wei Jingsheng's own arrest towards the end of March on charges of subversion, and the leaking of state secrets (which he denied) to a foreign journalist; Wei was sentenced to fifteen years in gaol. On 1 April all posters were banned from Democracy Wall, and although not all posters were removed immediately, henceforth only authorized posters were permitted, and these had to be placed in a prescribed area far from the centre of the city. The Beijing Spring of early 1979, as it had come to be known, had come to an end. The implications of the Democracy Movement will be explored more fully in another chapter (see Chapter 11). When Deng Xiaoping set out on his ground-breaking trip to the United States in late January, he would do so with a clear mind on the issue of democracy: for now, indeed for as far ahead as one could see, it would not be a part of China's modernization.

Tiananmen and after

Yet as the process of engagement with the outside world gathered pace in the early 1980s, China's economy grew, and social structures flexed and changed to accommodate the imperatives of that process of engagement, it became increasingly difficult to see how foreign influences and political ideas could be kept out. The Party was faced with the same challenge as the Qing dynasty when it had tried to use Western learning for practical application while preserving Chinese learning for the fundamental principles. Increasing numbers of foreign experts and business people came to China in the course of the ever more rapid implementation of technology transfer. Chinese people went abroad in ever greater numbers, sent there by the Government to obtain the skills that China now so desperately needed. The widespread new passion for learning English enabled those determined enough to find sources of news and developments abroad sufficient to challenge long-held beliefs derived from the Party's orthodoxy about political matters.

Officially the bounds to debate had been set by Deng Xiaoping at the end of March 1979, when in an address to the Party's conference on theoretical work he identified four "cardinal" or "basic" principles which people genuinely loyal to the Party should observe: continue to follow the socialist road; support the dictatorship of the proletariat; uphold the leadership of the Communist Party; and adhere to Marxism, Leninism, Mao Zedong Thought.[3] However, in practice the 1980s were characterized by cycles of reform and repression in politics, just as they were a time of experiment, then retrenchment, then innovation once again in the economy, and the four cardinal principles seemed to have progressively less relevance as China's circumstances changed.

In 1979 and 1980, the opening up to foreign investment was a time of great optimism, and even of some political promise despite the failure of the Beijing Spring. Yet in 1980, also, the film *Bitter Love*, in which the scriptwriter Bai Hua sought to air the excesses of the Cultural Revolution, was suppressed. From 1981 to 1984 it is possible to discern a greater emphasis on stability, following the first flush of enthusiasm, and this was accompanied for a time by a campaign against "spiritual pollution." From 1984 to 1986 there was once again a period of relative relaxation, but it was accompanied by overheating of the economy and inflation. In 1987 and 1988 there was much discussion of separation of the state from the economy, and the Contract Responsibility System was introduced for management of industrial enterprises (see Chapter 9); but there was also further overheating, a degree of panic in government, and a measure of repression.

Most significant from the point of view of events leading up to the Tiananmen crisis of 1989, though, was the renewed discussion of democracy in the latter half of 1986. In particular, Fang Lizhi, the eminent physicist and Vice-President of the University of Science and Technology in Hefei, one of China's leading scientific institutions, and the writer Liu Binyan had both been pressing the case for democracy, and had for several years criticized the Party for failing to listen to "loyal opponents." In December 1986, student demonstrations in support of democracy broke out in Hefei, and soon spread to other cities. In January, both Fang and Liu were dismissed from the Party, and in other ways humiliated. Soon afterwards Hu Yaobang, Secretary-General of the Party, was forced to resign from that position, taking the blame for allowing a situation to develop in which calls for democracy could re-emerge. In the spring of 1987 the Party sanctioned a further campaign to glorify the self-sacrifice of the model soldier Lei Feng around whom a propaganda campaign had been built in the 1960s, setting itself against any further discussion of democracy, socialist or otherwise.

Through 1987 and into 1988 the hardliners in the Party held sway, while those who may have felt differently kept their own counsel. Among them was Premier Zhao Ziyang. In early 1989, a series of events began to take place that would lead inexorably to the confrontation in Tiananmen Square on 3–4 June.

Forty years on from the Liberation, and ten years after Democracy Wall, discussion again began to take place among intellectuals of the prospects for democracy. On 15 April 1989 the former Secretary General Hu Yaobang was taken ill and died of a heart attack. Two days later a memorial rally was held in Tiananmen Square by students from various universities in Beijing, to honour Hu and to call for more democracy and less corruption. This turned into a sit-in the following day. Hu's funeral was held on 22 April, by which time students had occupied the square, beginning to boycott classes shortly afterwards.

The square remained occupied and demonstrations and rallies continued over the next month. In mid-May the Soviet President Gorbachev came to China on a long-planned visit; students used the occasion to highlight the reforms he had brought to the Soviet system. In the event, the visit was disrupted by the presence of so many demonstrators in the square, and the Chinese government was further embarrassed. Some 3,000 students went on hunger strike, and numbers in the square swelled to more than a million at times. The Chinese press became increasingly bold in reporting developments.

On 20 May the hard-line faction within the Party, led by Li Peng but with the apparent support of Deng Xiaoping, declared martial law. For two weeks, local troops ordered to clear the square by force if necessary, declined to resort to force and made little headway. Art students erected a large plaster statue to represent the goddess of democracy and freedom. Many ordinary citizens became involved in erecting barricades in the streets leading to the square, as the protest spilled out of Tiananmen and engaged people all over Beijing and in other cities all over China.

Then, on the night of 3 June, the troops struck. These were not troops from the Beijing garrison, reluctant to fire on fellow residents of the city, but rather seasoned soldiers brought in from other parts of China, and loyal to the hard-line military commander Yang Shangkun. In front of the world's press, the People's Liberation Army converged on Tiananmen with tanks and guns and by morning had crushed all resistance. Estimates of the numbers killed range from 300 to 3,000, with many thousands more injured, many of them ordinary citizens who had sought to intervene. The Party was back in control.

Li Peng in particular was credited with the decision to use force, though the authority undoubtedly came from Deng Xiaoping, who had lost all patience with the students. Zhao Ziyang, who had visited and shown sympathy for the students on 19 May, was dismissed and replaced as Secretary-General by Jiang Zemin, until then Party Secretary in Shanghai. Deng was quoted as saying that China must achieve reform in its own way, and not by "importing evil influences from the West."[4]

There can be little doubt that the call for democracy in this instance had been an expression of discontent stemming from a number of causes. The movement was undoubtedly complex, and the reasons for it, and its significance, are discussed further in another chapter (see Chapter 11). In its aftermath, the government cracked down on dissent everywhere, imprisoning as many student activists as it could find, and dealing harshly also with workers and other citizens who had intervened on their behalf. The leading universities which had spawned much of the activity, Beida, Renda and others, both in Beijing and in other cities, were subject to strict supervision and control over the next two years or so. Ties with foreign institutions became suddenly more difficult. The Chinese media were strictly monitored once again, and some journalists who had actively supported the students paid with their lives.

The Chinese government and Communist Party in turn paid with their reputation in the international community. The World Bank immediately suspended all new loans to China. Other multilateral bodies did the same. Many countries ceased bilateral aid and funding for joint projects, and most loans from foreign commercial banks were also frozen. For a period of two to three years, outside funding for China's further modernization all but dried up.[5] Moreover, foreign businesses, many of which had invested heavily in joint ventures in China in the belief that the Party had set aside ideology in favour of pragmatism once and for all, were severely shaken by the events of June 1989. Foreign business activity in China plummeted, and it would be a more sober group of investors that gradually started to return in 1991.

In time, of course, almost all sanctions were lifted, but the dimension of political risk is now taken far more seriously by foreign institutions than it was before Tiananmen, even at the time of writing, almost twenty years after the event.

'Going for growth'

Making money is glorious

It is said that in the 1980s Deng Xiaoping, when asked whether it was acceptable that some people would be likely to become rich if the trend of China's new policies continued, responded that, "Making money is glorious!" Or more precisely, "Don't be afraid to be rich. Let a few get rich first, then the rest will follow suit."[6] The 1990s, following the recovery by around 1992 from the consequences of the Tiananmen massacre, were the decade *par excellence* in which the dream of wealth would come true for a small but significant number of Chinese citizens.

From the early 1980s, the statistical evidence points to a rate of economic growth unparalleled at the time, even by the much smaller "tiger" economies of East and Southeast Asia. That this growth should continue unabated, except for a downturn following Tiananmen, through the 1990s into the new century, and up to the present day, shows that it was not simply a consequence of starting from a very low base; rather, the growth was both exponential and comprehensive, as China, for the first time ever, fully engaged with the rest of the world.

The statistics point to an average growth rate of around 8% per year in GDP for the whole twenty-five-year period from 1978, when the modernization programme began, up until 2003, with 7% being the target figure from 2004.[7] In fact this target has been easily exceeded. While in some years the rate of growth was lower, such as immediately following the Tiananmen incident,[8] in others it was substantially higher, as in 1992 and 1993 when 13%[9] was attained. China's GDP in 2007 stood at 24,953 billion yuan,[10] and according to the World Bank China has the world's third largest economy, after those of the US and Japan. In 2009, growth in GDP was reported as 8.7%, despite the world recession. Inflation skyrocketed in 1994 to 24%, but it was down to 2.8% by 1997 and has remained relatively low.[11]

Much of this success is a consequence of China's trading activity and manufacture for export. China's exports increased in value on average by 19% annually between 1986 and 1998.[12] In 2007 the value of its exports stood at US$1,218 billion, 95% of which were commodity exports, while its imports stood at US$956 billion.[13] Trade between China and most developed countries, including most of Western Europe, the United States and Japan is substantially in China's favour, and a cause of some friction. With Australia, Canada and certain other suppliers of raw materials, the situation is different.

With this dramatic rise in economic activity has come a similarly startling rise in average income. By 2007 China's GDP per capita was already officially 18,934 yuan.[14] By 2006 the average wage had reached 24,932 yuan.[15] However the distribution of this income is the critical issue here.

The first parts of China to benefit from this new prosperity were the Special Economic Zones, especially Shenzhen on the border with Hong Kong — which mushroomed from a fishing village to become within twenty years one of the largest conurbations in South China. Other coastal areas of Eastern China to benefit were major cities like: Guangzhou, Shanghai, Ningbo, Amoy, Tianjin, the capital Beijing, and the areas of adjacent provinces that were drawn into their heightened economic activity through the provision of food, services and labour for new industries.

Within these geographical locations, economic development and its benefits outpaced those in the rest of China. But even in these areas, not everyone profited in the same way from the new activity. Workers in the SEZs were paid at a much better rate than their counterparts living in areas that did not have this special status, even in coastal cities like Shanghai. Workers in joint venture companies, or in the small but growing number of privately-owned Chinese companies, generally enjoyed much better terms and conditions than those in struggling state-owned enterprises. Industries like construction, as they began to flourish, offered rural migrant labourers new opportunities to earn money, but often at the expense of health and safety considerations and with no job security.

Educated professionals — teachers and academics, scientists, engineers, doctors and other health workers, journalists and specialists of all kinds — also fared quite poorly as for the most part they remained outside the whirlwind of money-making activity, stuck on fixed incomes determined and provided by the state, while prices continued to rise around them, reflecting the increasingly market-driven economy.

Government and Party officials too ostensibly lost out under the new arrangements, as their salaries climbed only slowly. Yet unlike most professionals, they were able to cushion the effects of the market economy on their way of life through having access to goods and services in consequence of their official positions. These might include subsidized or free accommodation, numerous meals and entertainment, domestic travel (including for leisure purposes), medical attention, child care, pensions, even in some cases the sole use of a car and driver, and frequent access to free overseas trips. These were the "legitimate" perks of office. Beyond this emerged a pattern among some officials of personal involvement in questionable money-making ventures, the taking of bribes in exchange for permission for projects to go ahead, the peddling of influence, and general corruption.

The heightened economic activity in the coastal cities, therefore, generated wealth benefiting some very much more than others. Elsewhere in China, in the 1990s, as a general rule the further inland one travelled, the less was the obvious impact of modernization, and the poorer the rural communities. While the household responsibility system in agriculture had by now become widespread, the market mechanism, which had made rural communities close to the coastal cities more prosperous, failed to work in the same way in the remote regions of the hinterland where the cities were fewer and poorer. In these areas, where conditions on the land were often harder in any case, the loss of the collective approach of the old Commune system was felt more acutely. Peasants were now all too often alone against the elements. Moreover, because the cities themselves were poorer and had attracted little investment, the opportunities in industry and in construction were simply not there for migrant workers from the countryside.

The Northeast of China faced particular problems of its own. With an industrial infrastructure originally laid down by Japan during its occupation of the area in the 1930s, and built upon further with Soviet assistance in the 1950s, the Northeast had seen little development since. Its by now antiquated state-owned mills and factories were grossly inefficient and incapable of attracting foreign investment. Its geographical location was awkward, quite some distance from the main domestic markets, and hindered by out-of-date port facilities from playing a full part in international trade. Moreover, in the view of some officials, its population was disinclined to play its full part in the modernization of the country, and had set itself against change (a view perhaps conditioned in part by a longstanding antipathy to Manchus among Han Chinese).

In China as a whole therefore, the result of the situation described was a degree of inequity in the distribution of the benefits of modernization, depending on where one lived, what one did for a living, and how much influence one derived from one's position both at work and in society. This inequity extended well beyond the "normal" disparities of a market economy to encompass injustice often rooted in arbitrary old policies, arbitrary new ones, and the absence of an effective legal framework to govern the transition between the two. In its long history, China's successive ruling regimes had almost always in the end succumbed over the issue of how to secure the people's livelihood. The growing wealth gap in the China of the 1990s contained within it the seeds of conflict yet again over this issue, an issue that continues to be of concern in the new century.

Meanwhile, as the world approached the millennium, visitors to China who had known the country in earlier times could only marvel at the evidence of dramatic change in its major cities, which were the destination of most visitors. Massive marble and concrete hotels appeared along Jianguomenwai in Beijing, demolishing the *hutong*s and courtyard houses from which the citizenry had emerged to engage the troops in 1989. An entire new city centre across the river in Pudong appeared in Shanghai, a place whose time had come in the 1990s and whose skills and style were once more in vogue. Foreign and, increasingly, Chinese business people and officials criss-crossed the country in new aircraft, flying to new terminals in cities where money was to be made. Below them, more slowly, migrant workers travelled back and forth from the countryside to the nearest big city, no longer constrained by laws restricting freedom of travel, and hoping to supplement the family income with whatever work might be available, just as they had before the Communist era. Towards the end of the decade the private car, that totem of modernity, began to appear on city streets in ever-increasing numbers. China had arrived.

Preparing for take-off

As the process of engagement with the international economy and norms of political behaviour became increasingly irreversible, China came face to face with issues of global concern. Among these of prime importance were the environment and global warming, human rights, the regulation of international trade, and the pursuit of peace and global security.

On environmental matters, China's record had, like that of most countries, been patchy. A decade of Soviet-style development in the 1950s had left major problems of pollution and degradation which still had not been addressed by the 1980s. During the most complete period of isolation in the 1960s and early 1970s, however, some farming techniques had been widespread which were notably sound from an ecological point of view, such as the extensive use of night soil and other natural fertilizer on crops, while the expansion of small-scale industry was often less degrading than the continued construction of very large plants. Yet these approaches were not universal in China, and their environmental benefit was only incidental as far as the Chinese government was concerned; in reality they were adopted out of economic necessity. Questions posed in 1972 by a representative of Greenpeace during a visit to China by a delegation which included the present writer showed only a dim perception of the environmental issue, no more but no less than was the case in the West at the time.

The decision to embark on modernization following the death of Mao placed economic development at the top of a list of priorities. In the 1980s and 1990s it became very difficult to obtain a hearing for environmental concerns. The Director of Research for a leading Chinese steel company argued to the writer as late as 1995 that environmental standards belatedly put forward by Western governments were part of a plot to undermine China's economic development. Yet throughout the two decades the problems of pollution mounted: rivers were poisoned by the excessive use of chemical fertilizers and inadequate attention to industrial waste; by the mid-1980s cities like Beijing and Chonqing were subject to frequent smog; clouds of acid rain formed and dropped their loads on Eastern China and Japan; in the countryside the new market economy caused land productive for rice to be abandoned while elsewhere grazing land was ploughed up for other crops, causing the topsoil to be blown away and desertification to increase.

By the late 1990s, however, a change in attitude had begun. In part this must be ascribed to the return from overseas study and assignment to positions of responsibility of new, younger and better qualified senior managers, in some cases thirty years younger than the people they replaced. Their understanding of development often encompassed an understanding of the need for sustainability and environmental awareness. At the same time government environmental protection bodies began to have more power, and other bodies were set up to elaborate and enforce new regulations. By no means is the argument fully won, and China's attitude to the Kyoto Protocol, for example, remained ambivalent, but as China prepares for take-off this dimension of global concern at least is more firmly on the official agenda.

On human rights, China continues to stress, even in the new century, its emphasis on economic and social rights over political rights, a position that goes back to the founding of the People's Republic. While dialogue is now maintained with interested foreign governments and non-government organizations on Western-style human rights issues, largely in response to considerable pressure from overseas, the record in recent years has not been particularly good. The treatment of Wei Jingsheng and other dissidents at the start of modernization, the catastrophic breakdown of the Tiananmen massacre ten years later, and even, less dramatically, the determined deportation back to the countryside of people protesting at their lack of rights outside while the National People's Congress was discussing human rights inside, which occurred in 2004, all signal a lack of real progress on this issue. Outside Beijing, of course, out of sight is out of mind.

The Chinese position has always been that political rights are essentially a Western contrivance that may not be suited to China. They are seen as closely linked with calls for democracy, which can be permitted only in carefully-controlled circumstances, and in a Chinese way, so as not to invite degeneration into chaos in such a large country (see Chapter 11). Far better to concentrate on creating the conditions for universal prosperity which, it is felt, is the true goal of all people (a view that coincides with that of opponents of democratic reform in Hong Kong in the 1990s). While limited experiments with democratic mechanisms at the most basic level have been undertaken, political rights are at the discretion of the State, and are likely to remain so for the foreseeable future.

The regulation of international trade has become progressively important as the process of globalization has advanced over the past thirty years. GATT — the General Agreement on Tariffs and Trade — which regulated trade somewhat selectively from the 1960s onward, has given way to the World Trade Organization (WTO), to which China was admitted finally in 2002. In joining, China has accepted all the obligations of membership, with some dispensations over a transitional period. Yet some problems persist, which could, if they are not resolved, undermine the organization completely given the extent of China's involvement with the international economy.[16] These include the very serious cumulative trade imbalances between China and its major trading partners, the issue of intellectual property rights, hidden subsidies for Chinese-made goods, a still restricted domestic market, and imperfect laws governing foreign investment.

There is every likelihood that foreign trade, through manufacture for export, will continue to be the engine of growth for the Chinese economy; it is all the more important, therefore, that outstanding issues should be resolved. But if, as seems likely, China encounters in future increasing competition from new manufacturing bases with cheaper labour and perhaps a less challenging business culture, the incentive for China to comply with WTO requirements may not be so great.

In foreign policy terms, or with respect to peace and security, China's willingness to engage and the world's willingness to accept China into the international community have been the hallmarks of the past twenty-five years. Indeed, the Vietnam War artificially prolonged China's isolation by the United States, but other countries began to recognize China in the 1960s, and in 1971 it was admitted into the United Nations in place of Taiwan. As noted above, the Nixon visit to China in 1972 began a thaw in US-China relations, completed with full diplomatic recognition in 1979.

China also wished to see the resolution of injustices dating back a century and a half to the Opium Wars. Discussions began with Britain in 1984 on the retrocession of Hong Kong, part of which, the New

Territories, was only leased from China until 1997, leaving the remainder effectively unviable. After long and difficult negotiations, it was agreed that China would resume full sovereignty over Hong Kong in 1997 under a mechanism to be known as "one country, two systems," which enabled Hong Kong to keep its political, economic and legal systems for a period of fifty years. The handover was effected peacefully on 1 July 1997, despite the major trauma of the Tiananmen incident, and despite the democratic reforms of the last British Governor, Chris Patten, in the 1990s. China negotiated a similar arrangement for the return of Macao by Portugal, effected on 20 December 1999.

Taiwan and Tibet were more intractable issues. Despite ever greater flows of trade and investment between Taiwan and the mainland from the mid-1980s, China's confident expectation that Taiwan's government and population would eventually see the logic of reunification with the mainland proved unfulfilled, as sentiment in Taiwan moved ever further away from any accommodation. The danger here may lie in an inability on the part of mainland leaders to perceive the difference in circumstances between Hong Kong and Taiwan: in the first case a small city-state geographically a part of China, militarily indefensible, heavily dependent on the mainland for economic prosperity and such essentials as water; in the second case a self-sufficient island far from the mainland, militarily defensible, very well-equipped, and protected by powerful allies, with a sizeable and ethnically diverse population, and at no point in recent history effectively controlled by China. China's yearning to "reclaim" Taiwan may yet prove a threat to peace in the region as China's military might, and its naval power in the region especially, expand.

The status of Tibet, and China's human rights record there, remain of concern to governments and interested parties around the world. With China in effective control, however, and given the geographical remoteness of the territory, it is unlikely to be a focus of international conflict at any point in the near future. Whether this remoteness will serve it better domestically at any point in the future remains to be seen.

Apart from these issues, China's diplomacy as it prepares for take-off is directed towards a much more active engagement with international bodies of all kinds, the cultivation of allies on particular issues (different allies for different issues) as they are debated and adjudicated in international fora, the search for national security through sophisticated weapons systems, and the pursuit and consolidation of access to natural resources, notably oil under the South China Sea.

China's military forces ultimately provide the capability underpinning its foreign policy. Though reduced in strength over the past twenty-five years, they are now much better equipped and anxious both for co-operation with their counterparts overseas, and to acquire the latest technology from a variety of sources. In the longer term, it is the impetus to deploy those forces that will be critical. In traditional times, and indeed until very recently, China really had no foreign policy outside its borders to speak of, beyond achieving conditions in the world that would secure domestic peace and prosperity. It may be asked whether China's decision to modernize through engagement with the world, taking on the imperatives of sustained rapid development (which its population has been persuaded is the key to personal prosperity), may ultimately change that for all time.

5

THE CONFUCIAN HERITAGE
IN THEORY AND PRACTICE

In a society as long-lived as that of China, it is almost inevitable that observers will look to the particular nature of its culture to explain its longevity, and the ways in which it has adapted and survived. Attention has been drawn in previous chapters to the central role played by Confucianism in this process. In this chapter an attempt will be made to identify those aspects of Chinese culture, and especially of Confucianism, stemming from the pre-modern period, which have had a major and continuing impact on Chinese society. Reference will be made to the role of the family, to the individual's attitude to education, to commerce and to the outside world, to the principal themes of Chinese literature, and to the Chinese language itself. The "political culture" of pre-modern China — the Confucian state and its governing principles, the legal system, and paths of social mobility — will be dealt with in a subsequent chapter (see Chapter 6).

'Confucianism': how central to Chinese culture?

Confucius lived, we are told, from 551 to 479 BC — towards the end of the culturally prolific Spring and Autumn period of the Eastern Zhou Dynasty. By this time the pattern of China's development as a technologically advanced agrarian society with a large population was well established. Confucius looked back to, and was much influenced by, a body of thought proceeding out of the so-called legendary period of China's history, principally concerned with the shared morality which would be necessary for large numbers of people to live together in harmony.

Confucius therefore saw himself as the synthesizer of the wisdom of the ancient sages. By now, China's system of writing had settled down almost into the form in which it would endure over the next 2,500 years. Thus, although Confucius himself left no body of written philosophy, his disciples could and did dutifully record his thoughts and teachings for posterity. The best-known compilation of his thought is the *Analects*, twenty chapters and 497 verses which contain the core beliefs that would come to influence China so profoundly.[1]

Confucius was, as might be claimed of almost all Chinese philosophers before and since, acutely aware of the political potential of philosophy. To secure peace and good government remains a *sine qua non* for the Chinese authorities to this day, and this was Confucius' primary goal. Confucius himself hoped to become an administrator in one of the Chinese states of his day, and for a time indeed was employed in this capacity by his native state of Lu. It may therefore seem strange to treat the moral and social prescriptions of Confucius separately from their political end. However, to do so may help us to perceive the pervasive influence of Confucius over so many aspects of Chinese culture and life, while recognizing that these prescriptions all related ultimately to the need to achieve harmony for political reasons.

It has been observed elsewhere that in the Chinese philosophical tradition what was important was not the truth or falsehood of a statement or belief, but rather its behavioural implications.[2] As Charles Moore put it, writing of the humanism of Chinese philosophy as a whole, "People come first in China."[3] Arthur Wright has observed some thirteen separate "approved attitudes and behaviour patterns" distilled from the *Analects* of Confucius. These are:

1. Submissiveness to authority — parents, elders and superiors
2. Submissiveness to the mores and the norms — *li*
3. Reverence for the past and respect for history
4. Love of traditional learning
5. Esteem for the "force" of people
6. Primacy of broad moral cultivation over specialized competence
7. Preference for non-violent moral reform in state and society
8. Prudence, caution, preference for a middle course
9. Non-competitiveness

10. Courage and sense of responsibility for a great tradition
11. Self-respect (with some permissible self-pity) in adversity
12. Exclusiveness and fastidiousness on moral and cultural grounds
13. Punctiliousness in treatment of others[4]

So how could a society embodying these values be achieved in reality?

The family

Central to Confucius' view of how society should be ordered was the importance of the family unit. The family defined its members in a way in which even the most family-centric cultures in the more individualistic Judeo-Christian tradition did not. The hopes and fears of individual Chinese were enshrined in the family. Male heirs sought through their labours and alliances to advance the family. Women were expected to serve and promote the interests of the family by keeping house for their men, through bearing and raising children, males especially, and urging judicious marriages on their daughters. The family was the Chinese state in microcosm, with the male head of the family exercising absolute authority within his domain, echoing the authority exercised by the Emperor throughout the Middle Kingdom — or at least such was expected to be the case.

In support of this authority was the doctrine of the "five relationships" intended by Confucius to order relationships within society. Of these, three were relationships within the family, between husband and wife, between father and son (sometimes referred to as "filial piety"), and between older brother and younger brother. These were all relationships of a superior to an inferior, as was also the relationship within society between ruler and subject. In all these cases the inferior was expected to show obedience to the superior. Only the relationship between friend and friend could be one of equality.

Apart from obedience, other cardinal values to be exercised within the family and within society as a whole included "brotherliness, righteousness, good faith and loyalty,"[5] and "humanity, optimism, humility and good sense."[6] Moreover, the practice of traditional rites and observances should be followed scrupulously, relationships should be characterized by decorum at all times, and both the family and the state should be led by moral example and personal virtue.

Of particular importance was humanity. Challenged to say what he meant by this, Confucius indicated that the pursuit of humanity involved the practice of five virtues: courtesy, magnanimity, good faith, diligence and kindness. It was, however, a very broad term synonymous with the "goodness" which Confucius wished to see infuse all human activity. More than anything, it is the "humanity" of which men are capable in the Confucian view of life that attests to his optimism about the perfectibility of men.

The overall goal was a family, or a people, in harmony; from harmony would come peace, order and contentment. From the best families might be drawn future scholar officials. "Steeped in the Classics and in history, shaped by stern family discipline, tempered by introspection, and sobered by their vast responsibilities, these men were thought to have the power to transform their environment, to turn ordinary folk into the path of virtue."[7] The family therefore performed a critical role both in preparing such men to assume positions of authority, and in conditioning everyone else to accept that authority. This at least was the theory, and it worked in practice sufficiently well to ensure the survival of Confucian orthodoxy down to the twentieth century.

Confucian values in Chinese literature

Confucius' views of the importance of the family, and indeed of the primacy of ethics and morality in the ordering of society, have had a profound impact on the content of Chinese literature over the ages. Prominent themes have included duty, filial piety, male domination, bitterness, resignation, yet hope through looking back to a posited "golden age" when harmony prevailed. One commentator has observed that Chinese literature as a whole is marked by common sense, decorum, and personalities and moral judgements about them revealed primarily through action rather than ideas.[8] (He also notes, however, that if more evidence of vernacular literature had survived, such a generalization might not have been possible). Thus even in poetry, and certainly in novels and in historical writing, morality revealed through tangible actions is what counts, while exploration of the inner state is less important.

Among the earliest expressions of prose to have survived are historical writings. Chief among these are the *Spring and Autumn Annals*, or

Chun Qiu, probably from the late sixth or early fifth century BC, in the compilation of which Confucius may have played a part; the *Records of the Historian*, or *Shih Zhi*, written by the historian Sima Qian in the late second or early first century BC; and the *History of the Former Han*, or *Han Shu*, authored by the historian Pan Ku in the first century AD.[9]

There were some differences in approach. The *Chun Qiu* were set down principally as chronologies of what were presented as facts about events during the "Spring and Autumn" period, from 722 to 481 BC during the Eastern Zhou Dynasty. The *Shi Zhi* was largely made up of biographical studies of leading officials and military men. The *Han Shu* was a combination of sequences of events and biographical sketches. Running through them all, however, was the urge to moral judgement, the determination of individuals as good or bad, and the attribution of the pattern of history primarily to the behaviour of people in positions of power and influence. Historical writing carried on in this vein down through the centuries, with each successive reign or dynasty inevitably interpreting earlier events in a manner favourable to itself.

In Chinese poetry, on the other hand, the other ancient form of literary expression, there was a much broader range of themes. The *Book of Odes*,[10] or *Shi Qing*, normally taken to be the earliest extant body of poetry, is essentially a collection of songs from the period roughly between 1000 and 600 BC. These included songs of sacrifice and celebration, and accounts of affairs of state. Many touched on aspects of daily life, but while some deal with injustice or personal misfortune, there is no strong moral tone to this work as a whole.

By the third century BC, however, when the *Songs of the South* or *Chu Zi* were recorded, the focus had begun to change.[11] Although in poetry from this period deities and other mystical figures featured prominently:

...yet, much of this fantasy and lush imagery seems to be overlaid with allegorical meaning....subordinated to a moral or even political conception of poetry in which the final reality is not the fantastic world of the imagination but the sorrowing statesman and his protestations of loyalty.[12]

The introduction of themes of justice and injustice into Chinese poetry occurs here really for the first time. It is perhaps no accident that these songs postdate Confucius, and are contemporary with the growing influence of his disciples.

The Tang dynasty is perhaps most famous for its poetry, with Li Po (701–62 AD) and Tu Fu (712–70 AD) the greatest exponents of the art.[13] Li Po was known primarily for his romantic poetry, but Tu Fu engaged fully with the moral dilemmas of the politics of his day. A time of growing rebellion and uncertainty, the latter years of the Tang Dynasty provided fertile material for Tu Fu to comment upon in his unique and succinct way, but no opportunity, as he had hoped, to gain official position to help to rectify some of the evils about which he had written.

Prose literature, as opposed to historical writing, was given a significant boost during the Yuan (1279–1368 AD) and Ming (1368–1644 AD) dynasties with the emergence of "prompt books," *hua ben*, in which the tales of story-tellers were set down so that the stories could be passed from generation to generation. By their nature, these stories were told in the vernacular, and although the form in which they were recorded was more literary, their themes and the style of writing led in due course to the early Chinese novel.

Gradually, sets of stories involving particular characters became full-length novels. Among these were several which are regarded as milestones in Chinese literature to this day. *Romance of the Three Kingdoms*, or *Sanguo Yanyi*,[14] written during the fourteenth century, was set in the third century AD, and purported to depict life at that time. *Water Margin*, or *Shuihu Quan*, compiled at some point during the Ming Dynasty (1368–1644),[15] was set in the Song Dynasty and revolved about the theme of conflict between heroic robbers and corrupt officials.

Monkey, or *Xi Youzhi* (Record of a Western Journey),[16] believed to be the work of Wu Cheng'en in the late sixteenth century, is based on a journey to India made by a priest during the Tang Dynasty in search of religious texts; however, the characters and situations encountered may be seen as satirizing political life in contemporary China. The novel *Golden Lotus*,[17] or *Jin Pingmei*, from the early seventeenth century, graphically describes and criticizes corruption in a late Ming household. *Dream of the Red Chamber*,[18] begun by Cao Xueqin and completed by Gao E, and dating from the late eighteenth century, is a contemporary account of life in a wealthy family in the middle of the Qing Dynasty, and has been described as a tale of childhood innocence and its gradual loss.

What is striking is that in each of these novels, characters and situations are developed in such a way as to invite judgement by the reader, and indeed to direct the reader towards a particular point of view. Even *Dream of the Red Chamber*, one of the greatest novels of traditional China, still took Confucian morality among the routines and expectations of family life as its starting point. A saga of the Jia family, said to reflect in part the experience of its educated author, the book explores, as has been noted elsewhere[19] the family structure, politics, economics, religion, aesthetics and sexuality of life at a certain level in late traditional China. How people embrace, cope with, or get around the strictures of the roles which fate has assigned them — how they exemplify or rebel against Confucian values, indeed how those values may be corrupted in their application to real life — in addressing these questions Cao takes the reader some way below the surface of Confucian society, while still acknowledging the primacy of Confucian influence.

Taken as a whole, therefore, it has been observed of traditional Chinese literature that "...all serious writing, whether in poetry or prose, was expected to be edifying or instructive."[20] This didactic quality in literature, secured by China's effective cultural isolation down to the beginning of the twentieth century, both reflected and reinforced the centrality of Confucian morality in the life of traditional China. That a focus on morality and justice, or its absence, should form an integral part of China's transition to the modern world may therefore seem altogether less surprising.

Language and ideas in Confucian China

It was not only literature that served to reinforce Confucian values and the Confucian way of life in traditional China; the language itself played an important part. There has long been discussion of the complex relationship between, on the one hand, the Chinese language and writing system, based on short sequences and relatively simple grammar, represented in written form by pictographs, and on the other the nature of thought and ideas in traditional China. As Yu-kuang Chu noted,[21] number, gender, case, tense, voice and mood are frequently not indicated in Chinese, and there are no conjugations or declensions. Moreover, the reader must rely on the repetition of customary patterns of expression to impose order and meaning on a passage, whether it is one of prose or poetry. In traditional times, the Confucian assumption that only people well educated in the style of writing could (or should) be reading documents reinforced their exclusivity. The traditional writing style has been described as "elliptical and allusive....echoing and building upon the usages of the past....(permitting) great elegance.... (but) it also tends to inhibit originality."[22]

With the written language too, the long and arduous task of learning to read and write must be accomplished by memorizing each individual character. This reliance on rote learning seems to carry over more easily to other aspects of learning, creating a culture in which orthodox thinking was (and perhaps still is) inculcated into people in situations where a more questioning attitude might in the long run be more helpful.

The nature of the Chinese language, it could also be said, is such that it is not given to precision, but frequently conveys a general idea of something, leaving much to be inferred or imagined by the listener or the reader. This in turn could be said to be linked to one of the main purposes of discourse in Confucian China, and to some extent even to this day under the Communist Party — to find out enough about something or some situation to be able to judge whether it is good or worthwhile in some way. The detail could be left to those most closely involved, to technical experts, or to other specialists.

Until relatively recently the complexity of the Chinese written language has also meant that only a small proportion of China's population has been literate. The consequence of this has been that up until the twentieth century the main vehicles of expression for China's culture — prose and poetry, philosophical tracts, historical records — have been inaccessible to most of the population. Thus, China's people have until quite recently been dependent upon story-tellers, travelling players, and legends passed down from generation to generation for their knowledge of their own culture and history. The scope for manipulation due to the difficulty of the written language has therefore been all the greater.

One final point that must be made relates to the trouble encountered by a pictographic language such as Chinese, also heavily dependent for meaning on stylized syntax, in accommodating new philosophical concepts or developments in science and technology. The whole written language was geared to an evocation of the past, not to the exploration of new possibilities. While Chinese characters could, with some stretch of the imagination, be used to make new compounds to refer to modern items of technology (*qi che*, steam carriage for motor vehicle; *fei ji*, flying machine, for aeroplane), and for some purposes in the natural sciences, it would take the transposition of the vernacular style of spoken language to the written form in the early 1920s — during the so-called Chinese Renaissance — before Western ideas and new Chinese ideas on politics, literature, philosophy, history and science could really penetrate China, challenging and ultimately undermining the Confucian orthodoxy among China's intellectuals. Finally, the Thousand Character Education Movement, noted elsewhere, enabled the common man and woman to read about these new concepts in new mass publications of restricted vocabulary. Only then (and only for a brief time, as it happened) was it possible for the great bulk of China's population even to begin to take part in informed discussion of the many issues that modernization posed for them.[23]

The role of education

Through most of China's long history, education has been held in high esteem. This has been primarily due to the importance attached to it by Confucius himself, and by his disciples. Confucius observed, "By nature, men are pretty much alike; it is learning and practice that set them apart." For Confucius, a man with no formal education would have no basis for wise behaviour, no preparation for any position of responsibility within society, no capacity to contribute to harmony among his fellow men — in a word, he would lack any humanity.

The purpose of education for Confucius, then, was not only personal improvement, but also to meet political and social objectives. It was to prepare the next generation of leaders. From the adoption of Confucianism as the state orthodoxy around 150 BC, right down to the twentieth century, a system of examinations was progressively introduced and refined for admission to the bureaucracy; this depended of course on candidates first acquiring through education the knowledge to succeed in the examinations. This system was almost unique in the pre-modern world, and certainly effective in finding talented people to fill official positions. Confucius also said that in education there should be no class distinctions,[24] meaning that talented and intelligent boys from all classes should be taken and educated, and inducted into the bureaucracy, if China was to be governed by the wisest and brightest of men. The impact this had over the centuries on pathways of social mobility in China has been discussed above (see Chapter 2).

The nature and content of Confucian education evolved over the ages to reflect prevailing interpretations and points of emphasis, but certain core ideas were present down to the twentieth century. The values were those noted above, of humanity, filial piety, the practice of decorum in relationships, the observation of rites, the inculcation of a sense of duty, a strong sense of propriety or justice, and self-cultivation in personal virtue and the ways of the gentleman and scholar.

In practice, a young boy would often be taught by a private tutor, and perhaps later in a small school, where he would acquire first the ability to read and write the very difficult Chinese script. He would then go on to study the Confucian and other classics, works of history and philosophy, administrative tracts, poetry and other suitable material, which would give him a comprehensive grounding in Chinese civilization, and it was felt, prepare him for administrative responsibility. The progressive introduction over the centuries of the examination system for admission to the bureaucracy throughout China, noted in Chapter 2, gave a clear focus and incentive for education.

The method of teaching, which relied heavily on memorization of texts and the ability to recite them, mirrored the teaching of language itself, and again reinforced the orthodoxy of what was being taught. The content of education in China was generally not a matter for dispute; learning was to be absorbed, not argued over — somewhat ironic in the light of Confucius' rhetorical approach with his own disciples. There is resonance here also with the mass education campaigns which have taken place in China since 1949.

As noted above, Confucius is known for his assertion that in education there should be no class distinctions. Yet the acquisition of education required both money and the leisure time necessary for protracted study. Here the extended family came into play. A boy who showed promise, but whose parents were poor, might have the money put up for his education by a member or members of the extended family, or even of the kinship group. If he succeeded, and ultimately became an official, the favour would be called in and he would be expected to help his relatives. While this contributed to the pressure on an official to be partisan in various ways, it did mean that it was often genuinely possible for a boy from a poor family to achieve a position of power and influence (see Chapter 2).

One final point that must be made is that one half of the population were simply not addressed by Confucius' injunction to educate. Girls were excluded from education, just as women were excluded from positions in the bureaucracy. Only quite exceptionally, for much of the traditional period, was a girl taught to read and write, and then usually so that she could be a more cultivated companion to a man. China's only two women who were political leaders in traditional times — Empress Wu during the Tang Dynasty, and the Empress Dowager Ci Xi during the Qing Dynasty — were both regarded as usurpers.

Commerce in Confucian China

Confucius' attitude to the merchants of his day could perhaps find a parallel in other predominantly agricultural societies. Confucius tended to be unimpressed by wealth in any event, but he was particularly disdainful of wealth obtained through trade. His dictum that, "The gentleman understands what is right; the inferior man understands what is profitable," while it has more general application, is often taken as Confucius' judgement on the merchant class as a whole.

Of course, commercial activity in some degree was always present in traditional China, for as long as historical records exist. Local trade in produce and handicrafts was carried on from the earliest stages of agricultural society, was facilitated by moneylenders and early banks, and indeed was taxed in various ways by the same Confucian bureaucracy that held it in disdain. Just as some of the world's first canals were built, primarily for military purposes and the transport of grain, including the famous Grand Canal from Beijing to Hangzhou completed in the sixth century, so in due course other goods were traded between north and south China. This activity was supplemented by coastal trade, and from the Tang Dynasty by foreign trade conducted between south China, southeast Asia, India and East Africa, as well as by land along the Silk Road from Chang'an to central Asia and beyond.

There were, therefore, substantial numbers of people in traditional China who made money from buying and selling goods. Officially tolerated as a necessary evil, they were never really respected in an agricultural society where land, pedigree and education were the main routes to status and power; indeed many bought land with their newfound wealth, hoping to acquire respectability. This is an attitude not unknown in the evolution of Western societies — in both Britain and France, for example, the struggle for recognition by the bourgeoisie, most of whom had made their money from trade, was prolonged. In traditional China, however, no political accommodation was ever reached that would have admitted merchants to a share of power, even by the end of the dynastic era in 1911.

What did happen in practice, though, was a process of exploitation by Confucian bureaucrats of the financial opportunities that the merchants and their activity represented. Not only were merchants "squeezed" for additional taxes, which often went straight into the pockets of officials, in addition the state was apt to take over profitable operations completely: the salt monopoly is an early example of this, introduced, it is believed, as early as the sixth century BC, and maintained in some form right down to the late nineteenth century.[25] In the dying days of the Qing Dynasty the government imposed the regime of "merchant operation, government supervision" on a range of new commercial activities made possible by the introduction of new technology to China in the late nineteenth century. These included the construction and operation of steamships, mines, a railway, cotton mills, and arsenals. In a development that would critically undermine the spread of modern native Chinese capitalism, these enterprises were milked of their profits by a government and officials whose greed was undeterred by, perhaps even heightened by, their distaste for commerce.

At the same time, in traditional China the merchants themselves exploited the networks of family and kin open to them because of the Confucian character of society, to expand their business, generate capital, and bring in new talent whose loyalty to the family enterprise would be assured. Prominent merchant families (prominent through their wealth more than through their status) were often extended families. They feature in works of Chinese literature, such as the eighteenth century novel *Dream of the Red Chamber*.[26] What is striking, though, is that in China, unlike in Western countries or even Japan, no "merchant dynasties" developed based on particular families whose commercial activity succeeded over many generations, perhaps even over several centuries. There were no merchant cities, like Venice, London or Osaka, ultimately to challenge the political status quo. There was to be no investment in technology, no merchant-funded industrial revolution, ultimately no new era under the old regime.

The part played by religion

It was in the area of religion, rather than socioeconomic or political thought and practice, that there was really any effective challenge to the primacy of Confucius. He himself would perhaps in the present day be classed as an agnostic; asked about death, he said, "We don't yet know about life, how can we know about death?"[27] While he took part in religious observances, and sometimes spoke about Heaven, his whole philosophy was humanist in conception, and based on the inculcation of morality not linked to the threat of judgement and consequences in the hereafter.

Down through the centuries, however, Confucianism came to have a dual existence — as a social and political philosophy promoted especially by the ruling group, and as a set of expectations which, in the popular understanding, took on certain of the attributes of a religion; this said, the two were not mutually exclusive, and the average person might recognize the expectations in terms of social behaviour, while at the same time engaging in worship of deities or the spirits of ancestors.

The religious elements of Confucius have primarily to do with ancestor worship, which can be seen as an extension of the principle of filial piety. Ancestors are revered, and in some cases worshipped, and the souls of the dead are nourished, because they embody the wisdom of the old and of a former age and therefore deserve respect, because they remain a part of one's family, and because with deities they may intercede on one's behalf. Beyond this, there is no explicit metaphysical justification — certainly none in the thinking of Confucius or his immediate disciples — for Confucianism to be taken as a body of religious thought. Some would say that the Neo-Confucianism of the Song Dynasty came closer to embodying elements of religious belief, but even for the neo-Confucians the core message was a social and political one.

That Confucianism was so important, yet did not really occupy centre stage in any religious sense, meant that the way was open for other claimants to make their case. It has contributed to the eclecticism of China in religious matters, and its ability to accommodate elements of different religions side by side, and sometimes in the same person's belief. This has been true so long as that belief does not have significant political or social implications. It will be appropriate here to look briefly at the other two main belief systems in traditional China, as a counterpoint to Confucianism.

One such was Daoism.[28] Initially a mystical, transcendental philosophy associated with a legendary figure known as Lao Zi whose dates are unknown, Daoism sought to provide its adherents with an approach to life rooted in passivity and acceptance. The Dao, the Way, was the source of all life, and represented the unity of all contradictions (a concept that would emerge much later in the Chinese approach to Marxism). The Daoist focused on the natural world, and revered nature above all. With no really practical solutions to offer in the administration of a state, or any moral parameters for the ordering of society, the mystical quality of Daoism caused it to evolve over time into a religion, with cults and rituals and a search for immortality. It was believed that magic could be used to invoke the help of a broad range of deities with the problems of daily life. In due course, like Buddhism, it developed its own priesthood, monasteries and temples. It experimented with potions and remedies. In time it came to be a rallying point for people disaffected by the trials of life in traditional China, and fed the paranoia of successive Chinese governments down to the present day over organized religious movements. Yet on the positive side, Daoism has contributed much to the refinement of Chinese art and literature, and in its respect for nature may yet prove to have been very much ahead of its time.

The other main religious pillar of life in traditional China, Buddhism, was transplanted from India, probably in the first century AD. Central to the original Buddhist teaching was the doctrine of reincarnation, the cycle of birth, death and re-birth, from which the individual could only achieve release — *nirvana* — by perfecting his *karma* through a correct attitude to existence, through moral conduct, and through meditation. By the time Buddhism in its Mahayana form had reached China, it had evolved into something much more theistic, a religion according to which individuals had souls whose care could be assured by worship of not just one, but a wide variety of Buddha figures and *bodhisattva*s, beings who, on the threshold of enlightenment, turn back to help others to salvation.

In time, Buddhism in China developed all the trappings of an institutional religion, with priests, monasteries, temples and religious monuments and sites all over the country. Within 200 years of its arrival it had begun to exercise significant influence on the Chinese court, and during the early part of the Tang Dynasty it became for a time the state religion, and a privileged secular force with extensive landholdings and much wealth. Although its secular power was later sharply curtailed, Buddhism had established itself as the major religious influence on the Chinese population, and the practice of Buddhism has survived through all the changes of the twentieth century, including the Cultural Revolution, down to the present day.[29]

While Buddhism (in its Mahayana form), Daoism, and a version of Confucianism have together constituted the main indigenous religions of traditional China, there have been other influences. Centuries of trade conducted along the Silk Road to Central Asia, and some trade also by sea, brought numbers of Muslims to settle in parts of north-west and south-west China. Seen largely as interlopers with a record of rebellion, they have continued to practice their religion at the fringes of Chinese society, well away from the mainstream.

From the sixteenth to the eighteenth century the Jesuits established a small beachhead, seeking to win over China's elite to Catholicism through the demonstration of their scientific prowess. The number of their conversions remained insignificant, however, especially when compared to Catholic achievements in Japan in the same period, and in some respects they absorbed more of Chinese culture and ways than the Chinese absorbed of Christianity.

In the nineteenth century other Western missionaries, including many Protestants, came to China in the wake of the traders — both groups unleashed on China by the Unequal Treaties following defeat in the Opium Wars. Catholic converts came to number several million; the Protestant churches claimed far fewer adherents, but left behind an extensive record of social and educational work which would feed into the Communist Party's approach to problems of the people's livelihood.

Throughout China's long history, and especially in the nineteenth century, some form of religious belief would not infrequently become a rallying point for rebellion against authority — the Daoism of the White Lotus rebels of the 1830s, the quasi-Christian beliefs of Hong Xiuquan and the Taiping rebels in the 1850s, the Islam of the Hui rebels of the 1860s and 1870s — while the reaction against religious belief could be equally severe, as with the anti-Christian Boxer Uprising of 1899–1900.

Thus there was the apparent paradox of a society willing for its individual members to take an eclectic approach to religious belief, combining elements of different religions in a personal code of worship, while at the same time guarding jealously the social and political realm of the here and now for the state orthodoxy, Confucianism. Even the Communist Party, except at the time of its most radical phase during the Cultural Revolution, was relatively tolerant of private belief.

Perhaps the conclusion here must be that in China it has always principally been the here and now that mattered. The sheer numbers of China's population, and the overwhelming emphasis in tradition upon issues of state, may have served together to crowd out religion as a pervasive influence on people's lives.

Attitudes to the outside world

Finally, it is important to consider briefly the influence of Confucian thinking on attitudes to the outside world. From the earliest formation of the unified Chinese state, the term "Zhong Guo" in Chinese, or Middle Kingdom, was used to denote the territory inhabited predominantly by the Han race. The use of this term carried with it a set of strong messages about the self-perceptions of the people whose civilization began in the valleys of the Wei and Yellow Rivers. As has been noted above, the strength and early sophistication of agriculture in this area supported an unusually large population. The settled existence enjoyed by these people enabled them in turn to develop cultural, social and political arts and institutions well in advance of those of any other race in proximity to them, or of which they had knowledge. The Middle Kingdom therefore occupied both the best territory and the central position in human civilization.

These messages were reinforced by Confucius, interpreting and causing to be recorded the legends about the alleged progenitors of this civilization, Yao and Shun, and the long line of kings, princes, statesmen and philosophers who in one way or another embodied and defended its core values. When Confucianism became the state orthodoxy in the second century BC, the defence of those values both internally, and from challenge by foreigners, became a prime preoccupation of the state. The Great Wall, begun towards the end of the Zhou period in the third century BC, itself came to be a symbol not only of the military defence of China from barbarians, but of an entire way of life — indeed, it could be said, of a level of life — which could be found nowhere else.

The conviction that Chinese civilization was superior to all others was sustained over a period of many centuries by China's geographical isolation and an evident lack of curiosity about other places. The desire to Sinicize — one might say Confucianize — neighbouring territories through suzerain links (Vietnam, Korea, Tibet), or to make them sympathetic buffer states (Japan, Manchuria), was not always achieved, but was an assertion of a particular attitude to the rest of the world.

China had worked out how to achieve a society in perfect harmony, even if the present did not always match up to the posited "golden age" in the past; despite some degree of contact with other lands through communication along the Silk Road, through exploratory voyages during the Tang Dynasty, through Matteo Ricci, the Jesuits and the early Western traders, China — that is, its Confucian elite — remained unpersuaded. Ultimately, the incompatibility between Confucian values and the demands of a newly-industrialized outside world would prove all too obvious.

Confucianism and modernization

If the attributes of traditional Chinese culture, and especially of Confucian thought and practice, described above were significant in making China what it was, how were these ideas challenged during the impact of the West on China, and how do they relate to what has happened since 1949? Clearly these must be matters for intense speculation, and any insights into the answers to these questions may go some way towards explaining the nature of China's adaptation to the modern world.

The sequence of events following on from the opening up of China to Western influence in the mid-nineteenth century has been described in earlier chapters. In broad terms, the dynamic is one of fundamental challenge to the Confucian order on many fronts, the apparent inability of that order to adapt sufficiently to preserve itself, the collapse of its political institutions with the ending of the dynasty in 1911, and the overwhelming repudiation of Confucianism by intellectuals during the May 4th Movement which began in 1919. The power vacuum of the early 1920s was associated with the loss of any moral bearings for society, in China a critical loss never really made good by the Nationalist government that came to power in 1928. By contrast, the Communist Party picked up the role of moral leadership and relied heavily on it to engender support for its policies both before and after 1949.

So how did the presence of Westerners and Western thought impact on Confucian ideas of the family? In the Treaty Ports, and especially in Shanghai, the construction of modern factories, usually foreign-owned, from around the turn of the century induced migration from the countryside, not only disrupting ties of kin and extended family relationships, but often resulting in women and children as well as men becoming involved in industrial work. This meant long hours in often deplorable conditions, with minimal opportunity for family life and the observance of traditional family roles. In cities, workers often lived in dormitories, and were effectively the prisoners of their employers and subject to their abuse. In difficult times, men might join one of the many gangs and resort to crime, women could become prostitutes. Modern urban life left most people little scope for Confucian family values.

In the countryside, the long decline of effective administration over the last half of the nineteenth century, the proliferation of rebellion, and the political fragmentation of China followed by civil war in the first half of the twentieth century also undermined the "approved attitudes and behaviour patterns" noted at the beginning of this chapter. The breakdown of Confucian authority in large parts of China, and the decline into violence brought Confucian family life under threat. The cardinal values of brotherliness, righteousness, good faith and loyalty, humanity, optimism, humility and good sense seemed to have little relevance to life in many parts of China in the late nineteenth and early twentieth centuries. Even filial piety came to be seen more as a means of shoring up the past than as an expression of virtue. The May 4th Movement and its associated intellectual movement, noted in an earlier chapter, would challenge Confucian ideas of the family, find them wholly wanting, and discard them — leaving a significant vacuum for a time at the heart of Chinese life.

The repudiation of the authority of the family, and in particular the call for the emancipation of women given voice by the intellectuals of the May 4th period, would find expression in a somewhat different form after 1949. The Chinese Communist Party took the view that the family should in all things be subordinate to, and reinforce the values of, the Party and the state. The moral example of the ruling group was once again, as C.P. Fitzgerald has observed,[30] to be the standard of behaviour, but the values were those of the Party. Harmony of a kind was now to be achieved through class struggle and pursuit of the great project of national construction. The status of women, though, was to be drastically altered, with the Marriage Laws of 1950 laying the foundation for progress which, if by no means linear, would see changes to their professional and life prospects that would have been inconceivable a few decades before. By the time of the "Four Modernizations" of 1978–79, Confucian values were in most respects no longer a major force in family life.

In literature, the work of writers immediately before and during the May 4th Movement of 1919 was at the heart of the Chinese "renaissance" and its challenge to Confucian values. Writers such as Lu Xun, Lao She and others were starkly critical of the old order, and blamed what they saw as the backward-looking Confucian orthodoxy for China's inability to adapt to the demands of the modern world. They stressed the plight of the individual at the mercy of an uncaring political system, mirrored by the situation of China as a whole, at the mercy of foreign powers. The literature of the time impacted profoundly on China's educated young people, both men and women, and was an urgent call for action to which the formation of new political parties, and notably of the Communist Party, was a practical response.

For the first three decades after 1949 literature was placed at the service of the Party, performing a didactic role, emphasizing once again society over the individual, but inculcating the Party's values rather than those of Confucius. Since the opening up of 1979, new themes have been addressed, especially those of personal happiness for the first time, and of China's interaction with the world outside, even though these may sit unhappily at times with the Party's desire to retain its hold on power.

During the May 4th period, too, the Chinese script was identified by many as an obstacle to modernization. The Thousand Character Education Movement — started in the 1920s by the YMCA's James Yen — was at the same time perhaps the most significant piece of Protestant social work in China, and the inspiration for the Communist Party's own subsequent literacy campaigns on a much broader scale. Essential for modernization, widespread basic literacy achieved at an earlier stage than in other developing countries also enabled the Party's political messages to reach a much wider audience than would otherwise have been the case. There can be little doubt that without it, and without the various schemes of character simplification of the 1950s and 60s, China's extraordinary economic progress of the past twenty-five years would not have been possible.

In the event the language, freed from the constraints of classic literary style, and in more recent years of some of the other demands of orthodoxy, has not proved an insuperable barrier to the introduction of modern technology and ideas. Moreover, the process of rote learning still often used in teaching characters, is increasingly challenged in all other areas by a new generation of people who understand that analytical ability, rather than memory alone, is the key to productive intellectual activity.

Education was crucial in traditional society to the sustainability of the Confucian elite and of the social order — education based on the classics, abhoring change, and restricted to males. Even before the collapse of the Qing dynasty, new Western-style schools and universities had been established in China — introducing a modern outward-looking curriculum that included the sciences, economics, Western philosophy and foreign languages among other subjects — and were soon open to women. These were to be supplemented by technical colleges to teach engineering and other practical subjects. The graduates of these programmes featured prominently in the debates of the May 4th period, and their influence ended once and for all the hold of Confucian scholars over Chinese education.

After 1949, primary and then secondary education spread rapidly, and as will be seen in a subsequent chapter would be used as a vehicle for the Party's political messages. China's universities were for a time influenced by the practical and applied orientation of those in the Soviet Union. Following the traumas of the Cultural Revolution, a comprehensive pattern of contacts has been established with universities in other countries, and it is fair to say that higher education is, in the new century, one of the most fully globally aware and connected spheres of activity in China.

Confucius was hostile to commerce. Confucian bureaucrats in the late nineteenth century managed both to hold trade in disdain, and to profit from it. Western ideas of "free trade," self-serving as they were, challenged in no small way Confucian ideas of regulation, and indeed ultimately the whole sovereignty of the Chinese state.

The nineteenth century experience ensured that commerce enjoyed no great advocacy by any group during the May 4th period of the 1920s, though it is true that some bourgeois traders supported some of the aims of the movement. After 1949 for a short time merchants were used to run businesses on behalf of the state, but this soon came to an end. In line with Marxist parties elsewhere, the CCP took control of all significant economic and commercial activity, disdaining "what was profitable" just as Confucius did, but from an entirely different point of view. The extraordinary transition from this, to China of the twenty-first century, in which to "make money is glorious," is unprecedented.

The early impact of Western religion on China has been considered above. Christianity failed to take root in any serious way in China, but rather was partially absorbed and Sinicized as a minority belief system. Protestant missionaries left behind social institutions which have continued to have influence: the literacy campaign (the YMCA), the Women's Welfare Institutes and a campaign to improve factory conditions (the YWCA), the earliest industrial co-operative movement (the National Christian Council), many schools and a handful of universities.

Communist orthodoxy did not erase altogether the practice of Buddhism, or any other traditional belief system. In the Chinese way these beliefs continue to co-exist, and sometimes even in the same individual. In the new century the Chinese government remains relatively tolerant of private belief, but still wary of what it sees as rogue sects with political intent — Falun Gong being an obvious example.

Finally, it may be asked how the impact of the West changed Confucian China's attitude to the outside world. The manner of its first opening up during the Opium Wars, and the technological lead enjoyed by those foreign powers that had experienced the Industrial Revolution, ultimately left China's transitional aspiring leaders no choice but to recognize the country's backwardness. Much of China's twentieth-century history was spent in one way or another trying to address this problem. Yet throughout the traumas of the first half of the century, through the somewhat demeaning years of Soviet assistance, through the paroxysms and excesses of the Cultural Revolution, China's educated elite, having abandoned its faith in the particularities of Confucian orthodoxy, nonetheless retained its belief in the essential integrity of Chinese civilization.

In the new century, China's very substantial involvement with the global economy has brought prosperity to many parts of the country, though not all. Methods of communication have been transformed, and many younger Chinese people have travelled abroad for work or study. It is no longer possible to believe that the world outside China's borders consists of inferior people (an attitude in some measure prolonged even into the 1970s through the Party's insistence on its uniquely "correct" ideological position). Now China, it would seem, has abandoned the ethnocentrism of earlier times, to engage fully with the international community on issues of security, trade regulation, trafficking in drugs and people, health matters, and scientific collaboration among others — not as superior nor inferior, but as a sovereign equal.

This said, the exceptional scale and population of the Chinese state, the skills of its people, and the dynamism of its economy, heavily dependent as it is on exports for continued growth, are all factors making for a relationship between China and the rest of the world that is without precedent.

6

ORTHODOXY, IDEOLOGY AND LAW

It is frequently asserted that the role of belief systems in securing political consent from the population has been greater and more evident in
the case of China than in that of most other countries. Thus the prevalence of a sophisticated state "orthodoxy" in traditional China, and of
the ideology of the Chinese Communist Party under the People's
Republic, has offered a justification of government that has helped to
engender loyalty and obedience. The role of law, as it may be observed
in the Western tradition has until quite recently been less prominent.
This chapter will explore continuities and change in the political belief
systems of China, and the ways in which they may obstruct or facilitate modernization.

Orthodoxy in traditional China

The origins of the most basic beliefs about ethics, and social and political organization in pre-modern China are lost in the "legendary"
period of China's early civilization, around and before 2000 BC. In
this, China is little different from other societies. It is only possible to
speculate about norms of behaviour on the basis of archeological evidence of the structure of the family and society and patterns of life.

In some measure we are influenced to believe in the existence of
political and social structures for this early period that in fact only
evolved many centuries later — the projection back in time of institutions for which society had evolved a need when it had become both
more sophisticated and more sedentary. The beginning of the writing

system in China, whose date is itself disputed but is broadly considered to be about 1000 BC, helps to pin down the precise nature of the political system and commonly held beliefs in the early Zhou period (1122–771 BC).

It is already apparent at this time that the prevailing political institutions of the Zhou, both at the centre and in the constituent states, relied heavily for their legitimacy, if not for their control of the use of force, on a set of ideas which both derived from a view of the state as the extension of the family and encompassed a divine sanction passed down from the mythical Emperors Yao and Shun. These beliefs, at once an explanation of role and status in society and a justification of the way things were, were the cement of civilized life in the loose federation of Zhou China. Even so, they could not prevent conflict occurring both within and between states, and in the later Zhou, as the Spring and Autumn Period (722–481 BC) gave way to the Warring States (403–221 BC), the need for a codification of political ideas became more pressing.

It can be said of Confucius that if he had not existed, he would have had to be invented; indeed, to some extent his actual existence, and certainly his dates (frequently given as 551–479 BC), remain contentious. The role of his writings has been to offer to successive generations of Chinese down to the twentieth century a vision of what *might* be possible, based on an idealized view of what, even in his own day, was the legendary past. For rulers he prescribed a set of principles, for subjects a set of criteria and rules of behaviour. Yet Confucianism was much more than this, for its call to the population to *internalize* patterns of behaviour that would guarantee conformity to the goals of the state has striking echoes in modern times, and not only in China.

In what we shall call here the "writings" of Confucius — though he was more accurately a compiler, transmitter and editor of ancient texts and legends, and a commentator on them, and in fact it seems to have been often his disciples who actually wrote down his thoughts — the essential political features may be considered to be: the divine sanction accorded to the Head of State inherited from China's legendary period; an account of society which ascribes functions or roles to different groups, seeming to vary from the descriptive to the prescriptive, though not denying the individual the possibility of upward or downward movement between groups; a clear statement of the mutual moral obligations existing between ruler and subjects; and the control of thought as a tacit objective of government. Each of these deserves some further elaboration.

In asserting that the Head of State rules by virtue of the Mandate of Heaven, Confucius at once offers an incontestable justification for the exercise of power, and calls on centuries of mythology in support of the ruler's claim to legitimacy. His unequivocal assertion of this right to rule is indicated in his writings.[1] Confucius' invocation of Heaven is the more remarkable when his rejection of the supernatural elsewhere in his philosophy is recalled,[2] and it may be supposed that in part he was influenced by the need to take account of the widespread appeal of various forms of religion and primitive belief in the society of his day. The relationship between rulers and the gods was a matter of great importance in most early civilizations, while in Western society it is only very recently, relatively speaking, that the sanction of divine right of kings has been put aside.

The ascribing of functions to groups within society was, on one level, no more than a recognition of the distribution of economic tasks among different segments of the population, and therefore a statement of the actual situation in his own day. Confucius sought to provide means of stabilizing any tension within society, however, and his philosophy embodies a clear vision of a specific role for everyone in society, with justice and harmony prevailing when everyone does his or her job. The doctrine of the rectification of names, according to which the ruler rules, the soldier stands guard, the peasant tills the soil and so on, reinforces this, apparently offering no scope for change in the make-up of society or in the way economic and political tasks were performed. Yet there was no insuperable barrier to the movement of the individual between social groups, as Confucius also said that in education there should be no class distinctions. In later centuries it would be this freedom, unusual in pre-modern society, which would afford the social mobility that undercut any attempt to change the system.

The obligation on the ruler to rule wisely was another fundamental principle of Confucius' political philosophy.[3] The Head of State not only enjoyed divine sanction, as in the later experience of many Western countries, but also was supposed to represent the "will of the people," a concept with apparently surprising resonance in the experience of Western democracies, and even in China's own experience under the People's Republic. The ruler and his advisers were supposed, through cultivation of those virtues of study and contemplation which fate had assigned to them as their particular task, to have the wisdom to practise their statecraft in such a way as to bring order and prosperity to the common people, setting standards that they could emulate. In turn, the people were obliged to obey their sovereign and his officials in all things. Through mutual dependence and respect would come peace and good government. Confucius' later disciple Mencius (372–289 BC) added the proviso that if the ruler ruled unwisely, and the people rose up and deposed him, he would be held to have forfeited the Mandate of Heaven.

In all Confucius' writings on government there is an underlying expectation, not only that China's rulers would absorb the habits of mind and behaviour that would conform to and advance the purposes he expounded, but also that common people would do so too. There is the exhortation to cultivate "humanity," a desire to stamp out the coarse and the self-seeking, and ultimately to ensure as far as possible thought patterns that would make the task of governing China's large population easier. The education that Confucius advocated was in approved classics, the learning was by rote. The unorthodox was even at this very early stage excluded.

So what was Confucius trying to achieve through his insistence on these various tenets of political orthodoxy? Essentially, he and successive Chinese rulers who adhered to and promoted his philosophy sought to sustain the harmony and degree of social control that would make the maintenance of political order possible over such a large territory. The analogy between family and state was particularly important in achieving this, because through this link the authority of the state could be felt in every household. The sublimation of the individual will could be achieved through the inculcation of orthodox values from a very early age, very substantially reducing the need for coercion to be used to induce acceptable behaviour.

In this sense, it is possible to disagree with the assertion in Franz Schurmann's classic study on the early years of the People's Republic that "ideology" was new to China with the coming of the Communists;[4] rather, the core ideas that made up Confucian orthodoxy were the pre-modern "ideology" of China — the manner of thinking characteristic of the organization that was the traditional Chinese state.[5] Indeed C.P. Fitzgerald, writing soon after the founding of the People's Republic in 1949, was quick to spot continuities in this respect, both in form and in substance, in the new order.

The traditional ideology, the orthodoxy of Qing China was, it can be argued, in a conservative phase at the time of the most serious Western incursions in the last half of the nineteenth century. Despite a discernible dynamic of gradual change through the various dynasties up to this point, the threat of far-reaching change implied by expanded contact with the West, as Mary Wright has documented, saw a renewed invocation of Confucian values in an attempt to shore up the old order[6] during the Indian summer of the T'ung Chih Restoration, 1862–1874. Yet the impact of the West opened a Pandora's box of issues that could not be avoided. Ultimately, the old orthodoxy would prove inadequate to meeting the challenges of the new age.

Essential principles of Chinese Marxism

It has commonly been asserted that the progressive decline and collapse of the Qing Dynasty, accompanied as it was by the disintegration of the Chinese state over the years leading up to the May 4th Movement of 1919, marked a transition to a new pragmatism among those who were concerned with the country's future. Certainly, those who were active in the May 4th Movement, while they may not have agreed on the way ahead, were by this point almost united in their repudiation of Confucian thought as backward-looking and irrelevant to China's current needs. Yet the notion of ideology was still very much alive. The two main contending strands which emerged with practical programmes following the May 4th period were the "nationalism" of the Guomindang and the Marxism of the newly-formed Chinese Communist Party.

The ideology of the Guomindang had been formed gradually from its founding as the Xing Zhong Hui in 1894, through its transformation into the Dong Meng Hui in 1905, and into the Guomindang in 1912. Expressed in its clearest form as pursuit of the three principles of Nationalism, Democracy and the People's Livelihood, the ideology of the Nationalists addressed what were seen to be the three major problems facing China. The progressive dilution of this ideology in practice, and particularly after the death of Sun Yat-sen in 1925 and the accession to power in the party of Chiang Kai-shek has been well documented elsewhere.[7] It may be suspected that the need to create a Leninist-style party in order to retain power in the chaos of China in the early 1920s, which even Sun himself had to concede, was an early indication that the transition to democracy would not be so easy.

The collapse of the Confucian state, and the ideological vacuum apparently created thereby, gave rise to consideration of other alternatives during the May 4th Movement. The Pragmatists, an amorphous group of whom the most notable was perhaps Hu Shih, urged the goal of liberal democracy on China, with widespread popular education as the means of achieving it.[8] Yet this in China's circumstances could be no more than a long-term objective at best. Positing the democratic alternative begged more questions than it answered given the many political and economic imperatives confronting the country. What China needed were practical solutions embedded in the context of a new world view. Despite the efforts of some liberals to address China's economic problems,[9] on the whole the pragmatists were the least pragmatic of the contending schools of the May 4th period.

To a degree, the problems of the magnitude that China faced were a consequence of the erosion of Confucian values as the cement of the social order. It is scarcely surprising therefore that any group able to offer a programme of action reinforced by a social philosophy and political morality, but one that embraced and explained modernization in terms which seemed relevant to China's own experience, should have a strong appeal.

To many, Marxism appeared to offer just such a combination of practical and theoretical elements. The writings of Marx, Engels and Lenin arrived in China and became available in translation from around 1915, through the medium of *New Youth* and other publications. This was a critical time for China, and in some measure these years saw the nadir of its fortunes. The Qing dynasty had collapsed, the constitutional experiment of 1913 had failed, Yuan Shih-k'ai proclaimed himself President for life, and following his death in 1916 the country fragmented and deteriorated into warlord anarchy. Western influence over China was at its zenith, while Japanese pressure was felt more keenly with each passing month.

Marxism as further developed by Lenin seemed to provide for some young Chinese intellectuals both an explanation and a plan of action. Although traditional Chinese institutions hardly fitted Marx's understanding of pre-modern political structures, the old society could be rationalized away as "feudal" and cast aside. The suffering of the very great majority of poor peasants, and the new small industrial proletariat, could be understood in class terms and redressed through class struggle (though Marx himself had held out little hope for a radicalized peasantry). China's continuing experience of foreign dominance through the concession areas and the whole system of extraterritoriality could now be explained as colonialism, or semi-colonialism — imperialism being, as Lenin had said, the highest stage of capitalism. Added to this near-perfect fit, or so it was seen, of Marxism-Leninism to China's circumstances were the practical example of the successful revolution of October 1917 by the Bolsheviks in Russia, and the rise of nationalism elsewhere in Asia, notably in India after the Amritsar massacre of 1919.[10]

However, the Marxism which so appealed to Li Dazhao, Chen Duxiu and others, and on the strength of which the Chinese Communist Party was founded in 1920, was in some significant ways unsuited to China, and in need of modification. In the process of coming to terms with the Chinese reality, the Party would reinstate a form of orthodoxy that resonated profoundly with that which it had obtained in China for 2,000 years; in so doing it would succeed where others with different plans and aspirations had failed.

The mutual obligations of rulers and subjects

It is of course Mao Zedong who is generally credited with adapting Marxism to the Chinese reality, both by the Party and by independent historians. In particular, it was Mao's fortuitous trip to the Hunan countryside in 1924, so the story goes, that led him to realize — perhaps to rediscover as he himself was from a peasant background in Hunan — the capacity of the peasantry for organization and resistance to local tyranny. This, critically, would lead in due course to the assertion, when Mao himself came to take charge of the Party, that the peasantry must be the main revolutionary class in a largely rural country like China, of equal status in the Chinese Communist pantheon with the industrial proletariat.

In emphasizing the role of the peasants, Mao reintroduced an important element of the traditional Confucian orthodoxy. Confucius and his disciples also saw the peasants as dignified by their labour, and the natural partners of the Confucian literati who ruled over them in earlier times. For Confucius, the most important requirement for good government was the confidence of the people.[11] His disciple Mencius stressed that the Emperor represented the will of the people; if he ruled unwisely he would forfeit the Mandate of Heaven and lose the right to rule.[12] Usually peasant discontent was a critical factor in uprisings which led to the fall of one dynasty and the founding of the next, and sometimes these rebellions were even peasant-led. For Mao, the people were the sea, and Communist guerrillas were the fish that must swim in that sea.[13] Similarly, for the Communist Party failure to take heed of the needs of the people, more than four-fifths of whom were peasants, would mean in the Chinese context that it could neither retain power nor even take it.

The struggle for supremacy of Mao's view on the importance of the peasantry to the Chinese revolution took more than a decade, and paralleled his own struggle for supremacy within the Party, which most commentators would say lasted until his confirmation as Chairman in 1937. The sheer numbers of the peasantry in China, coupled ironically with the military failure of the Communists to take the cities or to foment an uprising of adequate proportions there, contributed to Mao's success. Yet it can reasonably be asserted that this was a victory of Chinese traditionalists over Marxist-Leninist modernists within the Party who had wanted to focus on the cities. By re-invoking the implicit social contract between peasants and rulers, and the right of peasants to expect good government which he claimed the Communist Party could provide if they would support and fight for it, Mao was breathing new life into a fundamental tenet of Confucian orthodoxy that had endured over centuries.

Different roles for different groups

In other respects too, the evolving body of Mao's writings which would guide his policy, especially through the civil war and the first decade after victory, picked up on cues, habits of thought and custom-ary political organization which owed more to the traditional than to the transitional period. As the Party re-established itself in northern China following the Long March of 1934–35, passed through the Second United Front, and attracted progressively more recruits in its struggle against Japan, there is evidence that Mao began to turn over in his mind how best to incorporate groups other than the peasantry into the struggle for victory and his plans for the new society. Critical to this process were his essays "On New Democracy" (1940), "On Coalition Government" (1945), and "On the People's Democratic Dictatorship" (1949).

It is of course possible to argue that each of these writings was a response to the exigencies of a particular situation — the need to rationalize the United Front with the Guomindang in 1940, the prospect of a coalition government following the defeat of Japan in 1945, and the perceived imperative to reassert the supremacy of the proletariat, defined as workers, peasants and soldiers, over other groups in 1949. Yet what is striking, if one looks beneath the classical Marxist veneer of the invocation of the existence of classes is that as with Confucius, Mao is ascribing a role or function to different groups within society, and that as with Confucius these roles vary from the descriptive to the prescriptive; indeed, in some cases, proscriptive might be a better term.

Thus in Mao's new society, the peasantry would continue to be the main producers, and have the task of ensuring — subject to the vagaries of the weather and the seasons, and the need to guard against corrupt officials — that the granaries remained full. They would be complemented by the new small industrial proletariat, who, just as the artisans of old were the virtuous providers of the tools society needed, would make power machinery and equipment that China would progressively require to develop (though there is no frequent use until the "opening up" of the late 1970s of the term modernization).

Intellectuals would have a role in the new society, but just as in traditional China would be expected to eschew individual thinking on matters of political theory and organization especially. As in Confucian times, the role of the intellectual would be to internalize the principles of the state (or Party) orthodoxy and to practise them and promulgate them at every possible opportunity. In return for this, just as in traditional China, an intellectual might hope to become a member of the ruling group, and to enjoy power, privilege and not a few material advantages in consequence of his or her position. The fact that some peasants and workers also became leading members of the ruling Communist Party in no way invalidates the comparison; in traditional China, as has been noted, in education there were no class distinctions, and even within a single generation a family could rise to prominence through educating a male scion who would subsequently become an official. That intellectuals have, as has often been noted, had a difficult time at the hands of the Party, that their ranks were frequently purged, does not change the fact that they have played a central role in it from the beginning.

The other main group of what, in today's terms, we would call middle-class people that Mao addressed were the commercial bourgeoisie. In Party histories of the period leading up to the Communist victory, this group is often identified with the Guomindang, yet the available evidence suggests that even the wealthier capitalists in Shanghai and other cities, having been very heavily taxed to support Chiang Kai-shek's successive campaigns against the Communists in the 1930s, and having been effectively abandoned to the Japanese in the 1940s, had little love for the Guomindang.[14] Through much of the 1940s, Mao saw a role for progressive elements of the bourgeoisie, notably the groups whom he described as the "petty bourgeoisie," the "bourgeoisie," and later on the "national bourgeoisie." Only the "bureaucratic bourgeoisie," those with close links to the Guomindang and its state apparatus, were to be completely excluded. Mao did not at this stage adequately define these different groups.

With the publication of "On New Democracy" in 1940, therefore, Mao began to address the question of the commercial bourgeoisie's role in the revolution. He sought to encourage that group to support the Party in the struggle. The formation of the Chinese People's Political Consultative Conference in 1949[15] gave them a limited opportunity to influence policy, while managers from this group were widely used in the process of restarting China's albeit small number of factories in the early years after 1949, notwithstanding the nationalization by the mid-1950s of all significant commercial activity. Moreover, individual members of this group, such as Shanghai capitalist Rong Yiren, were used intermittently for several decades after 1949 in an effort to develop trade with Western countries in the face of the US policy to isolate and contain China. Only for a time during the Cultural Revolution, it can be argued, was the commercial bourgeoisie in complete eclipse. When that period came to an end with the death of Mao, the imperatives of modernization meant that commercial skills were at a premium, and actually came to be positively encouraged by the Party.

Confucius, for his part, believed that the merchant knew only "what was profitable...,"[16] yet despite this commerce generally and both internal and external trade formed significant activities in traditional times, and major sources of tax revenue for most dynasties, however ineffectively it may in practice have been collected.[17] Despite its rejection of Western incursions into its territory, the Qing Dynasty accepted help in setting up the Maritime Customs in 1861 to ensure that it would benefit from the sudden increase in the volume and value of its international trade. Through the principle of "official supervision, merchant operation" leading members of that Dynasty profited from commercial activity even while deploring it, while individual compradors grew rich — much as they had always done from possessing commercial and linguistic skills that were in short supply. Mao, just like the Emperors before him, saw the opportunities that a *modus vivendi* with the merchant class could offer. His decision to assign them a role was both critical and in line with the practice, if not the theory, of Confucian China.

It was in his treatment of the landlord class that Mao parted company completely with China's traditional past. While in traditional China the dynasty identified closely with the interests of the landlord class, and saw it as the natural bulwark of stability and the social order,[18] Mao in contrast viewed landlords as the principal oppressors of the peasantry, and the chief obstacle to revolutionary change in the Chinese countryside. In one sense, Mao's task of isolating and undermining the landlord class was made easier by the fact that in twentieth-century China there were no natural ties between the intellectuals and the landlords as there had been between the scholars of Confucian China and the landlord class; in pre-modern China a scholar who became an official might well in turn himself become a landlord, if he was not already from such a background.

In this case as well, though, it can be argued that the role assigned to the landlord class, that of victim, the scapegoat on whom most of the ills of rural China could be blamed, was important. The Party took advantage of the opportunity to consolidate its hold on the countryside through the redistribution initially of landlord-owned land, and by means of campaigns directed against the landlord class.

Divine right

Another aspect of Confucian orthodoxy which had its counterpart in the early years of the People's Republic was the divine sanction accorded to the Emperor in traditional China. Confucius himself claimed to be an agnostic, but the political philosophy which bears his name, and which came to underpin successive dynasties, drew heavily on Chinese mythology for justification of the power and authority of the Emperor. Confucius' disciple Mencius further developed this concept so that in ruling China the Emperor was held to be carrying out the Mandate of Heaven.

For Mao, control of the Communist Party was some time in coming, and coincided with broad acceptance of his views on the importance of the peasantry to the success of the revolution in China. Once this was achieved, however, and with the consolidation of his position following the victory over the Guomindang in 1949, Mao was able to draw legitimacy from a belief system, Marxism-Leninism, which sustained one world superpower, had now liberated China, and appeared to be spreading rapidly throughout the world.

Marxism was, in the way it was presented by the Communist Party to the people of China, the one great new source of universal truth, and the modern scientific equivalent of the divine sanction of old. Although Marxism as a body of theory, and particularly under Mao, would continue to develop, and indeed had its own mechanisms to supposedly enable resolution of differences of view, it was not possible to challenge beyond a certain point the actions or decisions taken by Party officials acting in its name. Indeed, it conferred on Mao, China's ultimate ruler, a legitimacy comparable to that afforded by the doctrine of divine right.

Significantly, though, while in Confucian China the Mandate of Heaven could pass from the Emperor to the leader of a successful rebellion against his rule, or would pass naturally to the Emperor's male heir upon his death, in China under the Communist Party legitimacy attached directly to the person and the writings of Mao himself as both ruler and prophet. This diminished the scope for consideration by the collective Party leadership of policy alternatives not favoured by Mao. It also gave rise to serious abuse of power by the Gang of Four as Mao began to lose his faculties in the early 1970s, and offered no prescription for succession to the top position within the Party after Mao's death.[19]

The control of thought

Just as in traditional China, under the Communist Party unanimity of understanding and of purpose among the population has been considered essential to the maintenance of order and good government. The mechanisms used to inculcate in China's people the truths of the new regime, and to monitor and pre-empt opposing views, have been varied and far-reaching. They have included mass campaigns, public meetings, political discussion groups in the workplace, the dissemination of Mao's works in various forms, the publication of other political propaganda, of literature, poster art, the use of theatre, film, dance and other performing arts, and the exposure of the population to official doctrine through involving them in mass organizations such as women's groups, trade unions, and youth organizations. In addition political study has been an important part of the curriculum in schools and universities for much of the period since the Party assumed power. The media have also been widely used to convey official truths and interpretation of events to the populace at large.[20]

The Chinese people have not simply been seen as the passive objects of this propaganda effort, but rather have been required to become actively involved, internalizing the beliefs offered by the Party, and helping to further promulgate them at work and in society. James Townsend in particular[21] has explored the theoretical underpinnings of individual acquiescence in People's China. Townsend found that political participation was based on a series of principles derived from Mao's writings, notably the concept of the dictatorship of the proletariat (whose goal is to bring into play the full initiative of the masses), the supremacy of the collective interest (the idea that the interests of the state and the nation are taken to be synonymous, and that the interest of each individual is subsumed in this collective interest), the leadership of the Communist Party (because it has the scientific knowledge and political experience to perform this task), the mass line (the Party depends on the masses, and needs to be in constant contact with them), activism and its relation to political consciousness (the belief that zealous involvement will lead to greater awareness and understanding, and that non-activity equals opposition), and the conviction that socialist democracy is served by mass participation in the discussion of laws and policies as they are being made (that it is not solely dependent on elections and the work of representative bodies).[22]

This body of theory then provided a justification for the monitoring of popular attitudes in China under Mao Zedong. The great variety of means used by the Party to remain in touch with people at every level of society, and to convey to them the orthodox view of the issues of the day, meant also that those who deviated from the Party line could be relatively easily identified. For Party members, that organization had its own Discipline Inspection Commission and other means at its disposal to deal with offenders. For the population at large, the Party could, through its members in the workplace and elsewhere, observe, remonstrate with, and ultimately report and have punished, individuals who would not accept the Party's view of the world.

Arrangements could be made to spy on people through neighbourhood security organizations. Ultimately, in the case of recalcitrant individuals the Party had at its disposal all of the organs of government and national security, including the legal system, the police and in the last resort, the PLA. The penalty for resisting the accepted view on any issue could be severe, and during political campaigns and the even more fraught period of the Cultural Revolution, could sometimes be death.

The overall approach, if not the actual methods used to exact compliance with the orthodoxy of the state, was not unfamiliar. The traditional Chinese state very early developed mechanisms of control which were intended to guarantee not only conformity to the law and to accepted norms of behaviour, but also to monitor the population for expressions of dissent.

The Legalist Qin dynasty, for example (221–206 BC), in its total dedication to the creation of a state in which the whole people would contribute to military strength and prosperity, developed the "*bao jia*" system of mutual responsibility. According to this system individuals within a family were responsible for each other's behaviour, and groups of households were responsible (and could be punished by the state) for the behaviour of any household within the group. Although the primary objective under the Qin was to mobilize the population for economic or military effort, the Qin was also wholly dedicated to the control of thought and the eradication of philosophies in conflict with its own — including Confucianism. The "*bao jia*" system could equally be used to identify and root out opponents to Qin rule. The Qin dynasty was known for its spasms of book-burning, during which Confucian classics were seized and destroyed, and not a few Confucian scholars were put to death.[23]

The essential elements of the "*bao jia*" system were revived by more orthodox, Confucian, dynasties at other times in the course of China's history, notably during the Song Dynasty under Wang Anshi, and under the Ming and the Qing. John Fairbank, referring to the means by which the traditional state maintained its hold over people, points to "...the military arrangements of the Ming and Ch'ing, to which were added measures of local control by fear of punishment, as well as by moral exhortation."[24]

In addition to the "*bao jia*" system of mutual supervision, the traditional Chinese state had at its disposal at the centre a conventional Ministry concerned with offences against other citizens and against the state — in the Qing Dynasty the Xing Bu, or Board of Punishments — and the so-called Censorate, largely but not exclusively concerned with monitoring the behaviour of government officials, which could include lapses in orthodoxy. At the prefecture level, throughout China government officials known as magistrates, in addition to trying cases brought locally, would also have responsibility for maintaining order and for reporting and taking action to prevent any outbreak of activity unnacceptable to the state. In this sense they were the central government's eyes and ears in the countryside.[25]

Any evidence of thinking that was heretical, in the Confucian context, would immediately attract attention. In particular, the activity of religious minorities, such as the Muslims, or later the Christians, or of secret societies (which would frequently be active at times of dynastic decline), or of any individual or group appearing to challenge the legitimacy of the dynasty would be of interest. Local magistrates, sometimes with ties to local landlords, could also be expected to be alert to any talk of peasant rebellion.

The "*bao jia*" system and the threat of punishment, augmented by the moral exhortation to which Fairbank refers ("*lu*" — law, augmented by "*li*" — rites and ethics or morality) together afforded the traditional Chinese state one of the most sophisticated systems of thought control of any pre-modern society. Lao She saw this clearly in his play *Cha Guar* about China's early modern transition. The message on the board on the wall of his Teahouse echoes back and forth from China's past into her future — "No Political Discussions Allowed."[26]

Ideology and information in conflict

The injunction to "seek truth from facts" is not new. Mao himself first used it in his essay "On New Democracy" in 1940. It was, he indicated, the scientific approach, but he went on to say, "The only yardstick of truth is the revolutionary practice of millions of people."[27] Almost forty years later Deng Xiaoping revived the injunction, but in an appeal to the Chinese people to put aside the strictures of an ideological interpretation of every aspect of their lives, and to rely on common sense in judging every situation on its own merits.

The potential conflict between accurate information and ideology has perhaps been most explicit in the representation of events by the media in China over the years, though it has also been present in almost every other sphere of activity. As has been noted elsewhere,[28] the tension between the news and propaganda functions of the Chinese news media has since the 1930s always been a characteristic of their work. The New China News Agency (Xinhua), even now the major source of news for most of China's media, is itself responsible to the Propaganda Department of the Communist Party. Thus "...news work is...an important medium of communication between the Party and the masses, an important means of propagating the general and specific policies of the Party, of making the masses understand quickly, (and) of turning (the policies) into material strength..." At the same time, journalists "...must acquire a style of work of penetrating deeply into the realities of life, carrying out investigation and research..."[29] These two injunctions may in practice often contradict one another, and in consequence, the task of the journalist in China has long been a difficult one.

For our purpose here, the issue is the extent to which the Party's commitment to its own ideological parameters got in the way of a recognition of what others might see as objective reality. In the early years, before and immediately after the Long March, the Party could be said to have had little choice but to recognize reality, for its survival depended on it. The broad acceptance of Mao's view of the role of the peasantry in any revolution in China was an indication of just this, and a repudiation of the more strictly ideological view of the purer Marxists who had wanted to create revolution in the cities. The implementation of modest land reform in the base areas, the introduction of basic education, of elements of modern medicine, and the strict code of discipline for the Red troops — all these were policies that clearly responded to needs acutely felt by the population under Communist control. The nascent Party propaganda and media organs could report and promote these achievements without any crisis of conscience, as did also Edgar Snow, Agnes Smedley and others, presenting them as pragmatic policies to the audience overseas.[30] The Second United Front with the Guomindang to fight the Japanese, short-lived though it was, and the effort to appeal to progressive non-Communists in the latter stages of the civil war were also indications of the flexibility of the Party while it was still on the road to power.

As the Communists approached ever closer to victory in the civil war, however, a range of problems loomed larger, which Mao felt could not be resolved without a stricter imposition of more orthodox solutions. The critical factor here may be the transition in the Party's role — from that of a Leninist style organization, at the head of a popular movement to overthrow what many saw as a corrupt and discredited Guomindang government, to that of a new national government, unsure of itself, and facing the need to maintain control of the world's most populous nation, many of whose people were likely still to be deeply hostile to the Party's rule.

It is difficult to exaggerate the scale of the problems confronting the Party as the victory was declared in October 1949. Among the most pressing were the need for reconstruction following many years of civil war and war with Japan, the need to introduce modern industry into China on a much larger scale, the need to transform and increase agricultural production, the need to somehow break out of the diplomatic isolation and containment soon imposed by the United States, and the need to introduce widespread social, educational and health reforms.

Because of its scale the task facing the Party was qualitatively different from that of governing a much smaller and geographically more discrete base area whose people for the most part already supported the Party. The difficulty of promulgating doctrine and implementing central Party decisions across China after the Communist victory brought a new insistence on the rectitude of that doctrine and those decisions, and called for the new methods of spreading this truth which have been noted above.

While most of these methods involved active participation by those whom the Party was trying to reach — and indeed this was not so much an option as a requirement — the ideological rationale for this, the principle of "to the masses, from the masses," was seldom heeded in the actual observance. Thus the opportunity was lost for the Party to "learn from the masses," and the "transmission belts" between the Party and the masses, which the mass organizations, the discussion groups, the media and other institutions were supposed to represent, transmitted expectations and advice in one direction only.

At the root of this lay a problem within Mao's own epistemology. In his "On Practice" written in 1937, Mao first set out his own interpretation of Marx's conclusions on the relationship between theory and practice. Understanding of the true situation in any particular case, he affirmed, came from acceptance of the principles of dialectical materialism. Thus the truth of any knowledge or theory was to be determined "...not by subjective feelings, but by objective results in social practice."[31] From a series of perceptions of a situation, at a certain point a conceptual understanding will be reached. On the basis of this, through judgement and inference, logical conclusions may be drawn about the action or practice that would be appropriate in the circumstances to change the existing reality. This practice will in turn help to reveal the scientific laws that govern nature, society and so on, and will enable the individual to further modify the theory.

Discover the truth through practice, and again through practice verify and develop the truth. Start from perceptual knowledge and actively develop it into rational knowledge; then start from rational knowledge and actively guide revolutionary practice to change both the subjective and the objective world.[32]

Yet despite Mao's belief in the scientific nature of the theory he espoused, clearly it could all too easily be captured by those (including Mao himself) pursuing a political or personal agenda of their own. In the essay "On Practice" Mao makes the point that to be completely sure of whether the (new) theory corresponds to objective reality or not, one must again apply theory to practice "...and see whether it can achieve *the objectives one has in mind*."[33] The point here is that in the understanding of Mao and of the Party under his direction, there were, certainly by the time this essay was written in 1937, pre-existing objectives for the transformation of society and of individual consciousness which would be impossible to ignore, whatever the dialectic of theory and practice apparently revealed. There is, therefore, an agenda that is broadly fixed, tactics that must be followed, and truths on which all but those who have not yet been reached, or who are obstinate, or who are counter-revolutionary, are agreed.

Those who had risen to a higher level of consciousness — trusted Party cadres up until the outbreak of the Cultural Revolution (an assortment of radicals from a proletarian background during the Cultural Revolution) — were responsible for orchestrating the explanation of Party policies to the masses, and involving them in debate and action in support of Party objectives. In this they made use of all the institutions and techniques described above. However, as political campaign succeeded campaign, as the Party wrestled with the need to compel people to follow its orders in the marathon task of feeding and governing the population, any genuine discussion of policy alternatives in the fora provided, if it ever had been possible, was now out of the question. Doubters could be dismissed as having a low political consciousness, as being in need of re-education, or, worse for them, as attempting deliberately to obstruct the progress of the revolution. Debate came to be impossible; the Party was trapped in a cycle of uncaring acquiescence and received truths.

This conflict between the free flow of information and ideas necessary to the maintenance of a vibrant and responsive administration on one hand, and the Party's determination to act only within the parameters of its ideology, and on the basis of pre-conceived truths came to a head with the Hundred Flowers Movement of 1956–57.[34] Widely regarded as a response to the unease of intellectuals, who felt that the Party should be more responsive to constructive criticism, the movement began with Mao's invitation to "let a hundred flowers bloom, a hundred schools of thought contend," an allusion to the culturally prolific "Hundred Schools" period of China's ancient past.

The official encouragement given to the new movement could be seen either as a genuine attempt to address the concerns raised by intellectuals which got out of hand, or as a cynical ploy to expose opponents of the regime. Either way, it has aptly been described as being more akin to the "loyal remonstrance" permitted to the Imperial Censor of a traditional dynasty than to the sanctioning of a "loyal opposition" of the kind one might find in a Western political system.[35] The outcome, as is widely known, was a decision by the Party to crack down on dissent, with many intellectuals suffering harsh punishment as a result. A simultaneous rectification campaign within the Party, though directed against errors in the "work style" of cadres, contributed to an atmosphere of rigid and stifling discipline. Mao's attempt to distinguish in his 1957 essay "On the Correct Handling of Contradictions Among the People" between conflict "among" the people, and conflict "between" the people and their enemies, did little to reassure potential critics.[36]

Following the Hundred Flowers movement, even the Great Leap Forward of 1958, considered by many to have contributed to the major economic reverses experienced in the 1959–61 period, failed to produce any serious discussion of alternatives except at the highest level in the Party, where the espousal of different points of view came to be enmeshed with the political ambitions of individuals, and Mao's own determination to retain power.

Ideology and information in the Cultural Revolution

In mid-1966 China was plunged into the Great Proletarian Cultural Revolution. The reasons for this apparent rekindling of a kind of ardent ideological enthusiasm more usually associated with the early stages of revolution have been widely discussed elsewhere.[37] Instigated by Mao, the movement, as noted above in Chapter 3, has been described succinctly by James Wang as an ideological crusade designed to foster revolutionary spirit and to change China's culture, and especially its political culture. It was also a campaign to counter the bureaucratization that Mao could see spreading in the Party apparatus and in the state. It could be said to reflect fundamental differences of view between Mao and a number of his colleagues over the direction of economic policy, the rural/urban dichotomy, and issues including material or moral incentives. In addition to these genuine policy differences, the Cultural Revolution was clearly also a power struggle between Mao and those who now were keen to replace him. Finally, to a degree it was a response to the external stimulus of the Vietnam War which, rapidly escalating and involving ever greater numbers of American troops, Mao saw as a major threat to China, to which the country should respond by building up revolutionary ardour and further enhancing Mao's policy of self-reliance.[38]

In the context of this discussion, it is also possible to see the Cultural Revolution as a pre-emptive strike by Mao against those who argued that observation of objective reality should take priority over ideology as the chief determinant of national policy. Or, to put it another way, the conflict between ideology and information had reached a climax.

Mao's determination to seize back the initiative was marked by the publication at his instigation by the Party Central Committee on 8 August 1966 of its "Decision…Concerning the Great Proletarian Cultural Revolution" (the so-called "Sixteen Points"), and on 12 August of the "Communique," which approved all of Mao's policies over the previous four years.[39] The media, true to form, immediately began the task of promulgating the principles of the Cultural Revolution.

The "Sixteen Points" spoke of a "new stage" in the socialist revolution in China, in which all revolutionary cadres would be urged to do work in the ideological sphere. The people as a whole would be called on to "...use the new ideas, culture, customs, and habits of the proletariat to change the mental outlook of the whole of society."[40] A particular appeal was to be made to young people, who had no direct experience of the original revolutionary movement leading to the Communist victory. In their *dazibao* (big character posters) and debates they were encouraged to attack bourgeois intellectuals and "those in the Party taking the capitalist road." Workers, peasants, soldiers, revolutionary intellectuals and revolutionary cadres would "form the main force" in the new movement. Recalcitrant cadres and others resisting Mao's ideological prescription for China would be overcome through struggle. The masses were to be trusted, and relied upon, their initiative respected; cadres were urged not to be afraid of "disturbances."[41] The masses would "clarify the correct views, criticize the wrong views and expose all the ghosts and monsters."

Elsewhere in the "Sixteen Points," the first sanction is given to the setting up of revolutionary committees in parallel to the existing Party structures, and reference is made to the shortening and simplification of education at all levels, and its integration with productive labour; scientists would be helped to "transform their world outlook," while the armed forces too would be radicalized. Mao Zedong Thought would be the guide to action in all things.

It could be said that the Cultural Revolution constituted the high point for ideology as the main conditioner of thought and action under the People's Republic; neither before, nor since, has ideology been so influential. In a massive gamble, everything was henceforth to be sacrificed to Mao's new emphasis on ideological purity. This great consciousness-raising movement, however, contained within it the seeds of its own demise.

The history of the Cultural Revolution is well known. In its first and most vigorous phase, from 1966 to 1968, the closure of the schools for a time and the sanction Mao seemed to be giving to "creative anarchy" rapidly led to the cessation of production in many places as bands of Red Guards roamed the country fomenting revolution. Although the People's Liberation Army had been brought in to restore a semblance of order by late 1968, the campaign atmosphere of the movement remained its defining characteristic for the ten years until Mao's death in 1976. The death of Liu Shaoqi in captivity in 1968 and the disappearance in mysterious circumstances of Lin Biao in 1971 underlined the power struggle aspect of events, while successive short bursts of activity targeting various class enemies maintained the tension right to the end. Criticism of intellectuals and the transfer of many of them to the countryside for manual labour, and the overall subordination of expertise to political correctness, slowed China's economic development to a crawl.

The first casualty was truth. Accurate records of production were not kept, the true dimensions of a difficult situation would not be reported, negative news was not published, the well-intentioned views of experts would be suppressed because of their "bourgeois" background, the impact of the mass transfer of skilled people to unskilled work, or of doctors and scientists to manual labour in the fields for ideological reasons would be deliberately concealed. In the many "struggle meetings" held to inculcate Mao's revolutionary line, the dialectical mechanism for arriving at higher truth, involving remonstrating with those with other points of view, became in practice a means of rooting out unorthodox views and imposing pre-determined and fixed views on them.

In the end, as Mao became increasingly senile in the years approaching his death, the interpretation of his will and his doctrine fell increasingly to the so-called Gang of Four. Their often erratic attempts to infuse further radicalism into the movement had little impact on a population by now weary of constant struggle. Those with a fondness for historical allusion might see in this a classic case of the Emperor and his closest advisers in the process of losing the Mandate of Heaven. There was no great surprise inside China or elsewhere when, on the death of Mao in September 1976, a year which had already seen the demise of two other great leaders, Zhu De and Zhou Enlai, scores were very quickly settled, and it became apparent that China was on the threshold of a period of great change.

The Law or the Party as final authority

It is no coincidence that during the first flush of the campaign for the Four Modernizations in late 1978, Deng Xiaoping, having effectively inherited power from Mao, began to make reference again to the need to "seek truth from facts." Invoking Mao's call to do the same in 1940, Deng nonetheless recognized that the chaos of the Cultural Revolution had largely been caused by Mao's more recent obsession with ideology to the exclusion of all else. This approach had particularly limited discussion of alternative ways to take China's development forward. Now, as he is famously alleged to have said in referring to elements of capitalism that might be applied in China, it mattered not whether the cat was black or white, as long as it could catch mice.[42]

Above all, Deng saw that if China was to modernize, to catch up with the West and with Japan, thereby satisfying the widely-held nationalist aspirations of most Chinese, it would need to open up to the outside world and import new technology on a massive scale. This set in train a series of imperatives.

The previous pattern of aid and compensation trade which had partially funded the acquisition of technology from the Soviet Union in the 1950s could not be replicated in relations with the West. Much of the technology China needed would have to be purchased from abroad, and this would require hard foreign currency. To obtain this, China would have to sell much more to the West, yet at the time it had little that the West wanted to buy. What it needed to do was to develop manufacturing industry capable of making things to specifications and quality that would appeal to overseas markets. In turn, this would necessitate the injection of foreign investment and expertise, and this required the establishment of a legal framework within which business could be carried on, in the view of foreigners, reliably and profitably.

It is worth recalling here that Western traders had always insisted on a reliable legal framework for business with China, to protect both their persons and their goods. This had been a major point of contention with the Qing Dynasty, and was a demand subsequently met in part by the extraterritorial provisions of the Treaties of Nanjing of 1842 and Tianjin of 1860. The ending of extraterritoriality in 1943 was followed so quickly by the Communist victory in 1949, and the collapse of most trade with China under the isolation policy imposed by the United States, that the issue of a stable legal framework for renewed trade had not yet been addressed by 1979. The point should be made here that the modern expectation was not only for commercial law and regulations governing business transactions, but also for a whole superstructure of civil and criminal law which would, in the view of foreigners, bring stability to Chinese society and make it a safe place in which to invest their money.

Thus, the discrediting of a primarily ideological approach which was a major consequence of the ten years of Cultural Revolution, and the practical imperatives that followed in the wake of the decision to modernize China, were both responsible for a gradual shift to a new situation in China in which law would provide the new framework for nearly all areas of life.

Few people in China would have argued with the dramatic reduction in the role that ideology now played in ordinary people's lives; most were relieved no longer to have to attend interminable meetings, to couch every debate in terms of a dialectical approach to truth, or to rehearse the Thought of Mao Zedong. However, an unforeseen consequence of the decline of ideology, and the simultaneous rise of law, was that the Communist Party was now much more constrained in its ability to control people. This was immediately apparent in the unprecedented criticisms posted on Democracy Wall in Beijing in the spring of 1979, challenging the pre-eminent role of the Party itself. Moreover, if the Communist morality, the equivalent in some ways of the Confucian "*li*" — subjective, and open to *ad hoc* interpretation by the Party and its officials — was now to give way on all matters to a more fixed body of law, "*lu*" in Confucian terms, how could the Party be expected to adjust? Would it be only a matter of time before the Party would become irrelevant?

These matters will be taken up more fully in later chapters, but it may be appropriate here to reflect briefly on the major points of conflict over the thirty years since the opening-up process began. The earliest body of new law to be introduced after the end of the Cultural Revolution immediately followed the promulgation of the campaign for the so-called "Four Modernizations" — of Industry, Agriculture, Science and Technology, and National Defence — in the spring of 1979. This new code of law related to the governance of foreign investment in China, and the regulation of aspects of trade. This was in turn followed by the introduction of new civil and criminal codes by 1982.[43]

The new framework of commercial law noted above was received with qualified approval by foreign companies and governments anxious to see any measure of regularization introduced into the trade and investment process. However, China's legal framework for trade was (and remains) very much a work in progress, with many contingencies not covered well into the 1980s, and with abundant scope in practice for the Party to intervene and arbitrarily change or simply override the law when it considered the country's interests were at stake. Moreover the military were effectively excluded from regulation in trade matters, while other interest groups or influential individuals could often get around legal requirements as and when necessary. Many hoped that China's anticipated admission to the GATT, later the WTO, finally achieved in 2002, would force compliance through the law to international conventions for the regulation of trade.

Commercial law was of interest to only a minority within China, however, and it was the progress of civil and criminal law that would be of most concern to the man in the street. Here there was no clear utilitarian objective of winning foreign investment to motivate change (or at least the Party did not see things that way). Moreover there was the need to contemplate giving up an approach to governing society, based on morality, that was not just thirty years old, but 2,000 or more years old. To some Party cadres, the loss of the right (though as it was not enshrined in any law it can barely be called that) to intervene in the affairs of citizens wherever and whenever they chose in support of the Party's objectives was quite inconceivable. Indeed, the whole point of a Leninist-style Party was that it should take decisions and act in the name of the people, and should possess sovereign authority in doing so.

Up to this point, therefore, the law and the courts of the People's Republic had been marshalled in support of the Party's political and social objectives, and had been subordinate to them. Could this now change? Could the Party countenance a body of law and legal institutions sufficiently robust that it might afford protection to the citizen against the Party itself?

Initial signs were not hopeful. In order to try to persuade the outside world that times were changing, the Party in 1979 began periodically to invite foreign residents of Beijing to witness various trials. In one such trial witnessed by the writer of a man accused of murder, judged from anecdotal evidence to be not untypical in the way it was conducted, guilt had been predetermined by the police, the prosecutor rehearsed the evidence, the "defending" lawyer joined in haranguing the accused for his anti-social behaviour, the judge passed sentence, and the convicted man was executed the same afternoon. Around the same time, in the spring of 1979, Wei Jingsheng was arrested and given lengthy imprisonment for daring to challenge Party orthodoxy in his posters on "Democracy Wall" in Beijing.

Civil and criminal codes were prepared over the next several years. Yet, especially with regard to the criminal law a clearer codification did not bring a solution to the most pressing problems. Procedures with respect to the detention, indictment and trial of suspected offenders left much to be desired; in particular, anyone who reached a courtroom was presumed guilty, and was denied any effective means of proving themselves innocent. The determination of guilt or innocence effectively remained with the police, acting for the government and Party, rather than being conducted by an independent judiciary. Moreover, the police themselves, in choosing who to target in the first place, in practice continued to respond not to any legal framework, but to direction from the Communist Party.

In the event, it was interaction with the world outside China that would prove decisive in determining the peaks and troughs of progress in the regulation of Chinese life by law. Waves of Party morality continued to wash over China in the form of political campaigns in the early 1980s, conditioned by the degree of concern within the Party at the impact of new foreign influences as business people, students and tourists began to pour into China.

By late 1986, the top level of the leadership had been affected by these influences, as Hu Yaobang appeared to side with students in their demands for greater democracy, and was promptly detained and removed from his post early in the new year. It was Hu's death in the spring of 1989 that would lead to the wave of protest in Tiananmen Square which, on 3–4 June, triggered the event that more than any other illustrated the limitations of the rule of law in China. The Tiananmen massacre showed quite graphically the lengths to which the Party was prepared to go if it felt its authority was being fundamentally challenged. The law played no role in sanctioning the actions of the Party and the PLA that night, nor in the arrests and punishment which constituted the crude campaign for retribution over the next few months.

With political reform off the agenda, there have since 1989 been fewer occasions when the rule of law and the will of the Party might have come into conflict. Indeed, it could be said that the Party's moral orthodoxy has itself subsided in importance, as the old generation of revolutionary leaders finally passes from the scene, and the Party seems to put aside ideology and share in the almost universal pursuit of wealth which seems to characterize China at the beginning of the twenty-first century (see Chapter 10). Yet the role of the Communist Party in Chinese politics and society has still to be resolved. It is difficult to imagine a Party which, while continuing in existence, would cease to set the tone of political life, to dominate decision-making (even in a part-market economy), and to intervene in judicial processes whenever it felt its interests were threatened.

In the final analysis, it may be that so long as a consensus of support for the Party is sustained by continuing rapid economic growth and the appearance of economic opportunity, this matter will not come to the fore. The Party will continue to enjoy the Mandate of Heaven. Should the growing disparities of wealth at some point prove critical, however, or should some unforeseen disaster occur, the demand for a fundamental reform of the political system, and for the genuine rule of law, may become irresistible.

7

TECHNOLOGY AND POLITICAL POWER

It is widely believed both inside China and beyond that the acquisition or cultivation, and implementation, of advanced technology is critical to the country's sustained development. Science and technology constituted one of the "four modernizations" announced in late 1978, and as China has opened up to the outside world and engaged with the international economy, it has sought both to import technology from abroad through purchase and foreign investment, and to use its own resources to develop its own technology.

Yet despite much political fanfare and undoubted achievements in the expansion of economic activity, and especially in the area of production of high quality medium technology goods for export, China's approach to the development of technology — whether by acquisition from abroad or through the embedding of a culture of research and development at home has — it will be argued, been patchy and contained many inconsistencies. It is contended in this chapter that modern-day China has, in fact, inherited a mixed legacy of attitudes in some degree mistrustful of technology, and organizations that impede rather than encourage its spread. It is suggested that the strategy of the Chinese Communist Party has been to partially admit and partially exclude modern technology in a variety of ways, because despite a degree of progress in recent times, some in the Party continue to fear the consequences of more widespread access to technology and the new ideas that it brings, and associate it with their own loss of power.

This historical legacy will be explored, and observations then offered on the political constraints impeding technology development. First, however, it will be necessary briefly to review the recent literature on science and technology in China.

Chinese technology policy: some recent views

The central role of technology transfer in much trade and foreign investment activity in China since the "opening up" has ensured that attention has been drawn to the technology issue among both academics and practitioners.[1] Initially seen as a major market for foreign technology by trade practitioners, China continues to attract great interest in this way. As firms have become involved, however, the difficulties of effecting technology transfer successfully have become better understood, and this learning process has in turn stimulated more interest in China's own technology policy and the manner in which research and development activities are carried out in China. This interest has extended from practitioners to include academics from a variety of disciplines. Some recent views are expressed below.

Richard Suttmeier, discussing the impact of politics and society on science and technology in China, has put forward six propositions: that China's political economy is ill-suited to technological innovation; that the development of science and technology suffers from institutional fragmentation; that science and technology policy formation and implementation face indecision as a consequence of unresolved rivalries; that there is an observable technological nationalism, which has both political and psychological overtones; that there is a "maladjustment" in the relationship between theory and practice — a tendency to be oblivious to theoretical principles, and to employ instead a process of "trial and error"; and that China continues to experience widespread anxieties, insecurities, mistrust and "normlessness" in underlying relationships between people which have a significant negative impact on the successful operation of technologically complex enterprises.[2]

Suttmeier also sees in turn a variety of ways in which science and technology condition both politics and society, noting in particular that the illusion of the "technical fix," referred to by Manfred Stanley as the "cognitive conquest of technicism," may actually help to ossify and reinforce the static nature of Marxism-Leninism. The interactions give rise to a future that is fluid and unpredictable. Should it prove threatening, Suttmeier suggests, science and technology development may be jettisoned by leaders anxious to protect their positions of power.

Wang notes the proliferation of actors on science and technology matters since the reforms began in 1979.[3] He singles out the growth of personal, group and unit interest and involvement in science and technology projects as a major break with the past. Saich, however, highlights the difficulties encountered in establishing linkages in research and development matters between the old vertical structures inherited from the pre-reform period, especially anxieties over the sharing of inventions.[4] Zhao Ziyang's creation in 1986 of the Science and Technology Leading Group to lead and co-ordinate all organizations involved in science and technology both civilian and military was a step forward, yet its effectiveness, particularly after Zhao's own eclipse in 1989, was questionable. Saich sees the Communist Party's continued dominance of the science and technology sector as a key impediment to the sector's proper functioning.

Quan Li, asserting that the prime movers of technical innovation are "technology push" and "market pull," argues that in China the state often controls both the market the research.[5] Looking at the experience of the 1980s, he finds that most technical innovations are led by research units, supported by their production units. Both sufficient infrastructure and working capital are required on the demand side to facilitate operation of the market; there is a need to integrate market competition, planning and political interests.

Steward and Li, writing somewhat later, describe a three-tier research system in China in the 1990s, with the State Science and Technology Commission and other functional commissions drafting plans and performing a supervisory role, industrial Ministries with their research institutes, and provincial and municipal governments with their research institutes.[6] In addition to this hierarchy there is the sectoral organization of research and development capacities under the Chinese Academy of Sciences, the industrial Ministries, the higher education sector, the defence research sector, and the local research sector. These authors find the whole structure to be characterized by "complex replication, fragmentation and inconsistencies." Steward and Li observe that the gap between research and production is being narrowed by the cultivation of capabilities either within research organizations or within business enterprises, and not through collaboration between the two sectors.

Simon and Goldman highlight, *inter alia*, the gap that continues to exist in China between the enunciation of policy and its implementation, and the problems encountered in getting technology from the research institute to the factory floor.[7] These difficulties are compounded by frequent changes of political line which impact on technology policy, and by the illusion of the quick technical fix, noted above, to which many policy-makers continue to subscribe. Even more fundamentally, those authors make the point that Western values accompany the import of Western science and technology into China, bringing what the ideologist Li Honglin described as "decadent and degenerate ideology and culture," and triggering stultifying political campaigns which are counter-productive to the growth of an open research culture in China.

Richard Conroy, in a lengthy report prepared for the OECD at the beginning of the 1990s and based very largely on Chinese language material, finds *inter alia* that economic reforms introduced up to that time were "ambiguous" towards the need to persuade enterprises to make "appropriate decisions over investment, cost reduction, and the introduction of new or improved products."[8] This view is reflected in the later work of Porter and Forrester on management structures in China, which found these problems still apparent towards the end of the century.[9] Conroy, writing immediately after Tiananmen, also notes the worrying tendency of the Chinese government to be willing to forego foreign investment "in pursuit of wider domestic objectives."[10]

In the volume edited by Feinstein and Howe, various authors take a more positive view of progress in the mid-1990s, especially with respect to technological improvements in older enterprises.[11] Yet overall the editors conclude, in many respects the "objectives of technology reform are still not being attained," with many obstacles still needing to be addressed.

Only Q.Y. Yu among the recent work published outside China, notably takes a more optimistic view. Yu sees the decisions of the Communist Party Central Committee and the State Council of 1995 and 1996 on deepening science and technology reform as turning points in technology policy. Yet there appears to be little that is really new in the commitment to "take economic construction as the main battlefield," to speed up technological progress in agriculture, or to encourage enterprises, influenced by the market, to be the main focus of technological development.[12]

Taken as a whole, these views offer a picture of a technology sector in China experiencing significant difficulty, whether in terms of structures for formulating and implementing technology policy, the organization, aims and objectives of research and development, the intellectual atmosphere surrounding research, or the conditions governing technology transfer from abroad. Moreover, there is reason to believe these views are held in some degree by practitioners, both Chinese and foreign.[13]

Yet these problems have historical roots, both in the recent past and in the more distant past. These will be considered in the next two sections, before a return is made to the contemporary period and an analysis is offered of political constraints on the acquisition of technology. In this way it is hoped to shed further light on China's pattern of apparently conflicting technology policies.

The historical legacy

Traditional attitudes to technology

In traditional China, the application of technology evolved from two imperatives. The first was the need to feed a population that was, by the standards of early civilizations, very large, taking into account the water-based agricultural economy in the areas where Chinese civilization was born. The second was the need to provide military hardware and weapons with which soldiers could keep the peace, secure the position of the elite within China, and secure China's borders against attack from outside.

With regard to the first point, what developed was an agriculture based on the cultivation of rice, supplemented in some areas by other crops, and by animal husbandry. The technology used to control scarce water resources necessary to rice culture became progressively more sophisticated, while still depending on animal power and manpower. As skills and experience were accrued, it became possible to grow and harvest enough food, given peace and reasonable weather, to feed a very large population. Moreover, the need for employment, and work that needed doing, were broadly in balance. Thus there was no need to develop agricultural technology further — the theory of the "high level equilibrium trap."[14]

The state in traditional China came to be able to control this process in ways that are not generally apparent in other traditional societies. A class of scholar bureaucrats came into being to supervise water conservation and grain storage. The state was able to exact tax and tribute from its subjects in grain, which was shipped along canals it had ordered to be dug for the purpose. There was no rising class within China's borders which was excluded from political activity and would profit from exploiting new technology.[15] There was no real commitment to the practical application of scientific invention to China's economic life.

With regard to the second point, military need, from the Western Han dynasty (206 BC to 8 AD) the central Chinese state inherited the accumulated knowledge of military technology passed down from the tribal and feudal periods of China's history. This technology would henceforth be used to protect the Court, to keep the peace internally, and to secure China's borders. For this latter purpose military technology was used with indifferent success. Construction of successive Great Walls, and later the use of rocketry and cannon in battle failed to prevent invasion and extended periods of foreign rule even before the Western powers came to China in the nineteenth century.

Yet even here, where it might be thought that the need was most pressing, there seemed little impetus for traditional China to develop and build on its early technological lead. While the state was interested in the latest scientific developments in the West as they became known through the Jesuit presence in Peking, and was aware of their application to military technology, the implementation of this knowledge in China before the coming of the West remained very limited. Nor did China feel any need to mount voyages of conquest to distant shores.[16]

The attitude of China's traditional ruling class towards technology was therefore ambivalent to say the least. Confucian ideology, the orthodoxy of the traditional state, had little use for technology, while the ethnocentric character of the traditional Chinese state meant that it was disinclined to borrow new technology from overseas, even when it might have helped to save the traditional dynastic structures. The approach was to tolerate technology with reluctance, rather than exploit its possibilities and to dominate it.

The impact of foreign technology: China in transition

If the attitude of the court and the elite in traditional China towards technology was one of benign neglect, that of China's rulers after the impact of the West in the mid-nineteenth century became one of outright hostility. New technology was seen as irrelevant to the dominant mode of economic life that was agriculture, disruptive of the social order, and potentially capable of undermining the orthodoxy of the state and the legitimacy of its government. In setting its face against the wholesale adoption of new technology, it can be argued the government of late Qing China was offering a rational reaction to an irrational set of circumstances that it saw only too clearly as a threat to its very existence.[17]

The very nature of the pressure brought to bear on China was the consequence of superior technology. The Industrial Revolution in Western countries had inevitably brought with it great strides in military technology. The use of steam-powered ships by the British navy was decisive in the British victory in the first Opium War with China, and this advantage was matched on land in a contest fought between a British force equipped with the most modern armaments of the time and the ill-equipped traditionally organized Chinese troops. In this sense, the whole unequal treaty system that flowed from this military defeat for China was a result of the technological inferiority of its weaponry.

The new technology impacted on China in a number of ways. There was first and foremost the continuing military aspect. The response of the Chinese government to the crisis of the Western impact was not to embrace the new military technology, but rather to employ strategies designed to keep it at arms length. In consequence, it was not until almost the turn of the century, and a much greater loss of territorial integrity, that the central government agreed to form the small but relatively modern Peiyang Army. Such experiments as were undertaken earlier in the establishment of small modern arsenals and the acquisition of modern weaponry were ventured largely on the initiative of provincial leaders, whose relative influence in their own regions increased accordingly.[18] Even the demonstration effect of the arming of Chinese troops with foreign weapons under General Gordon, and the successful suppression at last of the massive Taiping Rebellion failed to move the court in Peking on this issue.

The court in consequence became progressively weaker, unable to defend itself effectively either from domestic rebellion or, as the century drew to a close, from further foreign encroachment. Militarily, the foreign powers maintained a stranglehold on China until well into the twentieth century.

Reinforcing the foreign military capability was the transport network which rapidly grew up using Western technology. From the mid-nineteenth century steamships began to ply China's many rivers and inland waterways, transporting people and goods with an ease previously unknown in the Middle Kingdom. Initially this was a sector in which Chinese participation was important through the China Merchants Steam Navigation Company, but from the turn of the century most steamships in Chinese waters came to be owned and run by foreigners.[19] From the last decade of the nineteenth century railways too were built, but up until relatively late these were often largely foreign-owned enterprises which in their routes and manner of operation conformed to the strategic and commercial requirements of the foreigners in China.

New technology enabled the commercial penetration of China by the foreign powers, providing the means by which trade could be carried on with increasing intensity, and giving rise to the formation of dynamic modern settlements in Treaty Ports like Shanghai in which foreigners lived and worked. From around the turn of the century modern industry began to take root in China. With some exceptions, this too was dominated by foreigners, with British investment in industry leading the way, overtaken by Japanese investment by 1930. Factories tended, however, to concentrate on the rapid production of readily saleable consumer goods such as textiles and tobacco products,[20] with the result that even by the outbreak of the Pacific War China still did not have "machines to make machines" — the heavy industry that underpinned the strength and independence of the Western countries and Japan. Moreover the distribution of modern industry, confined as it very largely was to China's coastal strip of Treaty Ports, was geographically lop-sided.

Together, the military and commercial penetration of China by the foreign powers in the late nineteenth century, facilitated by superior technology, and complemented by the rapid spread of Western missionary activity, constituted a very serious challenge to the social order, and contributed materially to the collapse of the Qing Dynasty in 1911. From the beginning of the twentieth century, the lure of wages in cash, and life in the Treaty Ports gave rise to unprecedented levels of migration back and forth between the urban centres and the rural hinterland, reflecting fluctuating degrees of economic desperation among working people in either place. Nationalist and Communist movements grew up, trade unions came into being to fight for workers' rights. The orthodoxy and certainties of the previous twenty centuries were swept away, to be replaced, for the time being, with nothing of any substance.

Thus China's experience of modern technology prior to the founding of the People's Republic in 1949 was very largely of the brutality of foreign armies, and exploitation of its people by largely foreign commercial interests. Only during the intermittent civil war between 1927 and 1949 were Chinese people in control of significant modern technology, and this was the technology of destruction. It is little wonder that after 1949 China's new leaders, and Mao Zedong in particular, continued to be wary of modern technology as a principal instrument of self-improvement.

Technology and power in People's China

China reconstructs: technology on the Soviet model

In the early years of the People's Republic, as we have seen elsewhere in this book, China suffered significant diplomatic isolation at the instigation of the United States. Eastern Europe's incorporation into the Soviet sphere of influence, along with the outbreak of the Korean War, generated a new hostility towards China in the United States and a strong desire to "contain" communism at any cost.

Talks with the Soviet Union led to a somewhat reluctant decision on the part of the Chinese leadership to import industrial technology and equipment from the Soviet Bloc, to be paid for with shipments of grain. China simultaneously introduced the Soviet system of central planning, with the first plan strongly biased towards the establishment of heavy industry.[21]

The industrialization process that took place is significant in several respects. First, the actual technology acquired by China, for iron and steel production, oil refineries and other chemical plants, locomotive works, truck plants, factories to make construction equipment and materials, arsenals and shipyards among others, was itself in many cases derivative and old-fashioned, either dating back to the early Stalinist period, or having come to the Soviet Union from the United States under Lend-Lease arrangements during the Second World War. While it was an improvement on having no heavy industry, it came with an inbuilt obsolescence that would increase China's difficulties later on.

Moreover, the thousands of Russian technicians who accompanied this vast project of technology transfer were in all too many cases as proprietorial about their installations and as dismissive of Chinese claims to control over them as the Treaty Port foreigners had been before the Communist era. Once again Chinese managers were expected to be grateful for imported technology, while having to endure repeated interventions on matters of its implementation and use.

The need to make payments to the Soviet Union in grain showed up the uneasy co-existence of agriculture and modern industry in China. For centuries, grain production has been an obsession of Chinese governments aware that failure to secure adequate provision of grain to meet the needs of the population usually produced political unrest, and in the worst cases rebellion. The need to mortgage any grain surplus to meet the cost of industrial technology disturbed China's leaders. It also threatened the socio-political objective of progressive collectivization in the countryside. While there had been substantial progress from mutual aid teams, through lower and higher stage co-operatives, to Communes by 1958, the grain export requirement combined with the first of several poor harvests to undermine initial support for the Communes in the late 1950s. Soviet domination of the direction of industrial development moreover had ruled out any possibility of socio-political experimentation on any scale in industry.[22]

Thus it was that when China's failure to keep up with the payments, and the growing ideological split between the two countries over the inevitability of war with the capitalist world, led to a sudden withdrawal of Soviet technicians and assistance in 1960, the project had probably, from China's viewpoint, already outlived its usefulness. The experience of acquisition of industrial technology had been very mixed. It could be argued that Chinese society, and perhaps even more so the Chinese leadership, had still not taken technology to its heart. Industrial technology had been acquired from abroad through deals between the Chinese and Soviet states. The idea of growing the country's own technology through assiduous attention to research and development was as alien as it had ever been.

Politics in command: technology policy in the 'sixties and seventies'

This inner conflict over the value of technology became more explicit in the early 1960s as China entered a period of even more complete isolation, this time both from the West and from most of the countries of the Communist Bloc. In due course this attitude of suspicion, coupled with the tendency to make a virtue out of the necessity of having to do without new inputs of high technology, became inextricably linked to the "red-expert" controversy which fed into the Cultural Revolution.

A case can be made that on the matter of technology some Chinese leaders saw an analogy with the Sinification of Marxism. In China revolution had not occurred so long as the Communist Party had followed the tenets of orthodox Marxism and tried to organize the urban working class; rather it had taken Mao's recognition that the vast masses of the peasantry needed to be radicalized before the revolution could succeed. So it was, some felt, with modernization and the introduction of technology; China's circumstances required that technology and industry should be diffused at an appropriate and affordable pace throughout the countryside, rather than concentrated at an advanced level in a few major cities.

The pedigree for this way of thinking may be traced back to the experiments with rural industrial co-operatives that were undertaken by Christian social reformers in the mid-1930s, and on a larger scale by the Industrial Co-operative Movement which functioned in much of unoccupied China in the early years of the Anti-Japanese War.[23] Mao himself acknowledged his debt to this movement.[24] The essence of this approach was that in a poor and populous country like China the concentration of relatively advanced technology in large factories in big cities actually produced more problems than it solved. It created a sharp imbalance in style of life and at times in standard of living between the city and its hinterland, encouraged uncontrollable migration of working people back and forth, placed impossible pressures on accommodation, health and hygiene and contributed little or nothing to the resolution of China's most pressing problems, which lay in the countryside. A bonus to the alternative proposed was that small-scale rural industry using locally available and relatively low-level technology could also be organized in a collective way giving people a measure of responsibility and control over their own production for the first time in their lives.[25]

These themes had been developed by the Communist Party following its assumption of national power, and implemented through the collectivization of agriculture, and gradual introduction of small-scale industry into the countryside throughout the 1950s in parallel with the establishment of heavy industry on the Soviet model, usually in the cities and larger towns. By the early 1960s, then, there was already substantial precedent for an alternative approach to industrialization, to the introduction of technology, and therefore to modernization.[26]

During the Cultural Revolution, beginning in 1966, one of the key issues on which pitched battles were, sometimes literally, fought was that of "redness" versus expertise — whether a correct and comprehensive understanding of revolutionary objectives, and an unwavering commitment to them, should have precedence over professional, often technical expertise. Mao had repeatedly asserted the importance of putting "politics in command."[27] It was but a short step further for some of his supporters to interpret this as a repudiation of any expertise and all advanced technology.

Although the educated professional people who were often the target of the campaigns for greater redness were generally singled out for class reasons, because in many cases they came from a middle class (bourgeois) or relatively privileged background, they were also in many cases the custodians of skills essential to China's technological modernization. The attack on them undermined China's capacity to move ahead technologically.

For much of the ten years of the Cultural Revolution, therefore, the Chinese government was under the influence of people who were, just as in Qing times, hostile to modern technology. This attitude was reflected in a widespread introduction of small-scale industry into the countryside through the Commune system, with an emphasis on local self-sufficiency in the acquisition of raw materials and the satisfaction of local needs. Since the beginning of the Second Five Year Plan in 1959, the rural sector had been given equal importance with heavy industry, and this shift now developed into an explicit rejection of the Soviet model of advanced heavy industrial bases in the urban areas.[28] China's most technologically advanced industries, generally those built up with Soviet assistance, were allowed to languish.

Science and technology: modernization and the age of reform

In 1979, all this was about to change. The death of Mao three years earlier had begun to pave the way for a fundamental re-ordering of priorities by his successors. The growing influence of the elder statesman Deng Xiaoping, and his determination to promote national reconstruction held the promise of a dramatic change of fortune for technology in official policy.

The proclamation of the "Four Modernizations" — of industry, agriculture, science and technology, and national defence — marked the most explicit commitment of any Chinese government to date to modernization in general, and to technological innovation in particular. As the policy unfolded it became clear that the Party meant to seek this new technology from the outside world, in particular from the capitalist West and from Japan; indeed, this would be the only way for China to acquire new technology quickly enough to enable it to catch up and achieve the rapid change it desired in its economy as a whole. Moreover, this would necessitate involvement in the international economy, both as a borrower and as an importer and exporter; this was involvement that the Chinese Communist Party had previously shunned quite specifically.

From 1979, new technology was introduced into China in a variety of ways.[29] Over the past thirty years technology transfer has affected almost every sphere of industrial manufacture in China, with prominent examples in the vehicle industry, electronics and information technology, household appliances, cameras and optical equipment, construction equipment, and — with somewhat less success to date — aircraft manufacture. Usually, the type of technology and the purpose for which it was required guided the choice of mode and framework for its transfer. The first enterprises affected were those able to attract foreign investment.

Early tentative enquiries about the scope for foreign investment and manufacture in China came from foreign companies encouraged by the lure of cheap labour and the possibility of a substantial domestic market for certain types of goods. This interest led to a growing number of joint ventures in which a significant element was usually the transfer of technology by the foreign partner to upgrade existing facilities or establish new ones in China.

In these cases the particular requirement for technology and the pace of its transfer were usually determined by the foreign partner. The decision on the Chinese side to go ahead with the proposal was increasingly taken within the enterprise itself, or within the group to which it belonged, but sometimes required approval from the central government's State Economic Commission, or later the State Planning Commission, if substantial expenditure of foreign exchange was required.[30] Implementation of the new technology was a matter for joint supervision by the two sides in the joint venture; disagreements between the

Chinese and foreign side were usually, but not always, over technical matters, as both sides had compelling reasons to make a success of the venture.

By the 1990s, China's legal and financial infrastructure having been substantially refined, some joint ventures were being formed very largely because of the tax advantages they offered, and in these cases very little technology transfer seemed to take place.[31]

In cases of sub-contracted manufacture of items by a Chinese enterprise on behalf of a foreign company, technology may have been transferred and equipment installed specifically for the duration of the agreement. In these cases the principal technology would not have been transferred permanently, though some of the related "know-how" could not of course be reclaimed at the end of the term of the contract.

The transfer of technology on the initiative of foreign companies also took place in the form of licence agreements to enable existing Chinese enterprises to manufacture items under licence from foreign companies, according to which they paid a periodic royalty to the foreign companies for the use of their technology. Because such arrangements usually required a greater capital input from the Chinese enterprise concerned, they were generally less popular than joint ventures.

Where there has been a clear foreign commercial interest, the transfer of technology to Chinese enterprises from abroad has been subject to relatively little regulation by the state, and has often been on the initiative of the foreign company involved, with the active collaboration of the Chinese side. Only if a substantial injection of capital was required of a Chinese partner in a joint venture, for example, would vetting and approval be likely to be needed from central authority.

There is of course another group of enterprises for which the Chinese government has played a much more conspicuous role in the introduction of new technology. These have tended to be enterprises engaged in manufacturing activity *not* geared to the production of readily disposable consumer goods, and which may find it difficult to attract foreign investment.

In many such cases, the need for new technology has been determined by the leadership of the plant itself, and the requirement met through a search for suitable technology overseas undertaken by the Ministry for the industry concerned. In these circumstances, the priorities and plans of the central Ministry have also been reflected in the decision taken over which technology was to be introduced, and how, and inevitably there has been some degree of compromise between the wishes of the leaders of the plant concerned and those of the central Ministry. The Ministry's power in the matter would depend on the state of the centralization/decentralization debate at the time (see below). Moreover, agreement for the release of foreign exchange with which to purchase the technology may have been needed from the State Planning Commission, or now from some other body.

In other cases, one of the Foreign Trade Corporations under the former Ministry of Foreign Economic Relations and Trade (MOFERT), later the Ministry of Foreign Trade and Economic Co-operation (MOFTEC) and now the Ministry of Commerce (MOFCOM), may have been asked to locate and negotiate the transfer of technology for the industry whose interests it represents, in association with the Ministry for the industry concerned. This approach may help to facilitate any compensation trade element necessary to enable the purchase of the technology.[32]

Within the Chinese external trade structures there are also several organizations concerned in a general way with the acquisition of technology and "know-how" from overseas. Prominent among these is the China National Technical Import Corporation, whose brief includes the research and acquisition on behalf of Chinese organizations of technology covering a broad range of productive activity. Usually, but not always, the request will have originated with a Ministry or even with a higher level of government.

Closer to the plant itself, in some cases one of China's many research institutes or universities attached to or with strong collaborative links with a particular large plant or industry may be asked to seek out or advise on new technology. The nature of the institute's involvement may vary from vetting the technical presentations of foreign firms, through preparing a justification to present to higher authority, to researching the available technology, locating a source, and negotiating the deal. Since the late 1980s it has become common for the staff of institutes to undertake commissions to provide technical advice of this kind to enterprises with which they have no connection, and this activity has become a necessary source of funding for many research institutes.

In all of the examples offered above, there has been no obvious commercial incentive to trigger the technology transfer through a joint venture or any other kind of investment by a foreign company. In these cases China has effectively been purchasing technology at its own expense.

Science and technology in the new century

The new century has brought new challenges. As China has become more integrated into the world economy, and the possibilities for substituting high-technology items for more basic exports have become ever more apparent, so have China's leaders begun to address some of the problems noted in the previous section. This process has been helped by the succession to positions of authority, in the most senior as well as middle management positions, of a new generation of more highly-qualified people, many of whom have obtained postgraduate degrees overseas.

The determination of the Party to grasp the nettle was due to a much more widely shared perception that structural divisions and interdepartmental jealousies, along with residues of old attitudes hostile to science, were slowing China's technical progress. Accordingly, in 1998 a new overarching Ministry of Science and Technology was set up to replace the State Science and Technology Commission. The new Ministry, known in English by the acronym MOST, was intended to embrace in its remit all scientific and technical activity under the direction of the government except for military research. It was to make policy, and be the main point of reference on science matters. It was also to be the principal channel for the distribution of research funds.

The creation of MOST has solved some problems, but not others. It should have served to reaffirm — or, it might be said, to establish for the first time in modern China — the link between applied technology and science, particularly as production evolves to take account of developments in high technology areas like biotechnology, nanotechnology, information technology, environmental science and space. Its authority over the choice of technologies to be prioritized for government spending means that other Ministries must listen to it and cooperate with it; this does not prevent them from pursuing their own priorities, however, sometimes in duplication of or in conflict with those of MOST, notably in relations with organizations overseas.

Moreover, MOST does not really control all the science that goes on in laboratories: many of the most important parts come under and are still funded by the Chinese Academy of Sciences and its sister academies. The funding situation is complex. Through the National High-Tech Research and Development programme (the "863 programme"), MOST funds research and development in key applied high-tech areas, while through the Key Basic Research Programme (the "973 programme") funds are provided for basic research. These funds are assigned by MOST to scientists working in any of the 100 research-active universities (out of an approximate total of 1,100) and 6,000 research institutes throughout China. MOST's "Torch programme" focuses on building research links with industry, and setting up science parks around the country.

The Chinese Academy of Sciences, however, runs a network of (currently) 108 research institutes and one university of its own, and is probably the leading source of expert scientific advice (as opposed to policy advice) to the State Council and to the Communist Party. The CAS receives funding for both its applied and basic research work directly from the government, as well as income from project grants from MOST. Other Academies (notably for Medicine, Agriculture and Engineering), while they lack the large number of institutes, are funded in a similar way. The Natural Science Foundation of China, a kind of Research Council, distributes funds for about one-third of the basic research done in China, and a small amount of applied research. Scientists may also seek and obtain research funds from local government or local enterprises. Relations between MOST and these other bodies are often tense and difficult, with each side continuing to protect its prerogatives with great care.

A further dimension to the problem concerns the rate of increase of government expenditure on science and technology. So far, this has not come close to the target figure of 5% of GDP projected in 1995.[33] Actual spending on research and development, which includes science and technology, was said to equal 0.5% of GNP in 1999,[34] but had climbed to 1.4% of GDP by 2006. Under the "2020" Medium to Long-term Plan for Science and Technology," that figure is projected to rise to 2.5% of GDP by 2020. This compares as a proportion of GDP spent on R and D to a UK figure in 2007 of 1.8%. However the actual sum spent by China, of 124 billion yuan in 2002, if the figure is accurate, is still significant.

It is claimed by the Chinese government that an increasingly significant proportion of funding for China's national R and D effort is contributed by private companies, yet there is no real evidence that this is the case. While some joint ventures do spend significant sums on R and D, the great majority of purely Chinese private companies are not high-tech in any event, and are primarily concerned with increasing turnover and maximizing profits for their owners or their shareholders.

This does not make for a climate in which investment in R and D is likely to flourish (see Chapter 9).

One development that is of particular significance is the encouragement given in recent years by MOST and by large municipal authorities all over China to the establishment of science parks, where academic researchers from scientific institutions can apply their knowledge to practical problems, "commercializing" the technology in which they have expertise. These science parks have incubated a very considerable number of impressive high-tech start-ups in recent years, which have contributed very substantially to China's strategic capability in high technology activity, and have rewarded the academic institutions, municipalities and private individuals who have invested in them. In one sense, this collaboration between academia and industry is not new; in the 1950s, following the Soviet model, many of China's industrial Ministries operated their own academic research and teaching institutions to train their own staff, and most of these are now universities in their own right.

Despite this successful initiative, there remain some areas of vulnerability in the operation of the science parks. There is to date relatively little active collaboration between Chinese high-tech start-up companies and their overseas counterparts, despite encouragement and incentives offered by foreign governments to enable this to happen. Also, in a good many of China's science parks, a large proportion of the facilities remain empty, or have been turned over to retail or office space.

Some indication of the direction of China's push for high technology is given by the priorities outlined in the 10th Five Year Plan 2001–2005, the "Technology Foresight Programme" of 2003, and the "Medium and Long Term Plan for Science and Technology," sometimes referred to as the "Twenty Twenty Vision," which will run from 2006 to 2020. Under the 10th Five Year Plan, a considerable number of priority areas are identified for science, indicating a desire for upgraded technology which will be useful in improving China's international commercial competitiveness; no real blueprint is offered for science, however. The Foresight Programme conclusions of 2003 take this commercial focus a stage further, identifying aspects of information technology, biotechnology and materials science as areas for future research investment. But it is the Medium and Long Term Plan that really brings together for the first time, however, the socio-economic needs of China over the next two decades and the ability of Chinese science and technology to address these needs. The extensive process of consultation that has produced this Plan, the opening references to developments overseas, and the attempt to include consideration of social, legal and other impacts of science policy make this document a milestone in the evolution of science and technology planning in China.

Yet despite these relatively clear indications of the role that technology is intended to play in China over the next several decades, some of the problems that have arisen with respect to implementation of technology objectives noted in this and earlier sections may be expected to continue to hamper progress. Among these are the transitional nature of the economy, the conflicting agendas of those involved, and the appeal of and belief in the "quick technical fix" — usually from abroad. Moreover the uncertain relationship between the Party and government on one hand, and the growing private sector — both Chinese and foreign — on the other, raises many questions about the country's high-tech goals. While the Chinese state is now fully committed to high technology, the particular nature of China's society and government will help to determine how that technology is used in the years to come. In the following section, the root causes of this uncertainty will be examined.

Political constraints on the acquisition of technology

Critical to the technological modernization of China has been the fact that throughout the twentieth century, through the reform period and right up to the present day, technology has been very largely acquired from outside rather than developed at home. The nature of China's past, and its more recent progress under Communist rule, have meant that the process of acquiring and implementing new technology has been highly political. Where the axes of technology and power intersect, difficulties and obstruction have all too often been the order of the day.

The 'half and half' economy

There are first those dilemmas caused by the fact that China remains a part-command, part-market economy. While the most desirable means of technology transfer from China's point of view, and often the most effective, is that undertaken through some form of private foreign investment, usually overseas investors are only prepared to become involved where there is a clear market and the prospect of a return. This is true for a range of consumer products that may appeal to the domestic market, or foreign markets, or both; in these sectors of manufacture the implementation of foreign technology through foreign investment of one kind or another has been most conspicuous. Yet there are other industries of perhaps greater strategic importance that operate in a free market fashion outside China, but are in no prospect of operating in a market fashion within China well into the foreseeable future.

Such a one until very recently was the vehicle industry, embracing cars, trucks, buses and their component parts. Here in the 1980s and 1990s there was no natural competition, as between Ford and General Motors in the US for example. Indeed there was no natural domestic market for a variety of reasons — lack of a developed road network, lack of money at the disposal of would-be consumers, the need for licences, permissions and often influence to be able to own and operate a motor vehicle, and the requirement imposed by some manufacturers that domestic buyers must pay for their products in scarce foreign exchange. Nor was there any significant overseas market in the hard-currency countries of the West, in Japan or East Asia, as China at that time made no effort to make its vehicles conform to internationally accepted standards, and in any case foreign joint venture partners in the industry, where they existed, moved to block China's exports in order to avoid undercutting their own export strategy.[35]

These anomalies, while they cannot all be traced directly to the Chinese government, were the consequence of the uncertain direction of Chinese policy, and its hybrid state. They clearly affected the industry's capacity to attract investment. Only now, in the early years of the new century, has there started to be a natural market inside China for the products of its vehicle industry, and it is still too soon to predict whether — because of road capacity, the environment, or some other pressing reason — the central government may not yet intervene to regulate output.

Moreover there are some industries that may never be profitable. These might include infrastructural industries such as iron and steel, chemical industries, the manufacture of rail transport equipment, and the operation of the railway network for example — those producing a product or a service on which the further progress of the country and its people heavily depend, but which they simply could not afford if the goods and services were priced according to profit and loss. In these cases the state has not abandoned the concept of social need, and it would be self-defeating for it to do so.

There has in recent times been a tendency to underestimate the continuing centrality of state-owned firms, many of which are loss-making, in China's economic life.[36] The problem is that these enterprises tend to be the least innovative technologically, and the most in need of new technology from overseas. Yet they often carry with them the immense and costly baggage of social provision for which state-owned firms in China have become famous — the provision of accommodation, subsidized food, education, health care and security in old age for their workers and their families. It is a widely recognized dilemma confronting the State that if these firms were to become more efficient and market-oriented they would be better able to afford new technology, yet they need the technology precisely in order to be more efficient. Moreover they would need to dispense with much of their social provision and put many people out of work, actions that would pose a serious threat to political stability. Thus many state-owned industries are caught in a cycle of high expenditure, low output, and technical stagnation.

Differing skills, conflicting agendas

There are other ways in which political concerns have impacted on China's ability to absorb new technology. Several of these have to do with the differing skills and agendas of people in power at this time of great political and economic flux in China.

Until very recently, it has often been the case that the closer it has been necessary to approach the top echelons of power in Party or state structures in China, the more remote has been the possibility that technical expertise necessary to assess the requirement for technology will genuinely be brought to bear on the decision over whether to import it or not. Following on from this, the skills of senior leaders have been likely to be political, and their objectives to be political objectives; in this sense the technical merit of a proposal may often have taken second place. Some senior Party and State officials may have associated new technology with the growth of entrepreneurial activity, and had very mixed feelings about the evolution of a society over which they no longer have full control.

Despite the growing trend since the turn of the century for engineers, scientists and other highly qualified people to occupy the most senior positions within the Party and government, new technology may still be seen by some power-holders at the centre as potentially threatening. Such people may still fear decentralization of control of previously centralized state-owned industries, and the growth of private enterprise in the economy overall. Just as in the nineteenth century, new technology is increasingly seen by prominent individuals in the regions as a way of reinforcing their power and influence vis-à-vis the centre.

On a simpler level, policy shifts on decentralization and on issues of privatization over the years of reform have made effective planning of any kind difficult, with most managers not knowing to whom they would be responsible or how much scope they would have from one month to the next. In such an atmosphere the important steps necessary to upgrade technology may well not be taken.

Finally, it should be recognized that the whole politicized context of daily life in China constitutes a hostile climate for rational decision-making, on matters of technology as on all else. Despite many outward changes, China remains a Marxist state, one in which there are still major conflicts over policy matters within the ruling party. Hidden agendas flourish, decisions are often taken in secret, and political and cultural imperatives intrude at all levels.[37] This is not to say that these things do not happen in other countries, but rather that their frequency in China is perhaps greater than in many other places.

In this way the attempt to introduce new technology becomes a political football. Modernization, dependent as it is on the widespread implementation of new technology, is in fact held up by the operation of the existing political structures and a heavy baggage of inherited political attitudes and behaviour. Genuine rational discussion of the technological choices facing China is thus rendered difficult, and for individuals sometimes even perilous.

While it is said that this situation will change with time, the evidence suggests that within the pool of better-educated and more outward-looking younger talent which might be the instrument of change, many are looking to the burgeoning private sector for a career, some are finding employment with Sino-foreign joint ventures, and not a few end up leaving China for good to seek a better life abroad. The hope is that at least some of those who have been abroad for further study will return, and will assume senior positions of authority in the Party and government, as they are starting to do. More than anything, this will bring change to the culture of decision-making on science and technology matters in China.

Attitudes to research and development

At the beginning of this section, it was suggested that China has as yet made only limited progress away from the wholesale acquisition of technology from overseas, and towards a policy of attempting to nurture and "grow" it at home. Why has this been so?

The explanation may partly lie in the habit of thinking of technological innovation as something that originates elsewhere and is provided by someone else. In support of this view it is true to say that for most of the period from the First Opium War of 1839 up to the Communist victory in 1949 China lagged well behind the West and Japan technologically, for which it paid a heavy price. As has been noted, technological inputs subsequently came from the Soviet Union, followed by a further period of isolation and experimentation with low technology solutions that were felt at the time to be suitable to China's needs.

However, Joseph Needham has offered conclusive proof through his multi-volume work on traditional Chinese science that, before the impact of the West, Chinese civilization was second to none in inventiveness;[38] as noted above, the reasons for the failure to move to application of the technological possibilities in traditional Chinese society were complex.

Since 1980, other factors apart from historical experience have influenced attitudes to technological development in China. The rapid development of the "free market" economy in China's cities and towns, and the widespread publicity given to a significant number of cases of personal enrichment, have tended to encourage the feeling that a quick return on a minimal investment was what free enterprise, and indeed the future, were all about. This attitude, which has its parallel in some Western countries, notably the UK, may be hostile to the assiduous investment and long-term view necessary to the successful cultivation of research and development.

Moreover, where large state-owned enterprises possessed research institutes, as greater pressure was placed on all organizations to adopt the techniques of profit and loss accounting, so enterprises sought to scale down or divest themselves altogether of what were seen as "non-productive" units. Research institutes were forced to cut staff, to seek and undertake commissions for cash from whoever might be persuaded to engage them, and to diversify their activity, sometimes even setting up small manufacturing sidelines of their own just to survive.[39] Needless to say, this had the effect of very substantially diluting the core research activity in the area of expertise of their staff.

Reinforcing these problems at the micro level has been an apparent inability at the macro level of government to translate the slogan supporting science and technology as a key element of the modernization programme into an effective policy to promote and develop technology. While the State Science and Technology Commission was intended to have a co-ordinating role in such matters, its practical influence over the degree or manner of introduction of new technology in fact proved to be very limited. Moreover it too tended to focus on the acquisition of technology from abroad, usually for major projects, rather than on defining a coherent policy for research and development at home.

Here again, conflicting agendas and interests, it may be supposed, played their part in practice in restricting the remit of the Commission and other macro level organs concerned with technology.[40] The comprehensive planning exercise for the whole of science and technology — outlining the so-called Twenty Twenty programme — completed by the Ministry for Science and Technology in 2006, may in this context be seen as a step in the right direction.

The role of central planning

Perhaps at the heart of the debate over technology, therefore, are some even more fundamental issues concerning the whole direction of China's political economy as the People's Republic travels through its second half-century. Fundamentally, it may be that the growth, or acquisition and dissemination of new technology can be best accomplished through a planned, centralized economy. Several arguments can be put forward in support of this view.

First, where state sector industries are responsible for a substantial part of China's output, yet are unprofitable, and for this or other reasons difficult or impossible to remedy are unattractive to foreign investors, it becomes clear that no organization but the state itself will be able to provide the investment necessary to upgrade their level of technology.

Second, foreign technology is invariably expensive, but in many industries needs to be purchased only once from one foreign supplier for application in a variety of locations within China. It is contrary to financial logic for state-owned firms claiming to be in competition with one another to each negotiate and purchase similar new technology from different foreign suppliers. This argument is supported by the economies of scale in production that can result when fewer factories are producing to achieve collectively a given required output.

Third, in order to achieve the rational introduction of new technology from overseas, a strong measure of central planning and supervision is therefore appropriate, both in determining what technology is needed, and in co-ordinating its sourcing from overseas and its allocation and implementation within China.

There are, moreover, compelling environmental concerns which support the case for effective central planning and control. Determination in some cases of the type of energy to be used, the allocation and transport of the energy supply, the elimination of waste and pollution in the consumption of energy by enterprises are all matters dealt with most effectively at the planning stage and through the supervised implementation of new technology.

In a general sense too, central planning should enable issues arising from the introduction of new technology to be resolved more rationally with regard to national policy objectives, presuming there is agreement on these. These might include the targeting of particular industries with export potential, appropriate regional distribution of technological investment, and preservation of the balance between city and countryside.

If it is accepted that new technology is indeed the key to China's modernization, therefore, there are many reasons why an integrated, nationally planned approach to its introduction may, in a country the size of China, be infinitely preferable to the competition and chaos resulting from half-adopted notions of a free enterprise economy. The political constraint here may be not that there is too much intervention, but rather too little intervention of the right kind.

It will be apparent from the brief summary at the beginning of this chapter that writers on China's technological development are frequently critical of what has been achieved in this respect over the past three decades. It is suggested here that many of these dichotomies and contradictions have historical roots, and may be traced to China's experience of technology acquisition in both recent and more distant times, an experience carried in the collective historical memory of many Chinese. It is further contended that many of those problems that have not derived from the past have been a function of current political constraints due to the manner in which the Chinese Communist Party has been carrying through the extraordinary transformation of the Chinese economy while still retaining its grip on power.

Thus the issues raised, for example, by Suttmeier, of institutional fragmentation, unresolved rivalries, technological nationalism, the neglect of theory, mistrust and normlessness; by Saich of Party dominance and obstruction; by Quan Li, of state control of both market and research; by Steward and Li of the complex "replication" and "fragmentation" of research structures; by Simon and Goldman, of the "quick technical fix" and the view among some top officials of foreign technology as a vehicle for the introduction to China of decadent Western ideology: are all conditioned both by unresolved issues from the past and by political conflicts of the present day.

It is suggested therefore that modern-day China may have inherited a legacy of attitudes at best ambivalent to technology. In traditional China, while science was valued, the applied science of technology was something which could be done without. In "transitional" China, the period of the foreign impact from the Opium Wars to the Communist takeover and beyond, technology was by and large something that belonged to the enemy, whether by virtue of his national origin or his class. In the China of the reform period, since 1980, technology has become much more widely regarded as necessary, but has still often been seen as something that can be purchased once, or acquired *ad hoc* from overseas, but does not need to be nurtured at home, or cultivated in the context of planned development at the micro or macro level.

In consequence, it may be that the strategy of the Communist Party over the years has been to partially admit and partially exclude modern technology in a variety of ways. Through the diffusion of technology a counter-elite begins to form, generating wealth, influence, and ultimately a desire for power.

There is no other example of a country on the scale of China, still committed to an orthodoxy rooted in Marxism, trying to modernize through engagement with the world economy. The outcome of such a strategy, from a perspective more than a quarter of a century after the reforms were begun, very much remains to be seen.

8

COMMAND STRUCTURES

In earlier chapters we have seen in outline how the Communist Party, following its victory in 1949, set up structures of government for the new People's Republic (Chapter 3), and determined the ideological content and parameters of its rule (Chapter 6). In this chapter we shall explore in greater detail the relationship between Party and state in China, the extent to which power is devolved away from the centre to local institutions, the approach to the formation and implementation of policy, and the structural and other reforms of recent years in the political arena. In this way we shall hope to shed further light on the overall policy process.

Party and state in People's China

Structure of the Communist Party

The conventional way of representing the structure of a Communist Party in countries in which those parties hold power is in the form of a pyramid. As has been seen, the Chinese Communist Party in the early 1950s took on a form of organization markedly similar to that of its counterpart in the Soviet Union. This placed the Central Committee of the Party, with its Politburo and the Standing Committee of the Politburo, at the apex of the pyramid, with the National Party Congress immediately below the Central Committee, and provincial Party committees, district and local Party branches and organizations below them. The principle of "democratic centralism" was said to apply, in which orders flowed down from the top, but supposedly democratic elections by lower Party organs of candidates to higher Party positions, coupled with consultation mechanisms, and a culture of frequent discussion down to the lowest levels, were said to counterbalance any autocratic tendencies. In practice, the power and influence of senior leaders in the Party was diluted very little by these supposedly democratic elements.

This was substantially the position until the Cultural Revolution began in 1966. That dramatic swerve to the left in Chinese political life, a consequence in part of Mao's wish to appeal directly to the "revolutionary masses" over the heads of Party and state officials, saw the whole Party organization go into eclipse for a time. From 1966, the normal activity of Party institutions was effectively frozen as Revolutionary Committees were created all over China to replace the Party and the state in the management of daily life.

These Revolutionary Committees were supposedly to be chosen in an unspecified democratic process in all organizations from the most basic work unit, as places of work were called, through the municipal bodies of big cities, universities, factories and communes for example, and the highest organs of national administration. Said by their advocates to be representative in the most effective way possible of the interests of the three truly revolutionary groups in society — workers, peasants and soldiers — in fact they were often a cabal of the friends of more senior officials, those with dominant personalities, people representing particular factions and interest groups, and those prepared to take the most ostentatiously ideologically correct position on any given issue.

The Revolutionary Committees were in their most dynamic, and some would say destructive, phase at the beginning of the Cultural Revolution. Following the Ninth Party Congress of 1969, by the early 1970s the Party was once again functioning, and held to be the source of ideological orthodoxy. However, in organizational terms it coexisted uneasily with the Revolutionary Committees, ostensibly state bodies, until after Mao died. The decision to strengthen the Party and reinstate its full organizational role in the governing of China came with the Eleventh Party Congress of 1977, and the Revolutionary Committees were finally disbanded as local organs of government by the Fifth National People's Congress of 1979.[1] From that point, the Party has evolved into what it is today.

In terms of structure, the Party has since 1977 been broadly restored to the model of before the Cultural Revolution. By the time of its Seventeenth Congress in 2007, it had more than seventy-three million members. So how does it work?[2]

The locus of actual power within the Party remains within the *Politburo*, recently twenty-two members, and its *Standing Committee*, seven of those twenty-two. The Politburo continues to function as a supreme "Board of Directors" for the Party, able to initiate and carry out discussion and take final decisions on any aspect of policy both for the Party and for the country as a whole. The Politburo meets at frequent intervals, while its Standing Committee meets normally on a daily basis.

The *Party Central Committee* holds the formal power to enact Party policy when the Party Congress is not meeting. Plenary sessions of the Central Committee are normally held annually to approve decisions of the Politburo and its Standing Committee. The Central Committee is elected by the Party Congress to serve for the five years or so between Congresses. The Central Committee elected by the Seventeenth Party Congress of 2007 has 204 members and 169 alternates.[3]

The typical profile of a Central Committee member in the new century is of a university-educated man or woman in their forties or fifties, often with a technical background and senior administrative experience, loyal to the Party but no longer unquestioning. In determining nominations, the Party Congress, acting on direction from senior leaders, addresses geographical and sectoral considerations, with provincial interests, mass organizations, the military and other groups all taken into account.

The Party no longer has a Chairman, a position created by Mao Zedong, but rather has a General Secretary at its head, whose principal task is to preside over the Party's *General Secretariat*. In 1987 the General Secretariat was reduced from ten to four members, nominated by the Standing Committee of the Politburo and approved by the Central Committee, a move to prevent it from becoming an alternative power base. In 1987 also the Secretariat lost the power to "filter" policy proposals passed by the State Council to the Politburo or its Standing Committee.

This central Secretariat is what might be termed the "functional" arm of the Party, with a substantial bureaucracy to support it. At the centre it has seven principal departments. These are responsible for organization, united front work, propaganda, liaison with communist parties overseas, policy research, the Party schools, and publication of the main mass circulation Party newspaper *Renmin Ribao*, or *People's Daily*. The functions of the Secretariat are replicated on a smaller scale at provincial and local levels.

In 1982 a *Central Advisory Commission* was set up to give a continuing voice to "retired" Party elders, but it was abolished ten years later, having intervened controversially during the Tiananmen crisis of 1989. In the new century old leaders continue to have influence, but as they are progressively replaced by a much younger, and in most cases more broadly competent, generation, their impact can be expected to diminish.

A more durable Party institution has been the *Central Commission for Inspecting Discipline*, reinstated in 1977, initially as a means of restoring order in the Party and redressing the cases of cadres wronged during the Cultural Revolution. The Commission has gone on to monitor the "work-style" of cadres, and to maintain "discipline" in the broadest sense — especially in the more prosperous current environment rooting out and pursuing cases of corruption, embezzlement, and influence-peddling.[4]

The Party has also most recently, and some would say belatedly, recognized the need for new skills among its members. The Central Commission for Inspecting Discipline also has responsibility for Party Schools, where future cadres are trained. In recent years these institutions have, at the tertiary level, shown interest in importing a variety of new subject matter into the curriculum to complement the traditional focus on ideology — such subjects include even Western approaches to Management Studies.[5]

Legitimizing the authority of all of these bodies is the *National Party Congress*, technically the supreme authority of the Communist Party. In a strange reciprocal relationship, the Central Committee, which the Party Congress elects as noted above, in turn supervises the process of selection to the National Party Congress by Party Congresses at the provincial and district levels. Although since 1982 this is supposed to have been carried out through secret ballots, the scope for nepotism and the promotion of groups with vested interests, in the face of any genuine intra-party democracy, remains considerable. The Seventeenth Party Congress of 2007 comprised some 2,217 members.[6]

The Congress is responsible for formally receiving reports from and approving the work of the Central Committeee and sometimes other bodies, for approving any revisions to the Party's constitution, for hearing and approving plans of work, and for electing new members to the Central Committee and Politburo. It is required to meet every five years, and usually does so for no more than two weeks, and often somewhat less.

Below the central Party structures, every province and autonomous region, city with province status, and municipality large enough to have district organizations has a Party committee, legitimized by a corresponding Party Congress, held every three years.[7] Each such Party committee has a Standing Committee with a General Secretary at its head, assisted by various other Secretaries and supporting bureaucracy as necessary. This level of Party committee is responsible for Party organizational matters, the supervision of economic activity, capital construction, women's and youth affairs, and policy development, all in the area under its control. Provincial Party Secretaries are supposed to implement central Party policy directives in their areas, as well as coming up with initiatives of their own, consistent with central policy.

Finally, at the most basic level, *"primary" Party organs* exist in the form of Party branches, each with a Committee headed by a Party Secretary, in towns, villages, city neighbourhoods, in co-operatives and on farms, in factories, shops, schools and universities, and throughout the PLA. These monitor the activity of the organization and the attitudes of its staff, and intervene to offer "guidance" both to those in responsible positions and to members of the organization more generally.

The fundamental purpose of the basic Party organs continues to be, as it has always been, to promulgate the Party line among the mass membership and among the population as a whole. They can sometimes be a forum for debate of Party policy, but always with a view to more effective implementation rather than offering any sort of challenge or disagreement. In the new century, some three and a half million primary units of the Party exist in China as a whole.[8]

These structures have been periodically reviewed and amended by new Party constitutions introduced at different times by the Central Committee, most recently in 1987, though with the exception of arrangements made during the Cultural Revolution these amendments have been relatively minor. Even in the new century, the Party retains, on paper at least, many of the structures and prerogatives to be found in the organization of any Leninist-style party.

State structures

In parallel with the institutions of the Party, China's institutions of State present a pattern of apparent decision-making on policy at the higher levels, with those policies flowing down for implementation through central Ministries and provincial and local organs of government, while the principle of election is said to be embodied in the choice of members of People's Congresses at various levels up to the National People's Congress — once again the concept of "democratic centralism" at work.

The highest state body in China is the *State Council*, made up of the Premier, currently four Vice Premiers, Ministers (and sometimes Vice Ministers) from the various Ministries, and heads of the central government's Commissions, themselves all formally designated by the National People's Congress. At any one time the State Council may have sixty to seventy or more members. A smaller operational group, broadly equivalent to a cabinet, comprising the Premier, the Vice Premiers, and a few of the most important Ministers, normally meets each week[9] to take essential decisions and to steer the work of the Council, which meets in plenary session rather less frequently.

The various central government Ministries, of which the most important have tended to be those concerned with the economy and specifically with production of one kind or another, are supervised and audited by the State Council, which must approve their plans. On certain specific matters, such as major new projects requiring significant expenditure, proposals must be submitted first to one of the State Council Commissions before the approval of the State Council is given. The bureaucracy under the ultimate control of the State Council was estimated at around 40,000 in 1988.[10] The State Council is chosen (or at least designated) by the National People's Congress, but not chosen from among members of that Congress, as it might be under a Western-style constitution. The NPC meets annually to approve the work of the State Council and its own NPC Standing Committee, receiving reports directly from Ministers as it chooses.

The *National People's Congress*, currently with almost 3,000 members elected for five years under the supervision of its own Standing Committee, meets annually, usually for two weeks. As China's parliament, it is the country's formal law-making body, though it would be more accurate to say that it enacts laws made by other organs of state at the instigation of the Communist Party. As it is so large, during its annual meetings there are relatively few plenary sessions, with most business transacted in smaller groups determined by geography or function. Delegates receive work reports, and are able to raise concerns and debate issues now with much greater freedom than at any time previously, and can question Ministers or Vice Ministers on matters for which they are responsible.

The NPC, as it is known in English (not to be confused with the Party Congress), is also charged with supervising the implementation of legislation by lower organs of state, amending the Constitution on the recommendation of the President of the Republic, designating or removing the Premier and other members of the State Council, and formally "electing" both the Chief Procurator and the President of the Supreme People's Court.

When the NPC is not in session, which is most of the year, its business is transacted by its own *Standing Committee*. Comprising currently 175 members, and elected by the whole NPC, the Standing Committee of the 11th NPC of 2008 broadly enjoys the power to enact and amend laws on its behalf when that body is not in session. It can also amend the Constitution, and declare martial law if it should so wish. The Standing Committee supervises the work of specialized committees of the National People's Congress concerned with a range of political, economic and social problems. It also supervises the functioning of judicial bodies concerned with law enforcement throughout China.

Below the central state structures are those at the provincial, city and county, district, town and "township" levels. All provinces and autonomous regions, as well as cities — including those such as Shanghai, Beijing, Tianjin and Chongqing enjoying province status — counties and districts within cities have their own People's Governments, which undertake administrative tasks devolved from the State Council. At each level there is also a People's Congress. Delegates to these Congresses are in each case elected by the Congress below, with the basic Congresses at the district, county and township level being directly elected by eligible voters. Provincial Congresses are elected for five years, lower-level Congresses for three years.

These People's Congresses at the provincial level and below are entitled to pass resolutions, and have a broad remit covering the will of the state in a particular geographical area. As Wang has indicated, their responsibilities include: the enactment of local statutes according to local conditions; enforcing the observance of and implementation of the state constitution, statutes, and administrative rules; approving plans for economic development, and related budgets; electing or recalling governors, mayors, and chiefs of counties and towns; electing and recalling judges and procurators; and maintaining public order.[11]

Formation and implementation of policy

The linking of Party and State

So how is policy formulated and implemented in People's China? To understand this we must first explore how what is often referred to as the "duality of Party and state" is actually achieved.

We should begin by reminding ourselves of the origins of this approach to government, which is unlike that of countries in which political parties are primarily seen as vehicles for the election of a government of one hue or another at regular intervals. The roots of this duality of course lie in the particular characteristics of the Party's rise to power through the three decades up to the middle of the twentieth century. A Leninist-style party, which the Communist Party of China aspired to be, was primarily intended as an instrument with which to achieve power in hostile circumstances. As the Communist Party of the Soviet Union found after the Russian Revolution of 1917, the transition to peacetime administration was a difficult one.

In order to implement the policies that it had fought the civil war to achieve, the Chinese Communist Party in 1949 broadly followed the approach of the CPSU. Thus it retained its role of defining and initiating policy on all important matters, and while passing it on to organs of state for formal enactment and implementation, still directed, monitored and evaluated results from behind the scenes. A number of mechanisms were put in place to ensure that the levers of power remained in the hands of the Party.

First, with the possible exception of the Cultural Revolution period, almost all important posts in state structures have been occupied since 1949 by people who are, simultaneously, senior members of the Communist Party. For example, in the late 1990s, during the tenure of the Eighth National People's Congress, every single Minister on the State Council was also a member of the Party Central Committee.[12] Other very senior state figures, such as provincial governors, may be members of the Politburo, for example. This principle has applied not only in the highest bodies of state but also in provincial and local government organs, on farms, in factories and state-owned enterprises, schools and universities, hospitals and other workplaces, and of course in the People's Liberation Army. Only in recent years, by some estimates since the mid-1990s, has this principle been relaxed somewhat, as the Party has begun to redefine, if not its role, at least the means of achieving its objectives.

The reason for filling administrative posts with Party members has been to try to ensure that Party directives are carried out effectively. Until very recently, the only real path to advancement for individuals in China lay through membership of the Communist Party. Thus an ambitious young person might join the Youth League in his or her teens, whether or not they felt genuine ideological commitment, and might in their early twenties hope to be admitted into the Party proper. From that point on, their career depended upon being seen to serve the Party loyally in everything they were asked to do for it. With or without commitment, therefore, a Party member could usually be trusted to follow the decreed policy unswervingly. Only very occasionally, at times when factions formed within the Party over certain issues, was this loyalty undermined.[13]

In addition, at the top the Politburo of the Party has a duty to guide and monitor the work of the various Ministries under the State Council, with particular functional areas assigned to particular Politburo members. The Politburo may also receive proposals from the Ministries for consideration, and possible approval and referral back to the Ministries. The Politburo in determining what should be policy is supported by the policy research arm of the Party's central Secretariat, as noted above. Generally speaking, the detail of policy to be implemented, and plans for the precise manner of its implementation, are left to the Ministry concerned.

At the provincial and local levels, the pattern is repeated for policy that is left to the discretion of these levels of government. Thus the Party committee at the level in question, and its Standing Committee and supporting bureaucracy, replicate for the matters on which they have delegated authority the role of initiating, directing, monitoring and evaluating policy performed by the Politburo at the central level. This policy is then enacted by the relevant local People's Congress, and implemented by the local People's Government bureaucracy.

At the most basic level, individual Party cells in workplaces, and individual Party members, promote, monitor and report on the implementation of Party policy by local government bodies, production units, and other organs of the state. There is therefore, in theory, a constant process of reinforcement and a flow of information up and down to facilitate the implementation of policy. In the more relaxed climate of the present day, these lower level Party units and individual Party members may propose to the level above them ideas for minor amendments to policy, or for detailed changes to plans for the carrying out of policy, which may then be accepted by the Party for onward transmission to the local level of government administration.

It will be appreciated that the role played by the Party in government in these ways is over and above the part it has played as ideological mentor to the masses, discussed in an earlier chapter. Indeed, the former has continued to be important, just as the latter has receded somewhat during the last quarter century of modernization.

Policy formation and implementation in
practice: some continuing issues

While these mechanisms integrate the Party fully into the decision-making process — and indeed it could be argued that in broad terms the Party is the executive arm of government, while the whole state structure performs the function of a massive civil service, charged with carrying out the Party's decisions — yet the duality of Party and state cannot ensure and has not always ensured the smooth functioning of government in China. In reality, there are numerous problems.

The Party at the central level may not see clearly or act appropriately or in a timely manner on a situation confronting it. It may fail to do so because of inadequate communication and reporting of the circumstances to it, or a failure to consult the expertise available to it, or, as sometimes happens, the conflicting personal or policy agendas of senior Party members. The same observations apply in the case of the government organs at the central level.

Local levels of both Party and government may not get their voice heard at the central or provincial level, or may not understand the bigger picture, or may not have the technical resources or skills available locally to assess the true situation. Regional or sectoral interests may intervene to slant the policy agenda at the central or local level, a matter to which we shall return below.[14] There may be a failure to convey appropriate or accurate statistical information up to the decision-making level owing to incompetence, or to a desire to avoid loss of face. Nepotism, or the practice of "*guanxi*" — the cultivation of special relationships between individuals, here meant in the negative sense — may subvert a rational decision process on a particular issue. Or there may be delays or negligence in the performance of tasks simply through pressure of work, a problem all too familiar to governments all around the world.

In the past, and up to the early 1990s, there has often been inconsistency and factional fighting in both Party and government bodies over ideological issues and their policy implications; this has now receded as a problem, but has been replaced by often intense debate over genuine policy alternatives as China integrates with the world economy.

Finally, in part because of China's experience over the past half century, during which economic development has been seen as inexorably linked with state planning exercises, there is still a tendency to "over-plan" and a lack of flexibility in response to evolving circumstances. The Party and state bureaucracies are very large, and are in proportion to the size of the country and its population; it is as difficult to turn around a failing policy as it is to implement any policy in the first place.

The impact of politics (in the general sense) and culture on decision-making is as profound in the actions of Party and State organizations as it is anywhere in Chinese society. To the "normal" problems of government are added, in China's case, the heritage of a Leninist-style party, enormous scale, cultural particularities, and the goal of turning the country from a command into a market economy. The difficulties are likely to match the dimensions of the task.[15]

Decentralization and devolution

To what extent is power, and therefore decision-making on policy issues, genuinely decentralized to any degree in China today? Can authority really be said in any sense to be devolved to lower organs within the Party and state structures? These questions are inextricably linked with and conditioned by the historical experience and scale of China, and linked also with the complexity of the economic transition that is being attempted, with the existence of regional power bases and inter-regional rivalries, and with the plans and policy preferences of leaders at the centre.

The whole approach to de-centralization throughout the sixty years of the People's Republic has been, and continues in the new century to be, influenced by a set of attitudes rooted in China's history. The intellectual elite, and in particular those among them who have occupied positions of power, have been acutely aware of the pattern of the rise and fall of central authority over the thirty centuries of China's recorded history, and the fact that it has usually coincided with the rise and fall of dynasties.

Decentralization, usually through the erosion of the central power of the state by rebel groups, has in the past not been a conscious act of policy, but rather has heralded the collapse of government, resulting in disorder and ultimately anarchy. This was the case in the period following the end of the Eastern Han Dynasty, at the end of the Tang Dynasty, and again towards the end of the Qing Dynasty and during the warlord period that followed. Indeed, in part it was this chaos that allowed the Communist Party to grow and prosper in the years before 1949.

There has therefore been, among senior policy-makers from Mao to Hu Jintao, some ambivalence of view at least towards allowing authority to devolve and spread throughout China's regions. In consequence, since 1949 the pendulum has swung back and forth on the matter of the degree of central and of local power, as central leaders have feared giving too much opportunity to local officials to go their own way.

The scale of China is another factor bearing on the centralization-decentralization debate. On one hand, because of China's size and population it was always much easier to formulate policy and to give orders than to have them carried out in the far-flung reaches of the Empire. This is only slightly less true today, despite the revolution in communications technology. Logically, this might have led to devolution of authority to local officials who understood conditions on the spot, and could decide what to do accordingly. Yet, on the other hand, it could be argued that the scale of China is so great, and the task of modernization so daunting, that only solutions drawn up and imposed nationally could actually work.

For this functional reason too the People's Republic has witnessed a fluctuation in approach, as successive leaders have experimented, imposing policy centrally at certain times, and granting the latitude to provincial and other local governments to formulate some policy independently at others. Normally the acid test has been whether the policy has achieved the result desired by the centre.

Related to this issue of scale is the complexity of the economic and social transition that the Party is trying to bring about, which is at the heart of China's process of modernization. The transformation of a command economy, largely isolated from the world, into a part-market economy fully engaged with the prevailing patterns of world trade has never previously been achieved successfully anywhere. There are therefore no precedents. How much of this process should be induced or regulated from the centre, and how much left to local forces can only be a matter of trial and error. The debate over "how much de-centralization," or "what is best at what level," as Breslin has observed, cannot be divorced from the evolving demands of the economic task at hand.[16]

Complicating matters further, aside from these rational considerations are questions of vested interest. Wealthy and powerful local officials, new and successful local entrepreneurs, and Party and state structures in the more developed provinces and cities constitute regional power bases from which pressure can be exerted on the centre. Some provincial and municipal officials indeed are themselves representatives on central policy-making bodies, enabling them to influence policy at first hand; they will often argue forcefully for a measure of local autonomy that reflects the power and wealth of their territory. Underlying these arguments may be a desire for policy parameters that will enable them to enhance their personal wealth and prestige. Often these struggles are manifest in inter-provincial or inter-regional rivalries which on occasion can become quite violent.[17]

Finally, leaders at the centre may themselves have agendas, plans and preferences of their own with regard to the various regions of China. For example, during the 1980s Shenzhen, Guangdong, and South China generally were favoured under Deng Xiaoping, with no fewer than five Special Economic Zones set up to encourage foreign investment and a more rapid pace of development; policy decisions were taken at the centre that granted a substantial measure of autonomy to the SEZs in particular, and helped to transform the economy of the South. In the 1990s, the appointment of Jiang Zemin, formerly Mayor of Shanghai, as China's President resulted in decisions being taken at the centre that favoured the development of Shanghai, and the decade saw a dramatic change in the fortunes of the city which had hitherto been out of favour.[18]

Taken as a whole, therefore, it is difficult to generalize about the degree of genuine devolution of policy-making power away from the centre. Certainly the process has not been a linear one over the period since the "four modernizations" were introduced in 1978. Trial and error has been the order of the day, and reference must be made to the particular area of policy involved, the time, the geographical location of the Party or state structure to which power is devolved, and the structural arrangements in force at the time.

In the economic sphere the transition from state to private ownership undoubtedly continues to bring much decision-making into private hands, effectively a devolution of power to the local level. The state is now much more concerned with regulation, however, and with provision of a regulatory framework for many areas of economic activity, often to conform to the requirements of the WTO. Thus there is likely to be greater central intervention in future on issues like intellectual property rights, product standards, and financial regulation to name only three.[19]

At the same time, in the political sphere, the Party's role has been changing subtly, and this in turn affects the decentralization question. In the new century the Party sees itself more as an institution that, while it still formulates the broad objectives at the centre, in the implementation has much more of a guiding role than one of hands-on administration. This has two effects: first, in the first instance, it gives provincial and local Party bodies more autonomy on most matters; second, these local Party bodies themselves tend to be less directly involved in organizing implementation, rather taking an approach of advising, monitoring, and finally reporting the results back up to the centre.

It should finally be noted that these changes do not necessarily mean that the Party has lost effective control over China. If there were to be any serious political challenge to the centre, it is entirely possible that many within the Party would seek a remedy consistent with its centralist Leninist roots. Such a response could also reflect traditional China's fear of chaos — "*yi luan, jiu zhua.*"[20] In this sense, the present trend to decentralization in many areas may be regarded as tactical on the part of the central Party authority; whether it turns out also to be strategic very much remains to be seen.

Political reform

The whole process of modernization, of opening up and engagement with the international economy has meant that the Party has had to become a more complex organization in order to address the new demands on it. Saich has observed that prosperity has brought social differentiation and new interests which the Party must successfully broker.[21]

One way of doing this, and perhaps the closest thing to a trend in the fitful process of political reform that has been taking place in China over the past twenty-five years, has been to experiment with the introduction of a degree of "democracy" in the state structures, and specifically in the selection of village assemblies — People's Congresses at the most basic village level — and as authorized by the Fifteenth Party Congress of 1997, at the township level. This experimentation began in a number of places in the 1980s, and has since spread throughout much of China. The critical aspect of this reform has been the new willingness to allow people other than officially designated people, those chosen by the local Party branch, on the slate of candidates.

However, despite the decision of the central Party authority to permit this change in procedure, in practice in many parts of China local Party cadres have visibly or clandestinely connived to ensure that only candidates acceptable to them could run for office as members of village or township assemblies. Moreover, local entrepreneurs and other vested interests have also been active, so that in some cases, as Dearlove noted writing in the mid-1990s, village democratic institutions have been "...captured by the rural rich."[22] Old habits die hard, and China has entered the new century with the issue of democratic selection, even at the most basic level, still effectively unresolved. It is noteworthy that all the main political party contenders for power in the May 4th period in the 1920s posited democracy as a goal, but all postponed indefinitely any real effort to work towards it. This issue will be taken up again in a later chapter.[23]

A less obvious change to the way in which state structures operate, but a significant one nonetheless, is the growing practice in assemblies from the National People's Congress down for delegates to challenge the accuracy of supposedly factual information presented to them in reports, and even to ask for amendments to proposed policy documents. In doing this they are behaving in a manner not dissimilar to that of opposition members of parliament in more genuinely democratic systems. What is striking is that the vast majority of delegates who do this are members of the Communist Party. Thus it can be claimed that in its desire to improve the effectiveness of government, the Party is monitoring and policing itself to a degree previously unknown, and in doing so is causing the policy-making process to become more transparent and open. This is a uniquely Chinese approach, resting ultimately on consensus, but no longer excluding the possibility of critical analysis of policy in the interests of efficiency.

Another development, this time on the Party front, has been the move to loosen the Party's grip on the state at all levels. At last it is becoming somewhat more common for individual officials even at quite a senior level not to be members of the Communist Party, though the numbers of such people are still limited. Moreover, as noted above, while the Party continues at all levels to advise on, monitor, and report back on the implementation of policy, often now it no longer dictates so directly to organs of the state how they should run their affairs. It is more widely recognized that in the much more complex economic situation of the twenty-first century specialist expertise may be required to implement policy effectively, and that this is more likely to be found among the broader state bureaucracy than in the Party, or may even need to be found outside either structure.

The Party itself has also recognized the need for greater expertise within its ranks. The days when sheer determination and charisma, bolstered by incessant propaganda, were sufficient qualities for leadership have long gone. The Central Party School in Beijing, and other Party academies throughout China, now actively encourage future cadres to study market economics, modern approaches to management, comparative law, international relations, sociology and a range of other subjects which would have been unthinkable even a decade ago. Furthermore, young cadres are encouraged to go abroad for postgraduate work, and to absorb and understand the customs and approaches to economic, social and even political issues in countries once considered to be China's sworn enemies. It becomes harder and harder to pick the Party cadre out in a crowd, as he or she will often have views and aspirations largely indistinguishable from other members of the public.

For the future, a major question mark hangs over the durability of the one-party state in China. Is it possible to foresee a situation in which the Chinese Communist Party will voluntarily accede to changes in the political structure such that it becomes simply one party among many in a polity within which political parties vie for power through democratic elections? This question will be addressed more fully in Chapter 11, but if such a thing were to happen the transition would be both unprecedented and not easy.

The experience of Eastern Europe suggests that where the political culture is more truly democratic — where for example there was evidence of successful democratic experience before the era of Soviet domination — as in the constituent parts of the former Czechoslovakia, communist parties are unable to regain significant influence or power. Where, on the other hand, there was a stronger autocratic tradition and no real previous democratic experience, as in Russia, the Communist Party will retain influence and may one day return to power, but political life will remain unstable, and the economy and civil society will be insufficiently developed. In China once again, the fear of "*da luan*," chaos, may militate against such a transition in the role and function of the Party, in the short term at least.

Taken as a whole, therefore, the command structures developed over the past eighty or more years of the Party's existence, and especially over the half century or more of the People's Republic, remain in place, though with modifications in the way in which they are used. These changes in practice represent the Party's pragmatic approach to the problems of administration and transformation thrown up by China's engagement with the international economy as a short cut to modernization. One thing has led to another. In the longer term the direct control exercised until quite recently by the Party (and the state) over the economy and over almost every aspect of life in China, which has begun to be eroded, may recede more completely. However, the role of the Party as arbiter of the wealth the market economy has generated, and the political processes that determine how chances and rewards may be distributed, may prove more durable.

9

POLITICS, CULTURE AND THE MANAGEMENT
OF CHINA'S ENTERPRISES

It is sometimes said that China at the beginning of the new century is well on the way to becoming a fully-fledged market economy; indeed, China's diplomatic initiative designed to persuade other states and the WTO that this is the case underlines its determination that its progress in this direction should be recognized. Yet such a transition from a fully planned to a market economy, it may be argued, has no success-ful precedent elsewhere. Certainly no single political grouping in any way similar to the Chinese Communist Party has achieved such a transformation.

It is the contention in this chapter that China's tens of thousands of enterprises, their function, their behaviour, and the nature of their management as it has changed over the past two decades, are key to assessing how much of a free market China has become.

Two issues with respect to the management of the enterprises as they undergo this transition are particularly relevant to any attempt to reach an understanding of how enterprises work in the new China: first, we need to examine the systemic attempts to reform enterprise manage-ment, and to assess where we are with this process at the present time; second, we need to look more narrowly at how decisions have been made within enterprises, and at the prospects for change. In this way, in the next two sections we can take account of both the political and cultural influences which, uniquely in China, impact on the way in which enterprises behave. This discussion will lead to a final section in which other factors will be brought into the balance, and some provisional conclusions reached through an analysis of the behaviour of China's enterprises, as to whether and when China will become, in the broadly accepted sense of the term, a true market economy.

Issues and incentives in enterprise reform

China commenced its programme of wholesale modernization of its economy in the late 1970s. The so-called Four Modernizations programme (for industry, agriculture, science and technology, and national defence) relied to some considerable extent on the import of technology from the West and Japan. This Open Door policy was ultimately bound to open up a debate on how the economy, at both the macro and micro levels, should be run. The decades of separate development, and the primacy of social goals achieved by political means, had left China still technologically and managerially backward in a comparative global sense. Such modernization was always going to be a radical and complex programme of events, especially given the time scales for change.

The logic of rapid modernization involved a sequence of imperatives. Fundamentally, the import of foreign technology could only be achieved by payment in hard currency (which was extremely scarce in China in the late 1970s), or through a variety of forms of foreign investment. In either case the export of goods to world markets on a scale hitherto unknown in China was likely to be involved. There was a major barrier to the increase in international trade: the quality of products produced for and consumed in the domestic market was not comparable with the quality of those produced in other countries and currently traded on world markets. So, to increase export trade, standards in design and manufacture needed to take a giant step forward within Chinese enterprises.[1] This meant that management techniques that had been in force for thirty years under the command economy needed to be thoroughly reviewed, as both the concept of commercial competition and the practice of profit and loss accounting were introduced in the People's Republic for the first time.

It was in this climate of discussion, and of challenge to long held beliefs about the economy, that the Contract Management Responsibility System (CMRS) was born. This sought not only to provide greater independence for the firm at the enterprise level, but also to install contemporary market-oriented management practices within the organization. In this process, the content of contracts extended to more than just profit sharing: it encompassed mechanisms for technical improvement investments and grants, and introduced a link between wage levels and company performance. Some contracts guaranteed an expansion of assets, whilst others were incorporated under an input-output system that laid down mechanisms for payments and deliveries between contracted parties.

The following discussion will offer a brief review of the CMRS — its origins, objectives, main provisions and impact — before going on to look at the Modern Enterprise System. The MES was seen as a replacement for the CMRS, having significant differences in substance and a number of broader provisions.

Objectives of the Contract Management Responsibility System

The various objectives of the CMRS emerged as part of the process of formulating the policy itself. It is noteworthy that the new contract system was never likely to offer a comprehensive set of strategic solutions to the felt needs of Chinese industry.[2] There was, and there continues to be, underlying disagreement over what those needs might be, and over the political costs of satisfying them. Thus, as we have seen previously, within the Chinese Communist Party even more than within most political institutions, ideological differences and factional strife may blight the formation and implementation of policy. This said, one objective certainly had to do with performance — a desire to see industry achieve higher output targets through the inducement of retained profits. Discussion of the possible reintroduction of material incentives in industry in some form followed in the wake of the Eleventh Party Congress in 1978, and experiments were tried in the early 1980s.

Another important objective was to increase the independence of state-owned enterprises (SOEs) with respect to operational decisions on a range of matters of concern to them.[3] These included: what to produce and how; sales; pricing; purchasing; the spending of company funds; disposal of assets; organizational matters; personnel; wages and bonuses for individual employees; and links with other enterprises.[4] The intention to extend greater autonomy in these areas to SOEs was stated explicitly by the government in 1984, and confirmed in the Enterprise Law of 1988, though there was a wide variation in practice even in the pace and nature of implementation of this policy. Local circumstances, including the size and type of an enterprise and the attitudes of its leaders, played a very large part.

171

Finally, the desire of the government to maximize its revenue from SOEs led to fiscal measures. These included the progressive application of a regime of income tax to all enterprises in place of the requirement to hand over all profits to the state. It was assumed that performance inducements, and the new autonomy to be given to enterprises, would be sufficient to ensure that, in the long term at least, the state would benefit from the new arrangements.

The government appears, then, to have been in pursuit of these three main objectives: improved performance in terms of output; progressive devolution of autonomy to SOEs; and increased income for the state. Experimentation with the CMRS commenced in the early 1980s.[5] The "factory director system," which placed the factory director's right to manage above the right of the Party secretary to intervene, was evident in places from around 1984.[6] The change from profit transfers to taxation of enterprises began around the same time. But it was really in 1987 that China began to see the widespread application of the CMRS to industrial enterprises. For most SOEs, the requirements of the contract provided that:

1. Enterprises must hand over to the state a fixed target of profit, negotiated with the enterprise, as "income tax," shortfalls to be made up by the company from its own funds, and additional profits to be shared between government and enterprise in a prescribed way. The enterprise would usually also be subject to a variety of indirect taxes, which would vary according to the nature of its activity and circumstances.
2. The growth of total wages and bonuses paid by the enterprise should be linked to any growth in profits and taxes paid.
3. Targets should be agreed for technological upgrading and for investment in this.

It should be noted that the CMRS usually operated at two distinct levels: the *state contract system*, which covered enterprise-level contracting with the state; and the *internal contract system*, which dealt with contracting within the enterprise's own business activities.

There were some minor variations in detail in these requirements as they were imposed on different enterprises. These were the basic principles of the CMRS, as they were applied in both its first (1987–90) and second (1990–93) phases.

The Contract Management Responsibility System in practice

The CMRS, while in operation, was judged by many, both within enterprises and by external analysts, as successful in bringing about a degree of enterprise and management reform in the state-owned sector of Chinese industry.[7] Individual enterprises developed more autonomy and were more responsive to change, as they could exercise some discretion in terms of investment decisions and organizational change.[8] Staff commitment to the enterprises increased, especially managers' commitment.[9] However, a number of "difficulties" were identified and these were deemed sufficiently serious to result in the gradual phasing-out of the CMRS.

The Chinese analyst Chen Derong[10] assesses the experience of four representative SOEs throughout the official six-year period of the CMRS. It is apparent from her work that the great majority of "issues" arising from implementation of the CMRS were conditioned or caused directly by the state, or by the regulatory position of enterprises — as Chen puts it, "between hierarchy and market." State-owned enterprises could no longer benefit from the structural certainties of the old command economy, yet they were not free to respond autonomously to market pressures in a whole variety of ways. Indeed, it can be further argued that in many respects, and for many of the products of SOEs, the market itself was not a proper market in the unrestricted sense in which that term would be understood in the West. This is so whether one speaks of the domestic market, subject to constraints and interventions, or the international market, where frequently, in the period in question, Chinese state-controlled import-export corporations often largely determined the terms of trade. In some cases, the issues raised as problems clearly signal a failure on the part of managers to understand the way a market economy functions.

It was also true that the CMRS caused confusion. This was because it tried to embody often conflicting goals of encouraging increased output from industry, giving enterprises a greater measure of independence, and reaping a bigger financial return for central government through a variety of taxes. Many observers close to the CMRS experiment commented on the short term behaviour it induced in managers.[11]

In implementing the CMRS, the government had believed that it would facilitate technological upgrading through progressive investment and inward transfer of technology from overseas. The evidence from Chen's and other studies suggests that, if anything, technological upgrading may have slowed down in many enterprises under the CMRS.[12] Although the government, except in the case of "key" enterprises, by and large no longer provided funding for new technology, it still set the parameters for investment. It had to approve all major building projects, its support was needed for critical bank loans, and it might hold things up by disagreeing with enterprises on long-term investment strategy. Even where investment targets were met, technical targets may not have been.

One way around this problem was to form a joint venture with a foreign company, but in this case managers stood to lose their overall control over the enterprise. Moreover, over all investment decisions hung the ever-present cloud of political uncertainty. On top of all this, the major advantage of the planned approach to the import of new technology from overseas, that unnecessary duplication would be avoided, was lost.[13]

On the financial side, while according to Chen state-owned firms generally benefited from the opportunities presented by the CMRS, some showed decreasing profitability or contrived to make a loss under the system. Many firms appear to have found that wages outstripped productivity over the six years or so of the CMRS. The application of income tax, along with a host of indirect taxes, to enterprises failed to yield the hoped-for windfall of revenue for the government, while the widespread variations and exceptions granted to many well connected enterprises only served to engender jealousy in others.[14] Many managers were unhappy with the complicated taxation regime and with the generally high levels of taxation.

Further empirical analysis has brought out a number of other, associated, effects in organizations that adopted the Contract Management Responsibility System. Among these were:

- Disparities between enterprises with regard to terms and conditions.
- Short-termism to the detriment of longer term, more qualitative objectives.
- Lack of incentive among managers to assume responsibility and create increased autonomy.
- Little improvement in the quality of management.
- The cost of replacing social provision, such as subsidized restaurants, hospitals, schools and housing, and the failure to address this.

The Modern Enterprise System

The MES was intended to tackle a number of issues not adequately addressed by the CMRS and other previous enterprise models. In the process it sought to clarify the position on property rights, provide a clearer definition of rights and responsibilities generally, distinguish between the role of the state and management functions, and introduce so-called "scientific" enterprise management. It was said to have a reform element (*gaige*) referring to the adoption of new management mechanisms and practices, a reconstruction element (*gaizao*) which comprised technical transformation and facilities improvement, and a restructuring element *(gaizu)* involving the reorganization and establishment of a legal framework for property rights and assets.

The MES has been implemented progressively since 1993 and has hinged on a division of enterprises into three groups, identified primarily by characteristics of current or potential ownership and the means of governance.[15] The first group have been "state-owned, limited liability corporations." These are exclusively funded, and wholly owned, by the state directly, and include most large state-owned enterprises in the metallurgical, mining and heavy manufacturing industries, as well as the railways, airlines and other capital-intensive enterprises of an infrastructural kind. It was estimated in 1996 that some 10,000 enterprises fell into this group.

Secondly, there are "shareholder corporations." These enterprises are owned by their shareholders, who may be employees of the company — both managers and workers. Alternatively, the enterprises may have issued shares on the stock exchanges in Shanghai or Shenzhen. Management frequently consists of senior managers and a board of directors. While the management enjoys much greater autonomy with respect to government, it is nonetheless responsible to its shareholders.

The third group comprises smaller enterprises designated "shareholder partner companies," in which the government has actively invited individuals to invest money. This approach appears to have been originally inspired by the success since 1987 of the shareholding co-operative system in agriculture. Their employees now own some firms in this group, while others belong to one or more outside private investors. Others are still collectives, waiting for a buyer. Management may vary considerably in such enterprises, and the state plays little role in them. It was believed that, particularly where enterprises are owned by their staff, the problem of motivation would be solved; no evidence has been adduced for this, however.

In practice, it is widely felt that the MES has been a substantial improvement over the CMRS. It has gone some way towards addressing the problems of ownership, short-termism, the complex negotiating environment, and the negative impact of earlier tax reforms. But other matters remain to be resolved. In particular, there are issues of governance (in the Western sense) that still need to be clarified further. These include the separate responsibilities of enterprise, state and Party. There are also management issues at the micro level concerning the respective roles of the Party secretary and the factory director.

The new system has not resolved the financial difficulties faced by many enterprises. It has been recognized that around one-third of all SOEs continue to be loss making. A related issue is the ongoing cost of social provision by larger enterprises, noted above. The MES does not address this, though some limited experiments have been undertaken with commercial provision of these services at certain enterprises.

While it is generally felt that the exposure of enterprises to market pressures is a good thing, there continues to be controversy over the employment consequences of heightened competition. A similar dichotomy of view exists on the matter of rewards and bonuses for managers in SOEs, and over the loss of clear delineation of managerial ranks of the old command economy.

Finally, the role of the Communist Party, and the extent to which it is willing to relinquish even part of its power over industrial activity, are of paramount importance. Reducing the role of the state would need a profound change in China's political culture which, it would appear, is unlikely in the near term. As one observer put it in 1996, the trend seems to be towards "capitalism with Chinese characteristics" under the auspices of what he terms "legal-person socialism."[16]

To sum up: in the context of the imperatives of modernization and the integration of China into the global economy, noted in the introduction to this section, various attempts have been made to implement management reform. The Contract System of the late 1980s and early 1990s in its different dimensions sought to address issues of enterprise management — especially the question of autonomy, improvement of performance and output, and the raising of profits that could then be subject to the new system of taxation. In most respects the Contract System was only partially successful.

The MES has, since 1993, focused on ownership and governance more than on issues of management *per se*, taking diversification of investment in SOEs and the divestment of loss makers as the twin keys to generating capital and offloading costs.

Taken as a whole, the recent pronouncements on enterprise reform have served to clarify matters to some extent from a structural point of view, but still leave some of the most critical problems facing Chinese enterprises unresolved. In particular, the complete integration of the SOEs into the economic and social provision for China's population in the past, and the state's guarantees of employment to its citizens — legacies of China's political system — have prevented any easy transition to a market environment for very many SOEs. The introduction of policies to enforce such a transition has so far proved politically impossible.

As noted above, outstanding problems include the provision of employment opportunities (and necessary retraining) for the very many workers made redundant by the process of slimming down. They also include the establishment of effective alternative institutions to make up for the social provision being stripped away from the SOEs — pensions, housing, medical care and educational facilities, among others. Moreover, there is no obvious reason to believe that the "collectivization" and the floating of shares in loss-making enterprises are likely to be an effective means of raising necessary capital for those organizations.

Again, it is not clear that there are any policies in the pipeline that will address the many practical issues of day-to-day management thrown up at the time of the failure of the Contract System. Many of these relate to the continued direct or indirect role of the state in the Chinese market. In part this may be because, despite assurances to the contrary, there is as yet no clear agreement among China's leaders on what should be done.

Significantly one observer, with final responsibility for the current national programme to expose up-and-coming Communist Party cadres to modern management techniques, insisted that whatever happened the interests of the state must come before those of the enterprises, and that the party controls the state. "Most managers are party members, and must follow orders."[17] There would ultimately seem to be no way to reconcile this view with that of those who hold that "the trend to a market economy is irreversible; in time, the mechanism of competition will spread to the political sphere, leading China toward a democratic system."[18] In this context, the MES, like the CMRS before it, may turn out to be no more than transitional.[19]

Politics, culture and decision-making in China's enterprises

In recent years China has embarked upon a programme to modernize every aspect of its economy and society. This follows a period of 100 years up to 1949 during which only the periphery of China was touched by modern ideas or economic activity, and a further 30 years up to 1980 when social need and political objectives were paramount in determining policy on most matters.

The new emphasis on economic development and the transformation of society using ideas from the West and from Japan has given rise to a need for management decisions to be taken to alter the status quo over a very broad range of issues both major and minor. In this sense, decision-making processes are key to the successful modernization of China, as the Chinese government itself defines that modernization, and a study of decision-making will help us to understand to what extent, and for what reasons, China will be able to achieve its goals.

In this section, some general observations will be made about the context of decision-making in China, and then specific political and cultural factors will be highlighted which, it is argued, have a major impact on the way in which strategic decisions are made.

The context

In this sense as for the many other dimensions addressed in this book, it is important to recall that China is still a Marxist state in which parallel decision-making structures of Party and state exist. Most obviously, this means that at all levels organs of government are shadowed and monitored by corresponding organs of the Communist Party, which have until very recently tended to dictate policy on all essential matters and supervise its implementation. It has also meant, however, that individual Party members and sometimes Party cells have performed a similar function within state-run enterprises. Although many of these now have much greater, or even complete independence, Party members are still active within them; despite the so-called director responsibility system, all too frequently decisions have been made with one eye on what the party might say if individual managers were called to account.[20] This has both restricted the actual freedom of action of enterprise directors and, where they have tried to implement significant change, may cause a lukewarm response among middle managers.

In addition, there are still major conflicts over policy within the Party, the residue of the extraordinary transition which has been under way since China started to open up to the West around 1980. The Tiananmen incident of 1989 served to underline these contradictions, and raised renewed doubts about whether they will ever be finally resolved so long as the Communist Party remains in power. Among the most important of these dichotomies have been those between state and private ownership, centralized or decentralized administration of state sector enterprises, "redness" versus expertise, skilled or educated versus unskilled or uneducated, and city versus countryside.

There may be, within the Chinese context, good reasons why a senior policy maker may advocate continued state ownership of certain industries, particularly those which are infrastructural in nature. In a similar way, there may be considerable logic in preserving a high degree of centralized administration of those particular state industries. There are some older senior cadres who continue to lament the loss of political instruction, and of "redness," among the workforce. Furthermore, while skills and training are now in vogue among a majority of senior officials and are widely perceived as desirable, there is much less enthusiasm for the kind of tertiary education that encourages discussion of a broad range of new ideas, including those of a political kind. There is still, moreover, a lingering doubt about the proper balance between city and countryside, and for a time after Tiananmen a lingering threat of reversal through policies of social engineering, of the massive movement of people and economic activity to the cities.[21]

A final point with respect to context has to do with Western assumptions about the purpose of decision-making in business, and their applicability in present-day China. It is commonly assumed in the West, though this may not always prove to be the case in practice, that decisions are made in a business organization to improve production or sales or business methods in some way so as to increase the effectiveness and profitability of the firm. It is suggested here that in many enterprises in China this may only apparently be the objective, or may be only a partial objective. It is not only social interaction for pleasure that is ritualized in China; much of the interaction at work is ritualized too, and this includes the routines and processes of decision-making associated nominally with improving production or methods. Hidden agendas exist at many levels and the pursuit of them, while it may be rational for the individuals concerned, may not be in the best interests of the enterprise. Thus a sequence of routines nominally related to importing technology and revitalizing production and profitability may in fact be a ritual whose real objective is the adjustment of position in the local party hierarchy of several individuals, none of whom may really care about the project for itself. It should not be assumed therefore that the commitment to problem solving which is the ideal of so much management science in the West, and which is still the thread running through most decision-making theory, is universally shared in China. With these broad comments in mind, it is appropriate to look at a number of political and cultural factors that inhibit rational decision-making in China.[22]

Political factors

On the political side, there is first and foremost the need for enterprises in China when making decisions at the micro level, to conform to policies of the state and the Party at the macro level. At a time when the country is attempting rapid modernization, and the economy is in transition from a command economy to a much more free market situation, it is often very difficult even for large state-connected enterprises to know where they stand. Over the past twenty-five years, policies have frequently been reversed in midstream, as when the move to decentralize decision-making power in much of industry was suddenly reversed in the mid-1980s, after duplication and waste made the government in Beijing feel it was losing control. Further relaxation was followed by a brief period of recentralization of control after the Tiananmen massacre of 1989. While there has been greater stability in this respect since the mid-1990s, the nature of the decision-making process offers no guarantee that this problem will not recur.

Compounding the situation for much of the early period of modernization was the culture of secrecy and just plain vagueness which was a legacy especially of the ten years of the Cultural Revolution. A great many middle and senior managers in China into the early 1990s still tended not to keep their staff or their colleagues fully informed, and themselves would not ask if they did not know something. For years it was simply safer not to know. Among some managers, the loss of education or training during the Cultural Revolution also meant that they had never been taught to analyze problems for themselves, and this tended to result in vague and imprecise answers being proffered or accepted where in reality a precise and detailed grasp of a problem was essential if an intelligent decision was to be made.

While the retirement of many older managers, and their replacement by men and women thirty years younger, and often with some post-graduate study abroad, has eased this problem very considerably, there are still pockets of activity where this type of managerial inadequacy persists.

The primacy of the Party, mentioned as part of the context above, is still reflected in a number of specific ways affecting the role of an individual in a decision process. Perhaps most notably, as has been indicated elsewhere in this book, it is still an important, possibly the most important, avenue of promotion in China, a sure route to power and privilege even if individual entrepreneurial activity has become the route to wealth. A young Party member working in an enterprise may therefore have divided loyalties; from the point of view of his or her career in the party it may be best to take a cautious view of a proposed business plan, for example, while what the enterprise may really need at that time is a more outward looking or entrepreneurial decision which may involve some risk. The discussion then will cease to be rational in terms of the information presented and the best interest of the enterprise, but will be hedged about with false premises and beset by straw men.

Cultural factors

On the cultural side, the need to satisfy imperatives with their roots deep in China's Confucian past also affects decision-making processes. Among the most widely recognized in both sociological and Western business studies of China is the need to save face, preserve harmony, and to avoid conflict in social relationships.[23] Where strategic decisions need to be taken to secure the continued successful operation of an organization, such a cultural predisposition is likely to discourage the consideration of contentious information which may nonetheless be essential to an informed decision. The facts of the situation may be too embarrassing, or it may be claimed that reliable information is to hand when this is not the case. Moreover, the wish to avoid conflict may incline the decision-makers towards an unsatisfactory or incomplete decision, or even towards no decision at all, where one is clearly required.

Another cultural imperative in professional or business life in China is the need to promote the interests of the family and even of the extended family. Under the dynastic system, which prevailed down to the early twentieth century as we have seen, China was ruled by scholar bureaucrats who in practice sought to advance the interests of their extended families alongside the performance of their official duties. Even down to the level of the lowliest peasant, comfort and favours were owed and could be claimed through the extended family.[24] The philosophical justification of this lay with Confucius, who maintained that the family unit should be the foundation of all social and political life. Classical Chinese novels, such as *Dream of the Red Chamber*, also very frequently take the family as their theme. Thus, far more than is generally the case in the West, family interests may impinge upon professional life, and create hidden agendas which can detract from the rationality of decision processes defined in organizational terms.

Related to this is the phenomenon known as *guanxi*, discussed in earlier chapters. Broadly this means having connections, or a special relationship, with important or influential people. Foreign business people became aware early on in the modernization process of the usefulness of *guanxi* connections.[25] Such a relationship may stem from personal friendship, from having attended the same college, from having once worked in the same workplace or from having lived as neighbours in the same town, for example. The relationship strongly implies a willingness to "help out," and acceptance of the right to ask favours, in return for which loyalty will be given. In a society that has always been heavily bureaucratic, both in traditional and in modern times, *guanxi* is the way most people get around red tape and solve day-to-day problems. The tendency to rely on and to function through the *guanxi* network undoubtedly still influences strategic decision making, determining sources of information on which decisions are based, the scope and nature of routines followed in reaching a decision, and to a large extent the actual choice made; once again, a systematic and objective approach to the decision will have been undermined.

Other culturally-rooted factors may also influence decision-making. One is a widely felt dislike of rapid change, and its association in people's minds with *luan*, or chaos. Until the twentieth century the notion of progress was unknown in China. The ideal was held to exist in the past, in a legendary "golden age" that pre-dated both Confucius and historical record. When faced with difficulties China's rulers always invoked this golden age, and sought to put things right by restoring the ideal past rather than by seeking out new solutions.[26] Moreover, in social and political terms, change was much less obvious in China in the 2,000 years leading up to the twentieth century than it was in the West. There was no transition, for example, from feudal to early capitalist and then to modern industrial society. Change, when it did come, was traumatic and inconclusive in the half century before the People's Republic was founded in 1949, and chaotic through the policy shifts and political campaigns since 1949.[27]

For many decision-makers, therefore, certainly in the early phases of modernization, the worry was that the consequence of novelty would be catastrophe. This fear of change, and of the chaos it may bring, undoubtedly imposes an additional constraint which has not entirely disappeared.

A final cultural factor which should be noted is a degree of xenophobia which still exists under the surface in China, the legacy of 3,000 years of separate development during which China was seen as the centre of all civilization. While the need for China to look to the West and to Japan for advanced technology has become apparent and widely accepted in the past few years, there is a residual distaste among some people for the need to borrow from other cultures. In this, China is markedly different from, for example, Japan in the Meiji period. This tendency has undoubtedly affected some managers and others in a position to make strategic decisions. A consequence of this may be a reluctance to accept technical advice, or to contemplate solutions to problems that may be seen to increase an organization's dependence on forces outside China, however temporary or tactically useful that may be seen to be. Once again, the options are limited and flexibility is reduced.

In sum, therefore, it is suggested in this chapter that in present-day China in any case of strategic decision making there may be many hidden personal or rival institutional agendas. It is frequently more difficult than in the West to see the process as essentially rational, defined in terms of the goals of the organization (though in Western business practice too there are of course many irrational factors). These hidden agendas are rooted in political imperatives outside the organization, imposed on all citizens of the Chinese state, and also derived from cultural influences and injunctions thousands of years old that have

183

survived into modern times. These combine in some measure to strait-jacket the decision-making process, rendering it less amenable to objective consideration of objective choices. In the worst cases, strategic decision-making becomes a lottery of external political imperatives, uninformed comment and vested interests. This can be a harsh environment for expectations of Western-style decision-making.

Western theory on decision-making as a rule makes no allowance for a hostile political context outside the firm, where routines of political decision-making have in recent memory, just thirty years or so ago during the Cultural Revolution, resulted in dismissal, imprisonment and death. Nor, it would seem can most Western constructs adequately allow for the influence of culture, and in particular of an all-embracing system of social relations, with its in-built provision for claim and counter-claim by individuals on each other, which can do so much to influence the decision-making process. At a time of great transition in the world's economies, it may be worth reflecting that expectations in terms of broad management processes may not be readily transferable across political and cultural boundaries.[28]

Dilemmas of the socialist market economy

From the foregoing discussion of management reform, and more narrowly of approaches to decision-making as part of the management process, it is clear that the transition from a socialist to a market economy in China will not be easy. The analysis has shown that in a whole variety of ways both politics, through the interventions of the Party and the state, and culture — the imperatives and customs formed over a period of thirty centuries when the market did not prevail — have severely tempered the effort to systematically reform management in enterprises (in itself a campaign derived in spirit from the planned economy), and are likely to continue to cast a shadow over rational decision-making according to the criteria of the market.

Apart from these issues, there are issues relating to the nature of the private sector in China, and other matters that condition the market environment in which China's companies, both private companies and the new freer state-owned enterprises, must operate. Among these latter problems are those related to intellectual property rights, the role of venture capital and related issues of financial regulation, fiscal policy, regional and local pressure and interference, issues of nepotism and corruption as they pertain to the functioning of enterprises within the market, and the prospects for continued high rates of export-led growth.

In recent years, the private sector has grown dramatically in China. Over and above the activity of small traders and entrepreneurs, many larger ostensibly private companies have also appeared on the scene, and the suggestion is often made that China is in process of a full-scale transition to a capitalist economy. However, most private companies, even large ones like Haier or Huawei, have not embraced high technology. Rather, they are seeking a rapid turnover of goods, either through supplying export markets or through selling to the growing domestic market; so long as this activity generates a profit, they have little incentive to alter their approach. Figures published by the Ministry of Science and Technology in recent years, claiming a very significant increase in research and development spending on the part of private companies, are regarded by some observers (and foreign governments) as unreliable.

Moreover, relatively few large "private" companies in China are wholly private in reality. Research very frequently reveals that government money has been given to promising companies, either through funding of schemes at the local, municipal or provincial level, or through covert investment of public funds by Government or Party officials. Thus the "private sector" is not really fully private as that term would be understood in the West. Nor indeed are the markets for certain major products or areas of economic activity, such as the vehicle industry or banking, fully de-regulated.

Respect for intellectual property is a key aspect of any advanced market economy. The issue of intellectual property rights has been to the fore since China first began to engage with the international economy in a serious way in the early 1980s. All too often Chinese enterprises, whether state-owned or private, have been accused by Western, Japanese and other overseas firms of copying designs and appropriating intellectual property without acknowledgement or payment, an allegation that has often turned out to be true. Here, it must be said that this practice has been far from unique to China, with other economies in the region especially having been guilty of this offence at an early stage of their export-led development, in part because they have in this way been able to take a short cut to the production of items to a design and specification that will sell in Western markets. In China's case, there has been the additional fact that until China engaged with the world economy, there was official political encouragement for units of the wholly state-owned structure to learn from (that is, to copy) one another.

China's membership of the World Trade Organization since 2003, with its attendant obligations, and its growing network of collaborative ties with foreign companies through joint ventures, licence agreements, and the presence of wholly foreign-owned enterprises in China, has done much to reduce abuse of intellectual property rights. However, perhaps most important of all has been the growth of new and sophisticated Chinese-owned companies with their own intellectual property to protect; they have themselves lobbied the government for clearer legislation and more uniform and effective enforcement. Here we may see political institutions beginning to respond to the needs of the market.

In the first decade of the new century it is apparent that China's courts are indeed beginning to enforce legislation on patents and intellectual property, but "the capital is a long way away" as the Chinese saying goes, and the extent and degree of uniformity of application of intellectual property law remains a matter of concern. It is likely in the longer term, however, that this issue will be resolved, as China has so much to gain from involvement in the international economy, and respect for intellectual property is ultimately a necessary consequence of that involvement.

The disengagement of the state from the ownership and running of many enterprises, and the diversification into activity dependent on high technology and significant investment in the newly emerging private sector, have increased the requirement for capital from other sources. In the first decade of the new century there is now much increased interest in the role that venture capital could play in funding the expansion of high-tech firms.

While there are private venture capitalists in China, many of whom have made their money from property speculation or from entrepreneurial involvement in the manufacture of cheap textiles for export and similar activity, there is a strong desire on the part of the Chinese government to attract venture capital from overseas, or from Hong Kong or Taiwan to take the process forward more rapidly. This capital would supplement that made available to spin-out Chinese companies, for example, by units of the Chinese government such as the "Torch" division of the Ministry of Science and Technology.

However, if foreign or overseas Chinese venture capitalists are to invest in China, they will wish to see the regime of financial regulation both tightened up and made more consistent with international norms requiring scrupulous book-keeping, transparency and accountability, and scope for exit from China without state-imposed penalties. Here the issue is ultimately the attitude of the Communist Party; will the Party yield on the matter of the terms for foreign venture capital so that China will be able to draw in the funding needed to match the possibilities generated by its very substantial advance in technical ability? Venture capital activity would have been unthinkable in the old China — abhorrent to the Party as the worst kind of profit-taking. Now, and for the moment at least, the trend seems to be towards recognition of the usefulness of foreign venture capital in achieving the Party's objectives for sustained growth.

The Party's approach to fiscal policy is another area where an about-turn may be in process. Until the 1980s, because of the way in which the command economy operated, there was little knowledge of or need for a sophisticated system of taxation. All units of production belonged to the state, and almost everyone worked for the state; resources were for the state alone to shift around as required by the central planning process, and as the Party thought best.

The introduction of taxation over the past two decades has seen frequent fluctuations in policy, especially as it has been applied to enterprises in the new "for profit" environment. It has also seen a vast array of local taxes introduced by lower levels of government across the country, exactions not unlike in principle those imposed by local administrators under the Nationalist regime before 1949, and before them by local officials under the dynasties over many centuries.

It must be clear that in order to provide a stable taxation environment within which enterprises, not least foreign-invested enterprises, can operate, the central government must settle on a policy which will both enable it to collect sufficient revenue to meet its needs and still offer incentives to enterprises and enable them to make a profit. Of course, schemes that encourage firms to plough back some of their profits into improvement and expansion will still be possible, but any attempt to require this by fiat would undermine confidence, particularly among foreign investors. Moreover, the Party needs to get a firm grip on the random imposition of taxes and levies by local and provincial authorities, a practice unsuited to the modern business environment which is all too reminiscent of the political culture of traditional China.

This leads naturally to a consideration of regional and local pressures, and the role they play in the new quasi-market economy. Here an important factor is the ambition of cities and provinces, and of individual officials within their administrations, to assert themselves. In this way, even in local Party structures, reputations are made and promotion is gained. The benefits visibly trickle down to the broader population, as they have done in Shenzhen, Shanghai and a host of other places, confirming the view that those responsible have done a good job. Beyond this, longstanding regional rivalries and the strong sense of local identity in most Chinese reinforce the desire for success in competition with other places.

This tendency, which contradicts the Party's approach over the three decades before 1980 of putting the nation first and levelling out the differences between regions, was first given significant impetus by the proclamation of the four Special Economic Zones in south China in 1980, continuing with the fourteen "open cities" and other areas with special privileges from the mid-1980s, and the clear preference with respect to resources for development given to Shanghai and certain other places in the 1990s. The abandonment of the steady, slow, "across the board" approach is all too evident.

Now it is routine for the regions to lobby aggressively behind the scenes in central decision-making bodies, while cities like Shanghai have their own plans and projects for the local economy which often seem to pay little heed to national priorities. Local hopes, fears and propensities to meddle make for a very variable context for business across the country, as foreign firms have become only too aware. Here the scale of China may be the prime consideration; there is a sense in which China, even in traditional times, has always been a series of regional economies, and it may be that the process of modernization will inevitably advance this tendency.

One aspect of this variable context which is of particular note is the trend towards nepotism and corruption. Throughout China's long history, official corruption has been a frequent cause of the decline and collapse of administration, even bringing about the fall of dynasties. Nepotism is the negative face of the importance Chinese people attach to "*guanxi*," the sort of special relationship that is as important to business as it is in all other areas of life. The sustained and very high rates of growth in China over the past two and a half decades have generated much more cash in the economy, and the payment of bribes to secure contracts or planning approvals, or just to get things done, has come to be all too common. Chinese business practice, and accounting procedures especially, have in the early years of the transformation often been completely lacking in transparency, and accountability as it is understood in a market economy has been almost unknown.

Procedures for financial governance, and more generally the introduction of the many aspects of a regulatory framework for a market economy, as required by China's membership in the World Trade Organization, recognition by many nations of China's "market economy status," and other external pressures should help over time to reduce the scope for and discourage these irrational and often essentially criminal interventions. So too will heavy penalties (such as the death sentence for serious cases of embezzlement), which nonetheless may cause concern outside China. It has to be accepted, though, that corrupt practices have been fuelled by the exponential increase in economic activity, and indeed may even have contributed in their own way to the growth rate; they will continue to need to be closely monitored, and are among the major fault lines affecting modern Chinese society, as discussed further in Chapter 10.

Finally, if the country's stability and the Party's survival depend on the achievement of conspicuous prosperity for ever greater numbers of China's population, what are the prospects for continued high rates of export-led growth? If we look about Asia, we will see that the wave of export-led growth has buoyed up a succession of economies — Japan, then the "four tigers" of Hong Kong, Taiwan, South Korea and Singapore, and more recently, and with rather less impact, some of the economies of southeast Asia, notably Thailand, Malaysia, Indonesia and the Philippines. India too is now starting to engage with the world economy.

Yet in each case the wave of high growth has passed, as the factors which gave each country in turn a competitive advantage — labour costs, a flexible workforce, a positive matrix of education and skills, high rates of personal saving, among others — have been duplicated or exceeded by another country down the line, and often with lower rates of pay. Without exception, all the earlier "miracle" economies of Asia have in recent years had to struggle to maintain their export markets, and have experienced much lower rates of growth; the Asian financial crisis of 1997 was symptomatic of their relative decline.

So how can China expect to be any different? As its population, especially in the Special Economic Zones and in other coastal areas most conducive to manufacture for export, comes to expect ever higher salaries, will it be possible to sustain GDP growth at an average of over 8 per cent, as has occurred every year since 1979, or even at more than 10 per cent, as claimed for 2004?

It may be suggested that manufacture for export will move inland, where wage rates are lower. Yet this is not easy: transport of finished goods becomes more problematic, and skill levels immediately go down — inland sites are much less attractive to investors. It may be proposed that the domestic market will sustain production if export sales at some point fall away; yet if Chinese goods become less competitive overseas because of higher costs, it may be unreasonable to expect that poorer domestic consumers can take up the slack. There can be little doubt that while exports will continue to thrive in the short to medium term, there will be much stiffer competition from nations such as Brazil, Bangladesh, and parts of Africa in the longer term.

The fact is that world trade for almost 200 years was predicated on the assumption that Europe and North America manufactured nearly everything, while other parts of the world sold their raw materials to buy those finished goods. The growth in trade of Japan and the other Asian economies challenged that assumption. The engagement of China with the world economy for the first time ever, beginning only in 1980, threatens to overturn it completely. There is no precedent in the history of international trade either for a situation in which modern manufacturing capacity is spread so widely, or for the involvement in manufacture for export of a country so large as China. These are uncharted waters, and neither individual governments nor world trade bodies seem willing to embark on a journey of exploration of the possible longer-term consequences.

In the final analysis, it is probably fair to say that the prospects for continued export-led growth will in the medium-term depend on the manufacture for export of higher value goods, requiring fewer people with more advanced skills to make them. Whether this will satisfy the Party's need to provide jobs and prosperity for all remains to be seen. Looking further ahead, it may be that a return to China's age-old self-sufficiency, but at a higher level, is more likely.

10

PUBLIC POLICIES, PRIVATE GOALS

What is the relationship between private goals and the political process in China? As noted above, the pre-eminent playwright Lao She in his play *Teahouse*, published in the early part of the twentieth century, summed up the tension between the two by setting his discourse on the many problems facing Chinese people against a backdrop of large posters saying "No political discussion allowed!". For all the changes that have taken place in China since 1980, the scope for free debate of policy alternatives inside or outside the Party, or for the realization by individuals of private goals which may run counter to public policy, is still quite limited. In this chapter and the next, these issues will be taken up more fully.

The state orthodoxy and social structure of traditional China have been outlined in previous chapters. For most people, expectations were constrained by the Confucian moral code and emphasis on the family. The state intervened to keep order, collect taxes, impose corvée labour for public works, and to recruit armies in times of emergency. Apart from these points of contact with officialdom, the average peasant, artisan or petty trader was free to make a living as best he or she could, within the context of accepted Confucian norms. Beyond this any activity — such as institutional religion, commerce on a larger scale, the introduction of modern machinery and equipment into China, or even attempts to render the traditional political structures more efficient, whether undertaken by an individual or by a movement — was seen as potentially threatening to the social order.

The erosion of Confucian morality, and the still more damaging collapse of the effective power of government during the transitional period between the end of the Qing Dynasty in 1911 and the founding of the People's Republic in 1949, removed some of the constraints on individual activity in pursuit of personal goals. Yet the new freedom was enjoyed in practice by only a very small number of educated and privileged Chinese who lived in the larger cities. For most people life became at this time a struggle simply to survive. Sublimation of personal goals in the effort to bring the Communist Party to power came to be proof of the worth and the patriotism of the individual.

From 1949 on, as we have seen, the Leninist-style Party continued through the 1950s, and through the Cultural Revolution, to require that personal sacrifices should be made both by its members and by the population at large in pursuit of the common campaign for socialist construction. To a degree, the evident poverty of most people and the urgent need to tackle the practical problems of feeding, clothing and housing such a large population meant there was substantial acquiescence in this approach. The beginning of the modernization programme in 1979, however, and engagement with the international economy and the world outside, and new means of communication — especially email and the internet — have brought new pressures, not least the need somehow to harness individual ambition to broad development goals.

Articulating private goals

So what are these new private goals? Can they be articulated through the system as it has evolved?

First, it should be recognized that people's aspirations in the new China of the twenty-first century vary more widely than before, and reflect the new influences on their lives. With great reluctance, the Party has progressively had to cede control over the information coming into China from the world outside, simply because it could not prevent it from happening. The flow of students and officials to the West and, in most cases, their subsequent return, the process of manufacture for export (involving exposure to the expectations in terms of style and quality of foreign consumers), the establishment in China of foreign-owned and joint-venture enterprises which employ Chinese staff, and finally access for some people to foreign print media and satellite television, and for all to more comprehensive coverage of the world in the Chinese press — these are just some of the developments that have stirred up individual passions about what people want out of life. The "four rounds" of the 1950s — the bicycle, the sewing machine, the wedding ring and the radio — to which everyone used to aspire, set in the context of acceptance of life goals set by the Party, now seem impossibly old-fashioned.

In part, the objectives of people will differ according to where they live, their level of education, and what used to be called their class background, though there are some aspirations shared by almost everyone. Thus, the peasants who make up most of the 65 per cent of China's people who still live in rural areas now want for the most part to work for themselves, to sell their produce in free markets without hindrance, to be able to afford to employ others to do the worst of the physical work, and to be able to acquire land and property and to pass it on to their children — their male children especially. If this is not possible they want to be able to go to a nearby city, or even overseas, to hire out their labour on a construction site, and to send money back to their families to elevate their status within the village.[1]

Officials, both in the cities and in the countryside want to be better paid and to gain more recognition for their work. They are concerned about their status and about the perks of office — subsidized accommodation, perhaps a car, frequent banquets with important people, and the right and the opportunity to travel abroad from time to time.

Entrepreneurs, whether in the new private sector or among the reforming state-owned industries, want to maximize their freedom to run their firms as they see fit, increasing their profitability and benefiting themselves in the process. Their staff want both job security and rising rates of pay which reflect the success of the enterprise for which they work. They are also increasingly coming to see better working conditions and shorter hours as reasonable things to expect from a modern economy — in some industries, such as mining, the case for reform cries out to be heard.

Intellectuals — professionals might now be a better term to use — including teachers and professors, lawyers, doctors, nurses, linguists, writers, artists, musicians and many others, hope for the creative freedom to pursue their profession as they see fit, and for better pay into the bargain. They are often particularly hopeful that their children will be able to travel abroad to study, reflecting their nagging anxiety over periodic spasms of orthodoxy in China, and the value they place on ideas.

Women, who are of course subsumed in all of the above categories, as a group still are concerned that they will be given equal opportunity in the new economy, and their rights will be respected within the family and in the courts. While some women have received recognition as entrepreneurs or as senior officials, the number is nowhere near what it should be, and indeed in the rural areas the status of women may even be in decline, with land ownership and the cash economy encouraging a return to a situation in which greater value is placed on boys than on girls.

Young people, by definition a transitional group, generally are much less compliant nowadays than in earlier years, a trend observable in most countries. As the first generations emerge who are unashamedly individualistic, interested in material acquisition and in style, the Party will need to redouble its efforts to appeal to the country's youth if it is to reproduce itself over the coming decades. There is the danger too that a future population influenced neither by the morality of Confucius nor by that of the Communist Party may have no fixed points of reference by which to judge its own behaviour.

Finally, in a world in which national minorities are all too often blamed for political instability, we must take account of national minority aspirations in China. Broadly speaking, the position of the minorities in China has since 1949 been the result of a trade-off between linguistic and cultural rights and real power — the latter being conceded to secure the former. In part this has been because with few exceptions the national minority populations are small in number. Minority leaders have also tended to accept symbolic positions in both the local administration and in central government. While there are no real signs of national minority restlessness in China for the present, Tibet aside, in the future this may change, especially with respect to the substantial Muslim population, and in the light of Islamic fundamentalism in some other parts of the globe.

These particular considerations aside, all Chinese people wish to see for their children opportunities for education, a continually improving level of affluence, freedom from the threat of hunger, freedom to travel — at least within China — and greater mechanization of their personal lives both for work and for leisure. Most aspire to upward social mobility in the new and more status-conscious society. Almost all value stability very highly — freedom from "*da luan*," the chaos and unpredictability of the recent past.[2]

Articulation of these goals through the Chinese political system is not an easy matter. Chinese citizens do not have available to them, as a rule, the electoral mechanisms which in many developed countries, though far from perfect, permit a degree of popular control over governments at different levels which may advance or obstruct the realization of their personal ambitions. But some progress, albeit limited, has been made since the co-opted participation described in Townsend's analysis of earlier years.[3]

To begin with, the whole socio-economic and political context has changed. There is a greater permissiveness in Chinese society, which is given implicit sanction by the decline in the pervasive character of propaganda, in particular over the last decade of the twentieth century and into the new century. Whereas previously ideology was everywhere — in the workplace, on the streets, in the classroom, in the media, and in every aspect of the nation's cultural life — what is striking in present-day China is the almost total absence of moral exhortation and encouragement to follow a strict line, to the average citizen who is not a Party member at least. To a much greater degree the man or woman in the street is free to think things through for himself or herself, and to decide on his own goals and those of his family.

The change in skill requirements is another contextual factor influencing the ability of the individual to follow his or her preferred life choices. China's engagement with the international economy, as has already been noted, has brought forth a requirement for people with a broader education and new skills. If the Party is to continue to be successful in bringing ever greater prosperity to China's population, and to keep itself in power in consequence, it must to a minimal degree at least tolerate the pursuit of professional and personal objectives by those who are instrumental in achieving this. It must still rely heavily on its intellectuals, but in new circumstances in which it can no longer simply coerce them into supporting its policies.

Moreover, China is much more in the international media spotlight than ever before. There is now a sustained appetite overseas for news of developments in China, and a small army of foreign correspondents reside in the country to satisfy it. Gone are the days when just two or three of the largest foreign news organizations had a single correspondent in Beijing, and when it was possible to delay the release of the final death toll of a quarter of a million in the Tangshan earthquake by two and a half years.[4] So too do foreign governments monitor more closely domestic developments, and lobby, sometimes quite noisily, for human rights, intellectual freedom, and curtailment of the death penalty.

So in this context, how do people articulate their concerns? Can they be addressed through formal means outside the Party? It very much depends on who you are, what you do, where you live and, more than ever before in the People's Republic, how much money you have.

In theory, the mechanisms of government described in Chapter 8 offer scope for influencing people who run for local office, or even the opportunity to run for office oneself. Two thirds of China's population still live in rural areas, and it is perhaps no coincidence that the first limited experiments in democracy have taken place in the villages. The acquiescence of the peasantry is still seen as critical to political stability in China, so any mechanism that might help to secure peasant support would be likely to appeal to the Party; furthermore, peasant demands, as noted above, are likely to be fairly straightforward and related to non-controversial material objectives. This said, as has already been observed, the existence of a mechanism for democratic election is not a guarantee of its unhindered operation, or (as in any country) that the democratically chosen representatives will listen to the expressed wishes of their constituents.

In the cities, officials tend to seek preferment, as perhaps civil servants do anywhere, by demonstrating loyalty to the government, and sometimes by demonstrating loyalty to a particular clique of more senior officials. "Elected officials" — as we may call those who have been chosen by the Party as representatives to the National People's Congress and other similar bodies lower down the scale — may possibly now quibble over the phrasing or intent of legislation, trying both to render it more effective and to push the envelope of their own influence.

Entrepreneurs, seeking to promote their business objectives, will tend to develop personal networks through which to lobby for the necessary state support to enable them to realize their goals. However, substantial numbers have in recent years sought and obtained admission to the Party in pursuit of this end.

Intellectuals have more complicated personal goals, and fewer resources through which to achieve them. Often lacking money or powerful connections, and with little direct political leverage, they tend to use professional networks, especially with colleagues overseas, to spread the risk attached to what they do, and to maximize opportunities. Despite the country's need of their talents, they are still perhaps the most vulnerable group, and the most frequently frustrated in achieving their ends.

Both women and young people have needs and objectives that in part are still met by the mass organizations. The official women's bodies, and the Youth League, which previously served as transmission belts between the Party and the individual, ensuring compliance with the Party line over a very broad range of matters, seem now much more genuinely interested in problems related to their specific constituencies. Whether women and young people are as ready as they may once have been to have their interests defined for them, and indeed whether their principal concerns are shared concerns, or in fact vary widely from one individual to the next, are matters of debate.

Trade unions too, among mass organizations, now for example do take up on workers' behalf issues of industrial safety, though it has to be said the Party itself is belatedly attempting to address this area of concern because of more widespread reporting of industrial accidents. At last an activist for a particular cause, so long as it is one broadly approved of by government, might hope to realize at least some of his or her objectives through participation in a mass organization.

The fifty-six officially recognized national minorities have formal representation through local administrations and on certain central government bodies, yet apart from serving as a safeguard for cultural and linguistic concessions made to them, these bodies cannot really be regarded as an effective means for realizing the individual objectives of national minority people. Insofar as most minority people still live their lives outside the mainstream of China's modernization, it could reasonably be said that their situation offers little scope for expressing personal ambitions. Despite occasional tensions, the lack of any practical alternative to Chinese rule, and a grudging acceptance that the benefits of being part of China may be greater than the disadvantages, tend to reinforce the status quo.

The two obvious exceptions are the Tibetans and the Uighurs. In traditional times, Tibet's tributary relationship to China only worked because, by and large, the Chinese Empire left Tibet alone to run its own affairs. China's invasion of 1951, and full-scale occupation since 1959, changed matters completely, and the exiled Dalai Lama's international diplomatic efforts to gain support for Tibet have brought substantial sympathy, especially on the question of obvious human rights violations by the Chinese authorities.

The Uighurs, China's substantial Muslim minority living mainly in Xinjiang, have (unfortunately for them) always in recent times been seen as a potential source of trouble, having been the cause of more than one major rebellion during the Qing Dynasty. Now, in the context of Islamic fundamentalism elsewhere, and the international reaction to it, Uighurs tend to get short shrift when their grievances are brought to the attention of the authorities. For both the Tibetans and the Uighurs, the scope to realize personal objectives under Chinese rule is all too limited.

So then, if the existing mechanisms of the state structure in China have only very partially begun to take account of the goals of the individual, what is the situation with the Communist Party itself? If the Party still holds the real power in China, how can the individual influence the Party?

The Party as a vehicle for private goals in the new century

The Chinese Communist Party from its founding in 1920 embraced the assumption that all patriotic Chinese should subordinate their personal goals and wishes to the good of the Chinese people as a whole. Through the struggle to take power, and in the thirty years or so after that, this assumption went unchallenged, although there was conflict over ways and means. With the coming of the campaign for modernization in 1979, however, new stimuli were brought to bear on the Chinese population, and for the first time large numbers began to think much more in terms of personal goals. Could the Party accommodate the implications of this change of direction that it had unleashed? Could a structure that had for so long decided on policy and given orders for its implementation be a vehicle through which people might achieve the private goals now emerging?

First of all, it should be recalled that the vast majority of China's people are not members of the Party. The old adage that "the people are the sea, and the Party are the fish that swim in that sea" carries little weight today, and unless non-members have money, connections, or some other means of exercising influence on it, their voices are in any direct sense likely to remain unheard in the deliberations on policy that may affect their lives. Moreover, the Party controls not only the government of China, but also ultimately its police, its courts, and its armed forces. In this sense, any serious conflict between the personal goals of the individual and the policy of the Party can only result in defeat for the individual. Finally, the Party has tended to become a self-perpetuating elite, is completely unaccountable, and cannot be repudiated at any form of election. For the average man or woman in the street, therefore, there may be no chance to influence the Party with respect to their private goals or anything else.

So what of the actual membership of the Party — who joins the Party these days, and how? Of the seventy-three million members, for most of them there can be little doubt that in twenty-first century China the composition and personal goals are to a degree different from those of Party members through much of the twentieth century.[5] For many, but not all, the route in is still through membership of the Young Pioneers and the Communist Youth League, a process that will require assessment of a candidate's seriousness and moral purpose, but the heavy emphasis on ideology of earlier times has been substantially diminished.

It is fair to say that the Party now looks for dynamic leadership qualities (and hence ambition) as well as loyalty in its new members, with the attendant dangers that this may bring. While there is still undoubtedly a core of young people from all walks of life who subscribe to the old ethic of service and patriotism, there are growing numbers who primarily see membership in the Party as something which, in one way or another, will be good for their careers — rather like joining the right club. Here again the cultural practice of "*guanxi*" — developing a network of helpful contacts — merges with the political.

Furthermore, the Party is now willing to bring in promising young entrepreneurs and others with a clear sectional interest who have not followed the normal approach to membership. The management of potential conflict of interest in these cases is in its infancy. Young Party members include some of China's best and brightest, the heirs of May 4th, and even of Tiananmen, but with entrepreneurial flair and ambition.

So can the individual Party member have any influence on the formulation or implementation of policy which will have an impact on private goals? Where those goals are part of a widely-expressed desire, shared by the Party, for sustained development and a continuing increase in prosperity, the individual can probably now trust that the Party through its policy formulation will consistently do all it can (within the limits of its understanding) to achieve these objectives, seeing their realization as the surest way to maintain itself in power. Individual Party members can work for the Party knowing that what is good for the Party is likely to be good for them. When it comes to implementation, on the other hand, where private goals might run counter to the Party's stated policy, in whatever way, the Party may often only be a vehicle for achieving those private goals if the power and influence it gives to individuals is illicitly used to promote personal interests.

Here the issue arises of the abuse of power by some Party members who respond to lobbying for favours by taking bribes in cash or kind — the peddling of influence, not unknown in other countries but particularly acute in present-day China because of the lack of transparency and the large amounts of new money circulating in the economy. Here the Party is acting as a vehicle for achieving personal goals in a way that was entirely unintended.

The matters on which a Party member's intervention may be sought are many and varied. China remains, for all its part-market credentials, a country in which permissions and approvals have to be obtained over a vast range of activity. For example, planning permission for property development, permission to release foreign exchange, permission to do a business deal over a certain amount, approval for investment, approval for withdrawal of investment, exemption from certain types of taxation, product approval, permission to hire and fire employees in certain circumstances — in these and many other cases of legitimate activity there are gatekeepers who are themselves Party members or who can be instructed by Party members. Beyond this there is straightforward criminal activity, such as embezzlement, which is tolerated by Party members, who may even be involved directly.

Thus, in sum, it would appear that the private goals of Party members can be accommodated in a general way in the Party's processes of policy formation primarily insofar as they coincide with the views of senior leaders. While the scope for the views of younger Party members to be heard and acted upon may expand in time, it must be remembered that the Party is above all a centralist organization which is hierarchical in its lines of authority. Private goals of Party members or their friends which are accommodated in the process of implementing policy are all too often satisfied through the transgression of established legal norms.

The primacy of the family in post-Deng China

In previous chapters, the role of the family in defining the life of individuals in traditional China has been the subject of some discussion. It is reasonable to ask, therefore, how strong the family is as a unit for forming, articulating, and achieving private goals in twenty-first century China. Have sixty years of Communism, nearly thirty years of contact with the West, a new economy, and urbanization changed things? Each of these factors that have impacted on family life may be taken in turn.

There can be little doubt that the Party's efforts to subordinate the goals of the individual, and of individual families, to those of the state both before and after the Communist victory in 1949 had for a time a significant effect on the public face of family life. As noted above, the rationale was that the interests of the individual, if they were legitimate, would naturally be subsumed in the interests of the nation as a whole. Thus, families and the individuals within them were expected to sacrifice their personal hopes and aspirations to the great common projects of nation-building and national defence, and might only very privately fantasize about a future defined independently of the Party's wishes. This approach reached its high point during the Cultural Revolution, when children denounced their parents and the family probably was less significant than at any time in China's history.

In part in reaction to the bleak attack on the family represented by the Cultural Revolution, most Chinese people have reverted to a position of respect for the family (and for the networking possibilities it may afford); even the Party has now embraced the family, and presents itself as the only possible guarantor of its prosperity and well-being.

Contact with outside influences, and especially with the West, has also affected the way families function in China. Through media reports, films, and sometimes foreign travel, people in China have become aware of the role the family plays in other countries — which, it is recognized, differs from place to place. "Individualism," which Chinese people had been led to believe was the principal driver of all activity in the West, has been seen to be tempered by devotion to the family in varying degrees, and by concern for the family's place in society not so dissimilar to that in China before the Communist era.

China's engagement with the international economy has also impacted on the family as an institution. The dramatic rise in prosperity in parts of eastern China especially has reinforced the common purpose of the family as a beneficiary of the new circumstances, and as a unit of acquisition. Thus a nuclear family or even an extended family may acquire a car, or a new house, or may have a member who holds an important position in a successful enterprise, for example; all of which reflect increased status on the family as a whole.

Demands on China to act as a supplier of manufactured goods to the world have also hastened the process of urbanization, so that now some 35 per cent of its people are considered to live in cities. Here, the effect has been similar to that observed in many other societies undergoing a process of modernization: where peasants have migrated from the countryside to the city, the extended family has often been broken up, and the family that survives is the smaller nuclear family (or, in the case of those labourers who migrate back and forth on a regular basis, a divided family, or ultimately perhaps no family at all). Urbanization, however, has by no means eliminated the role of the family in the formation of private goals; rather it has refined it, offering new and alternative forms of family life.

For these reasons among others, it is possible to assert that the family's role in society has undergone a revival in twenty-first-century China, even that it may form a cornerstone of an emerging civil society, and ultimately of a new democratic movement. This possibility will be dealt with further in Chapter 11. In terms of defining private goals, it provides a link with the past, and therefore a benchmark by which future success can be measured. It is the chamber within which positive attitudes to education are formed, dreams and ambitions are nurtured, and which increasingly in a society that becomes more affluent day by day affords the incremental surplus to enable individual plans and goals to be realized, to the benefit of all.

Thus the broad goals shared by most Chinese, noted above — increasing affluence, access to labour-saving devices, freedom to travel, upward social mobility, a politically stable environment — are often generated and communicated through discussion within the family, through sharing the experience of members of the extended family, and form a vision of the future conditioned by a kind of organizational memory of the family's circumstances in the recent and more distant past. Even the rebellion of youth, in the Chinese context, can be seen as a reaction against the conditioning received within the family, and may not last beyond the assumption of family responsibility.

What have changed are certain of the old family attitudes of Confucian times to gender roles, to the state, and to the types of activity now seen as acceptable in the struggle to move the family forward. In the cities certainly, women now frequently undertake paid employment, and with wages has come an elevation of status within the family. Contributing to this has been the one-child policy, which has meant that for the first time daughters have been encouraged to see themselves as the equal of sons, and have ambitions to match. With this change, women have continued to perform as a rule the task of ordering and motivating the family. In the countryside, the new market economy has had a somewhat different effect, the new right of peasants to acquire and bequeath land having revived in some measure the desire to have and to favour sons.

In Confucian times, the family saw itself — indeed was obliged to see itself — as being ultimately at the disposal of the state, while the state viewed the family, bolstered by Confucian morality, as the foundation of peace and prosperity. In the first decades after the Communist takeover, the state downplayed the role of the family. Now, by contrast, the evidence is that in the emerging market economy the power families have as consumers, augmented perhaps by half-formed notions of rights filtered through from overseas, has encouraged the formation of a new feeling of independence from the state, a view that the state is largely irrelevant to the achievement of the economic goals of the family. This is ironic in the light of the state's (and the Party's) desire to present itself as the author of the new prosperity.

Following on from this, most families are now happy to encourage sons and daughters to experiment with new types of economic activity, and there is no stigma or reticence attached to success in manufacturing, financial dealing, or commercial activity of any kind. The more entrepreneurial the better, seems to be the order of the day. Moreover, speculative activity is by no means limited to particular groups in society, or to particular parts of China; rather it is ubiquitous, and its consequences are everywhere to be seen. This is in marked contrast both to Confucian China, which tolerated commerce while frowning on it, and to the decades of communism after 1949, when commercial activity solely for private gain was effectively proscribed.

All in all, therefore, the family has gone a long way to re-establish itself as the significant unit in Chinese society, though some of the ambitions it nurtures, and the means of achieving them, may have changed.

The individual as subject or object of modernization?

When all the factors cited above are taken into account, can it be said that the individual is driving modernization in China now, or is he or she rather being driven by it? Do public policies reflect private goals and interests sufficiently to keep the Party in power?

There can be little doubt that the Party sees its ability to continue to generate high rates of growth, and therefore increasing prosperity, as its principal means of retaining sufficient popular support to enable it to stay in power. This equation is often fairly crudely put. It is true though that so far at least, in the first thirty years of the new phase of modernization, the Party has been able to counter any criticism of its stewardship by reference to the unprecedented rates of growth — an undisputed average of over 8 per cent per annum of GDP since 1979, over 10 per cent claimed by the National Bureau of Statistics in 2004, and over 11 per cent in 2007, with a peak of 13 per cent in 1994.[6]

Frequent assertions of the importance of sustained growth, however, beg a number of questions. The first must be whether it is possible to continue to achieve the rates of growth registered so far. China's upward spiral of development started in 1979 from a very low base: given this, and China's advantages of abundant cheap labour, a determined central administration, and an as yet untapped world market for its new range of manufactured goods, the achievement, although highly creditable, may not be possible to sustain indefinitely.

Moreover, China's hold over certain markets, in certain sectors, is now being effectively challenged by cheaper goods manufactured in Brazil, India, and the less developed parts of Southeast Asia. The competition from these and potentially other areas can only be expected to grow as labour costs rise in China. In this way, China may follow the well-worn path already trodden over the past fifty years successively by Japan, the "tigers" of Hong Kong, Taiwan, Singapore and South Korea, and then Malaysia, Indonesia, Thailand and the Philippines. In each case a strategy of export-led growth has produced an initial surge of prosperity and industrialization, followed by a loss of competitiveness and a lowering of growth rates. While a move to the manufacture of more sophisticated and less labour-intensive products has slowed the decline, it is clear that the extraordinary growth of the early phase has in each case been a transitory phenomenon.

The problem here is that expectations have been formed among China's population, which the Party in the longer term may be unable to fulfil. Indeed, if Chinese companies begin to behave as other multinationals do, they may be expected to shift production offshore to less developed economies to save money, preferring this option to the lower labour cost areas of China's own western hinterland where greater logistical problems would be involved for companies wishing to export. This prospect will sit well neither with the fairly deep-rooted notion that the activity of Chinese corporates should benefit China, nor with the Party's desire to take the credit for sustained prosperity. A feeling of what is sometimes called "relative deprivation" may set in, so that although people are more prosperous than before, they may feel deprived if rates of growth are not sustained.

There are in addition certain fatal flaws in the great project for China's future development which may serve to undermine the scope for the individual to achieve his or her private goals. In these cases, it is the ordinary man in the street who will bear the consequences most, and it becomes apparent that he may become a victim as easily as he may be a beneficiary of a process of modernization over which, when all is said and done, he really has little influence.

The first problem arises from the unequal distribution of the benefits of the new economic activity. This works on several levels. The inevitable consequence of the repudiation of the old economic regime, which critics derided for producing an equality of poverty, has been that some people have benefited significantly from the new prosperity, while others have not. In the part-market economy, the more entrepreneurial have seen their chances and taken them. This has resulted in a dramatic growth in the disparities of income, the formation of a group of *nouveaux riches* who ostentatiously display their new wealth, and a rising culture of contempt for those who do not have material possessions. The transition to a consumer society has been characterized by a rush to acquire colour televisions, mobile phones, washing machines, hi-fis, and most recently private cars by this group, many of whom are now also able to buy luxury private accommodation, take holidays abroad, and put their spare cash into investments, some overseas.

The conventional argument is that the benefits of rapid development will in due course trickle down into the wider society, and that a comfortable middle class will form which will be a pillar of social and political stability. This may happen, but in the meantime twenty-first-century China has begun to exhibit a gap in wealth between its richer and poorer citizens all too reminiscent of that which obtained in the decades leading up to the Chinese revolution of 1949.

It is also noteworthy that this discrepancy in wealth marks a fault line between cities and the countryside in their hinterland. While it is true that the abandonment of the Commune system in the early 1980s in favour of private production and agricultural markets led for a time to a significant improvement in the lot of China's peasants, in many areas this progress was not sustained into the late 1990s or the new century. This in turn has led to pressure for migration from the countryside into the cities, as rural people seek to address their relative poverty by working in cities as casual labour and sending money home to their families. This too is a familiar problem which recalls life in pre-Communist China. The implications for criminal activity and public order of large roving bands of poorly educated peasants travelling around China in search of work are all too obvious.

A further dimension to the wealth gap relates to the geographical distribution of the new prosperity. With certain exceptions, such as the cities of Chongqing and Chengdu, the further away from the east coast one travels in China, the poorer the country becomes. The explanation for this lies in several factors. The reluctance of foreign companies to set up joint ventures and stimulate economic activity far from the principal transport routes and the seacoast is one — location being a major concern for exporters, as noted above. That political figures from these areas have less influence in Beijing is another. The generally lower education and skill levels of the local workforce is a third. Yet this is to a degree a self-perpetuating situation: unable to attract investment because local conditions are not right, these areas are destined to remain unattractive because they cannot bring in the resources they need to make improvements. The consequence is endemic poverty, as people in the western hinterland areas of China, especially, fall further and further behind their fellow citizens in the East.

In these ways, the growing wealth gap creates and perpetuates divisions in twenty-first-century China which may yet prove every bit as disruptive to the social order as did the gap between rich and poor in the civil war period of the twentieth century.

Another major problem in an economy newly flush with cash and wedded to growth is corruption of all kinds and at all levels. Not only is there influence peddling on the part of some government officials and Party members, as noted earlier in this chapter — a phenomenon made worse by the many approvals needed for private initiatives left over from the old economy. There is also a range of opportunities for corrupt practice resulting from the absence of clear and clearly understood regulatory mechanisms governing private business, of a uniformly implemented body of commercial law, or in many cases, of mechanisms for enforcement and the will to use them. It is all too easy for the dishonest entrepreneur to double-deal with business contacts, to fail to supply agreed quantity and quality for personal gain, to embezzle money and falsify accounts, to neglect to pay taxes, and to form links with violent criminal elements in order to eliminate rivals.

Although the Party has not yet developed effective means of dealing with this new corruption, the drive for personal wealth and the corruption associated with it, it can be argued, may have more to do with pre-Communist China than with anything the Party has done or omitted to do. The distaste of the dynastic order for commerce had the effect of marginalizing commercial activity in traditional China, as we have seen. Thus it tended to develop in an anarchic way, and remained effectively unregulated right down to the Communist victory — one reason why foreign businesses preferred to operate under the legal protection of the foreign settlements. Indeed, the relationship between both the traditional (imperial) and the transitional (republican) state and the business community, if it may be called that, was itself corrupt; under the principle of merchant operation and government supervision, dynastic officials were accustomed to taking large bribes just to enable the activity to go ahead, while the warlord governments of the early Republican era, and Chiang Kai-shek's government, simply squeezed Chinese merchants for funds to support their armies and their military campaigns.

When the Chinese Communist Party came to power, it saw corruption as a particular characteristic of the bourgeois merchant class, and sought to sweep it away with the influence of that group. Corruption associated with opportunities for personal gain then remained largely dormant as an issue until the 1980s, when the new engagement with the international economy and the new scope for private business began to tempt the less scrupulous. Reinforced by the practice of *guanxi*, the cultivating of the special relationship, corruption is now rife in China, and despite recognition given to the problem in Party and NPC deliberations, the evidence suggests that the authorities have no real plan to deal with it.[7]

There are also the environmental costs of the private goals which the Party sustains in order to stay in power. The destruction of old neighbourhoods (and much of China's vernacular architectural heritage) to enable modern office blocks and luxury apartments to be built in

China's cities impacts immediately on the individual families who may have lived there for generations, and are now moved out to the suburbs with little hope of adequate compensation. Serious problems of atmospheric pollution from sulphur dioxide, carbon dioxide, methane and other sources have arisen from the much accelerated pace of industrial activity, as well as from exponentially increased traffic flows in the cities; despite growing appreciation of the impact on public health and climate change among specialists, the Party remains unwilling to sacrifice development goals in pursuit of a serious effort at ameliorating the problem. Contamination of the soil, and of canals and irrigation ditches in urban areas especially by industrial waste, is another dimension to the environmental cost of rapid growth.

In the countryside, the move to agricultural free markets, and the elimination of the Communes as units of production in the early 1980s, led to the abandonment of large tracts of land suitable for growing rice, including elaborate terraces constructed with great effort and ingenuity over the three decades before 1979. The motivation here has been the individual peasant's wish to maximize income by growing more expensive crops; the consequence has been that China must now import ever-increasing quantities of rice, and is no longer self-sufficient in this basic commodity. On the other hand, land has been brought under cultivation which is not suitable for this purpose, destroying grazing land, causing topsoil to be blown away, and rendering it unsuitable for any economic purpose within two or three years. Throughout northern China, many trees which were planted in the 1960s and 1970s to secure the loose fertile soil, and incidentally to counteract atmospheric pollution, have been felled to make way for property development and road schemes.

The ever-greater consumption of energy, and the demand for new supplies of energy, has also had environmental consequences. While some thought has gone into reducing the consumption of coal for domestic heating purposes and by industry, and this has had some positive effect, new hydro-electric schemes have often caused significant damage to the environment. The Yangzi Gorges dam project, the largest in history, has destroyed a world heritage site, caused a complete upheaval in the ecosystem of the Yangzi River, and triggered the enforced permanent removal of more than a million people from their homes.[8] A smaller but not insignificant scheme on the upper reaches of the Mekong River has devastated the ecology and the lives of communities downstream in Cambodia.

While all of these environmental issues are now discussed at least in China, there remains a reluctance to put attempts to address them ahead of the overriding goal of economic growth. Indeed, the majority of China's individual citizens would probably still support the government in this choice, and insofar as the West both historically and currently has been principally responsible for causing climate change this is perhaps understandable. Yet a recent Chinese government report suggests that if the trend toward climate change goes on unabated, by 2030 China's food production will have decreased by 8 per cent, and this during a period when China's population will almost certainly increase.[9] Security of the food supply has preoccupied Chinese governments throughout the centuries, and failure to achieve it has been a primary cause of political unrest. For this and other reasons, the whole range of environmental issues may yet prove to be the single most significant flaw in China's long-term modernization plans.

Some action has been taken. At its Seventeenth Congress in October 2007, the Communist Party for the first time made environmental protection one of its leading priorities. Early in 2008 it set up a fully-fledged Ministry for Environmental Protection, while later that year a comprehensive White Paper on climate change was published, acknowledging the urgent need to address this problem. Yet conflict over the importance to be attached to the environment as opposed to development continues behind closed doors at the highest levels. At the Copenhagen conference in December 2009, China still declined to accept any binding targets for emissions, and all the evidence so far suggests that it will be China's own perception of the urgency of the need to respond to climate change that will produce policies to tackle it, rather than any pressure from foreign countries.

One final problem that must be addressed in any discussion of China's future course of development is the continued lack of institutional frameworks through which to resolve issues and to shape the policies to come. This may at first seem a strange assertion when made in the context of a state that has had the habit of planning everything (for better or for worse) and is top heavy with political structures. Yet the point here must surely be that China's political and legal structures continue to lack transparency, remain very much influenced by the centralized decision-making model of the Communist Party, and are ultimately inaccessible to China's people.

The question may be asked, if the Chinese Communist Party has all but abandoned its attempt to inculcate Marxist political and social orthodoxy into the population, if it is no longer fighting to assert China's independence, to redress old feudal and bourgeois inequities of the past, and to eliminate social evils, then from where does it derive its moral legitimacy? We have seen that in practice it may try to persuade China's people that it is the best guarantor of their continuing prosperity. Yet this is a high-risk tactic, as it loses its force as an argument as soon as the present high rates of growth can no longer be sustained.

The Party almost certainly recognizes this dilemma: it cannot allow its political and legal processes to become too transparent for fear that citizens will begin to ask why the Party in the twenty-first century continues to enjoy unchallenged power and influence. Yet the lack of open institutions, of transparent government, and of a legal system which is independent, based on due process, and before which all citizens are equal — these are precisely the faults that may ultimately undermine political stability in China, and the Party's grip on power.

The Chinese Communist Party is at a crossroads. It could take a giant leap of imagination, and attempt to genuinely open up and pluralize political life, undergoing a metamorphosis of its own in the process. It could reinforce the independence of the courts, and take steps towards the impartial administration of justice. Or it could wait until it is no longer able to play the prosperity card, and must resort to force to sustain itself in power. The choice it makes will be critical for China and her people.

This chapter opened by asking about the nature of the relationship between the political process and private goals in China. While it may be somewhat easier for the individual to pursue personal goals in the China of the new century, the political mechanisms are still very imperfect. Where the individual confronts authority in China, probably the resort to *guanxi* is still the most effective route to a resolution. The great leap to the institutionalization of accessible and transparent political processes, uniform in their application, which could afford the individual greater control over his or her own life has not yet been made. This issue, and the major challenge to the system represented by the Tiananmen incident, will be dealt with more fully in the next chapter.

11

THE FIFTH MODERNIZATION

One final issue that must be addressed in any discussion of China's recent development and future prospects is that of the outlook for democracy — the so-called fifth modernization, as Wei Jingsheng referred to it in 1978.

Even before the advent of post-Second World War approaches to development, a gradual transition to "democratic" government in principal interlocutor countries overseas had been an aspiration of some Western governments, in part because it was believed to encourage peace and stability, and make those countries easier to deal with. In this way in Asia, from the 1890s and up until the end of the 1920s Japan was often cited as an example of a good student of Western democracy; Japan's constitutional progress in the 1890s must have made it seem more acceptable as an equal partner for Britain in the Anglo-Japanese Alliance of 1902.

By contrast, China during the final decline of the Qing Dynasty seemed to many Westerners a hopeless case — autocratic, backward-looking, with impenetrable and corrupt institutions of government. In the nineteenth century, as we have seen, China, unlike Japan, had largely declined to import or emulate Western practice in any sphere if it could avoid doing so. In the light of this, what would be China's experience in terms of practical attempts to implement democracy in the twentieth century?[1]

Historical antecedents: 1913, 1919, 1940, 1979 and 1989

China's first brush with democracy was the shortlived experiment of 1913. Following the collapse of the Qing Dynasty in 1912, the Guomindang had pressed for and achieved agreement among the rebels for elections to be held to a national assembly in 1913. These took place under a restricted and indirect franchise in February 1913, resulting in a Guomindang victory in all provinces in which they had occurred; however, when the Guomindang tried to assert its right to choose a Cabinet and form a government, one of its leaders was gunned down on the orders of the new warlord President Yuan Shi-k'ai. The President progressively assumed full authority, and China declined into civil war, and subsequently the warlordism for which it was known in the early 1920s.

The May 4th Movement of 1919, as we have seen, was triggered by China's poor treatment at the Versailles peace conference following the end of World War One. The Movement involved for the first time large numbers of Chinese intellectuals in open debate about their country's future, and the new possibilities both politically and in terms of social and economic organization.

Indeed, since the 1890s, and especially since 1915, owing to the spread of newspapers and the translation of core texts of Western political theory, including those of Karl Marx, Chinese intellectuals had become much more aware of developments outside China; this process was helped by the appointment of a liberal-minded intellectual, Cai Yuanpei, as President of Peking University, which subsequently became a focal point for discussion of current trends and alternatives. In addition Chinese intellectuals became aware of the growth of nationalism in India, another large Asian country. They also became aware of the Russian Revolution of 1917, and many were influenced by the example it seemed to pose for China.

One such was Chen Duxiu, who in January 1919 originated the terms "Mr Science" and "Mr Democracy" to describe the two institutions that China most needed if it was to enter the modern world. In time, most of the protagonists of the May 4th Movement claimed to be supporters of Mr Science and Mr Democracy, and it is notable that Chen was well on his way to becoming a Marxist when he made this comment; he would later be one of the founders of the Chinese Communist Party.

The problem was that science and democracy could mean different things to different people. For Chen, a scientific approach was the antithesis of Confucianism, with its prescribed truths and moral exhortations: "to explain truth by science means proving everything with fact. Although the process is slower than that of imagination and arbitrary decision, yet every step taken is on firm ground..." (1915) Linking science with the need for political change, he observed: "The contribution of the growth of science to the supremacy of modern Europe over other races is not less than that of the theory of the rights of man" (1915).[2]

Chen's concept of democracy evolved, from the early period of his writing for *New Youth*, when he emphasized individualism, to his later acceptance of the need for democratic centralism as expressed in the theory and structure of the Communist Party to solve China's problems. His idea of democracy no longer encompassed the structures of a specific political system, but rather seemed to elevate the social and economic requirements of citizens, and saw the satisfaction of those needs as of paramount importance — an approach echoed in the Tiananmen demonstrations as recently as 1989.

For Hu Shi, the prominent liberal writer and orator, science was the necessary antithesis to Chinese fatalism, and offered a methodology that Chinese people needed to adopt if they were to become modern. An advocate of the vernacular written language, Hu emphasized the place of science in education, and of a scientific approach to health issues such as birth control.

Democracy for Hu meant liberal democracy on the American model, reflecting his own experience during seven years in the United States; in a parallel with Chen Duxiu, Hu ultimately threw in his lot with the Guomindang under Chiang Kaishek, by which time that party had ceased to be in any sense democratic.

For the Guomindang under Sun Yatsen, democracy, first envisaged in 1905, had become one of the three planks of the party's platform, the so-called *Three Principles of the People*, when the party was reformed in 1924. For Sun, however, who had been trying to bring about radical change in China since 1894, the need to address the reality of China as it was in the early 1920s soon meant compromises with warlords and a reform of the party structure on the lines of that of the Communist Party of the Soviet Union, a process that had started in 1922. In such a climate, even Sun's personal commitment to the ultimate goal of liberal democracy was bound to be placed under strain; his death in 1925, and the takeover of the Guomindang by the reactionary Chiang Kai-shek in 1926, effectively killed off any remaining democratic ambitions the party may have had. It is worth noting that while the *Three Principles* made no specific reference to science, for Sun himself, as a doctor of Western medicine, a scientific approach to the solving of China's problems would almost certainly have been integral to his thinking.

Overall therefore, Mr Democracy, even in the May 4th period, was much misunderstood, maligned, and ultimately in practice abandoned by the immediate participants in the debate; Mr Science was seen by some as a methodology, an approach to life, and a range of disciplines which if taught could make China strong.

The next references to democracy came in Mao Zedong's essays "On New Democracy" of 1940, and "On the People's Democratic Dictatorship" of 1949.[3] By 1940, Mao was firmly in control of the Communist Party: the New Democracy he envisaged was a stage on the way to socialism, during which progressive elements of the bourgeoisie could take part in the process of revolutionary change alongside peasants and workers; the People's Democratic Dictatorship gave a theoretical rationale for a "people's democracy" in which the will of the people would be expressed through the Communist Party. Both notions fed into the theoretical underpinnings of the alleged legitimacy of Communist Party rule after 1949; however, neither had very much to do with democracy.

By 1979, the People's Republic had existed for thirty years. China had gone through the Cultural Revolution, Mao had died, political arrangements appeared ripe for change. From December of the preceding year, as noted in Chapter 4 above, a movement began to gather pace that would turn into the so-called Peking Spring of 1979. For a few months only, political dissidents led by a former soldier named Wei Jingsheng put up big character posters and secretly published political tracts demanding democratic reform in China. Wei was arrested in April, tried for treason and sentenced to fifteen years. Democracy Wall closed shortly thereafter.

In the late 1980s came the final and perhaps most significant of China's brushes with democracy. The beginnings of major economic and social change in China in the early 1980s, as it started to become integrated into the global economy, by the last half of 1986 brought renewed demands for democracy on the part of some intellectuals, led by the physicist Fang Lizhi and the writer Liu Binyan. The Party General Secretary Hu Yaobang was dismissed in 1987 for appearing sympathetic to this group, and the hard line was reasserted throughout 1987 and 1988. The death of Hu from a heart attack in April 1989, however, brought a major demonstration in Beijing in his support, which rapidly turned into the Democracy Movement of 1989, fanned by the visit of President Gorbachev, who had recently been responsible for *perestroika*, the reforms in the Soviet Union.

In Tiananmen Square thousands gathered to demand political reform, and a "goddess of democracy" was erected to symbolise their hopes. While the goddess of democracy subsequently became the focal point for the world's cameras, she was by then the symbol also of all that was wrong with China, and not just of an alternative political system. Demands for further economic reform on both a macro and a micro level, for measures to check unemployment, for constraints on the development of inequities in the distribution of benefits in society, for intellectual freedom and freedom of speech, for the elimination of imprisonment for political offences, for reform of political structures, for an end to corruption in government, and many other sometimes contradictory measures, are evidence of a widely felt sense of grievance in early 1989 by no means confined to the students of Beijing.

The ensuing course of events has been outlined in a previous chapter. The declaration of martial law by the Party hardliners on 20 May, with the apparent support of Deng Xiaoping, effectively sealed the ultimate fate of the demonstrators. The failure to clear the Square over the next two weeks could only mean that the crackdown, when it came on the night of 3 June, would be more severe. By this time, the protest had spread to many other parts of China.

What was particularly striking was the apparent willingness of the Party to sanction such a display of violence by the authorities in full view of the world's press. The Party was drawing a line which it made clear people were not to cross.

In its aftermath, the government cracked down on dissent everywhere, imprisoning as many student activists as it could find, and dealing harshly also with workers and other citizens who had intervened on their behalf. Since Tiananmen, there has been no further discussion of democracy in China, most people keeping their heads down on political matters, and putting their effort into entrepreneurial activity that will benefit themselves and their families.

The foundations for democracy in China

In the light of this brief summary of China's exposure to and engagement with democratic ideas over the past century, it may appear that
the prospects for democracy in China, the "fifth modernization," are
not particularly good. However, as this issue has been the subject of
such extensive debate both inside and outside China, it may be appropriate to explore further what democracy for China might actually
mean. The remainder of this chapter is therefore devoted primarily to
a review of how circumstances in twenty-first-century China would
meet two sets of criteria put forward by two leading political commentators. The first criteria are those devised by the political analyst David
Beetham for "measuring" democracy. The second set of criteria is suggested by the veteran China specialist Jack Gray as preconditions for
"sustainable" democracy.

There has for some time been discussion among students of politics
of ways and means of "measuring" democracy.[5] Much of the early
discussion was predicated on the Cold War assumption that the forms
of democracy to be found in North American, Western European and
certain other developed Western societies were normative, and a model
to which other "developing" countries could approximate in time.
Democracy was often defined in the narrow sense of the electoral system, the degree of responsible government, and the institutions and
patterns of political behaviour that reinforced them. Some work on the
measurement of democracy attempted through surveys and sampling
to project a quantifiable assessment of the degree of conformity in any
particular country to Western, often American, norms. In this way a
country could be assigned a figure, supposedly enabling it to be compared objectively with other countries in the extent of its democracy.[6]

More recently, account has been taken of the possibility of more
diverse forms of democratic expression, with allowance made for distinct cultural influences on the form democracy might take,[7] and for
the effect of the level of economic development on democratic institutions and practice.[8] The transition under way in the former states of
the communist world has in some degree forced this broader view.
Simultaneously, there has more recently been some disenchantment
with the quantitative approach to the measurement of democracy, and
greater experimentation with qualitative and experiential approaches
to assessment.[9]

The systematic audit contrived by the political scientist David Beetham and his team for application to the United Kingdom is broad and qualitative, and by and large avoids judgements about what is "normative" in political institutions. According to Beetham, "democracy" rests on the two related key principles of popular control (over political decision-making) and political equality (in voting and standing for office, in treatment by legislators, in simply making one's voice heard). The practise of these principles in any given society may be tested by the application of a series of thirty indices, expressed in the form of questions, in four groups.

It is not intended here to suggest that Beetham's methodology could be applied to China without some degree of adaptation. However, it does serve to focus attention on some of what many would consider to be the prerequisites for democracy. In the discussion that follows, Beetham's indices will be rehearsed in their essentials, and in the light of this, brief comment will be offered on the extent to which current Chinese political institutions may provide scope for further development of democratic principles and practice.[10]

The first group of indices concerns popular control over the legislature: the "reach" of the electoral process, its inclusiveness, its fairness, its independence. Following Beetham's approach, this would mean asking the following six questions or sets of questions:

1. How far is appointment to legislative and governmental office determined by popular election, on the basis of open competition, universal suffrage and secret ballot?
2. How independent of government and party control are the election and procedures of voter registration, how accessible are they to voters, and how free are they from all kinds of abuse?
3. How effective a range of choice and information does the electoral and party system allow the voters, and how far is there fair and equal access for all parties and candidates to the media and other means of communication with them?
4. To what extent do the votes of all electors carry equal weight, and how closely do the composition of parliament and the programme of government reflect the choices actually made by the electorate?
5. How far is there equal effective opportunity to stand for public office, regardless of which social group a person belongs to?
6. What proportion of the electorate actually votes, and how far are the election results accepted by the main political forces in the country?

In China, as we have seen, appointment to legislative and government office is determined in secret procedures of nomination and selection orchestrated by the Communist Party, of which most government leaders are members. Only at the village level is there some measure of popular election to positions of leadership, and here too the Communist Party may intervene if it disapproves of successful candidates.[11]

As there are no elections to high legislative and governmental office, there is no information disseminated about selection processes. The media are controlled by the Communist Party, and represent its views alone. The composition of the National People's Congress and the programme of government do not in any discernible way reflect the popular will, as there is no way of telling what the popular will might be.

The way to public office lies through membership of the Communist Party, and for many years after 1949 former landlords, capitalists, and many members of the bourgeoisie were excluded from membership on the basis of their social origin.[12]

As there are no national popular elections, so the issue of acceptance of election results does not arise.

The second group of indices addresses the degree of openness and accountability of government: political accountability of the government to the elected legislature, legal accountability to the courts, financial accountability to the legislature and the courts, and monitoring of government by independent bodies. This would lead to a further twelve themes for questions:

7. How accessible to the public is information about what the government does, and about the effects of its policies, and how independent is it of the government's own information machine?

8. How effective and open to scrutiny is the control exercised by elected politicians over non-elected executive personnel, both military and civilian?

9. How extensive are the powers of parliament to oversee legislation and public expenditure, and to scrutinize the executive, and how effectively are they exercised in practice?

10. How publicly accountable are elected representatives for their private interests and sources of income that may affect the performance of their public office, and the process of election to it?

11. How far are the courts able to ensure that the executive obeys the rule of law; and how effective are their procedures for ensuring that all public institutions and officials are subject to the rule of law in the performance of their functions?

12. How independent is the judiciary from the executive, and from all forms of interference, and how far is the administration of law subject to effective public scrutiny?

13. How readily can a citizen gain access to the courts, ombudsman or tribunals for redress in the event of maladministration or the failure of government or bodies to meet their legal responsibilities, and how effective are the means of redress available?

14. How far are appointments and promotions within public institutions subject to equal opportunities procedures, and how far do conditions of service protect employees' civil rights?

15. How systematic and open to public scrutiny are the procedures for government consultation of public opinion and of relevant interests in the formation and implementation of policy and legislation?

16. How accessible are elected politicians to approach by their electors, and how effectively do they represent constituents' interests?

17. How far do the arrangements for government below the level of the central state meet the above criteria of openness, accountability and responsiveness?

18. To what extent does sub-central government have the powers to carry out its responsibilities in accordance with the wishes of its own electorate, and without interference from the centre?

In China, the plenary meetings of the National People's Congress, which occur once a year, are public but stage-managed, while the Standing Committee and smaller steering groups meet in secrecy. More important, the plenary sessions of the Congress of the Communist Party, though widely reported, are also stage-managed. The real debates over issues and policy are carried on in secret by the Party Central Committee, its Politburo and Standing Committee. All domestic reporting on proceedings of state and Party organs is undertaken by New China News Agency, which is charged with the dual function of reporting news and disseminating propaganda.[13]

As delegates to both state and Party Congresses are not popularly elected, there is no control by elected representatives over civilian and military personnel.

While the National People's Congress technically has the power to oversee legislation and expenditure, it very seldom challenges the agenda set by the Party.[14] There is no monitoring of any possible clash between public and private interests, apart from occasional campaigns against corruption in the government and Party.

The judiciary in China is not independent of the executive, and indeed may be seen more accurately as an arm of the executive. The courts effectively rehearse the evidence and pass sentence on citizens deemed by the police to have committed a crime.[15] The judiciary does not monitor public officials, institutions, or the Executive to ensure that they obey the rule of law.

By and large, there is no means of redress available through the courts to citizens who believe they have been mistreated by government or by public officials or institutions. Appointments in public institutions are not subject to equal opportunities procedures; in many parts of China employees do not, in practice, have civil rights.

There are no procedures for government consultation of public opinion in the formulation of policy, and no elected politicians to represent electors' interests. Below the level of central government, administration is similarly secretive, unaccountable and unresponsive, although most recently elections at the village level to administrative councils hold out a small glimmer of hope for the future.

In the third group of questions, guarantees of civil and political rights and liberties are explored, which are crucial to effective popular democratic control over government. A further five questions would explore this aspect of democracy:

19. How clearly does the law define the civil and political rights and liberties of the citizen, and how effectively are they defended?
20. How equal are citizens in the enjoyment of their civil and political rights and liberties, regardless of social, economic or other status?
21. How well developed are voluntary associations for the advancement and monitoring of citizens' rights, and how free from harassment are they?
22. How effective are procedures for informing citizens of their rights, and for educating future citizens in the exercise of them?
23. How free from arbitrary discrimination are the criteria for admission of refugees or immigrants to live within the country, and how readily can those so admitted obtain equal rights of citizenship?

In China, while the constitution guarantees economic and some political rights, in practice decades of civil war before 1949, the revolution, and the Cultural Revolution have perpetuated a political culture of precipitate measures to resolve differences in which Western notions of the rights of the individual have little place. This is as true of China now as it was before the economic reforms began in 1979. The law therefore does not effectively define or defend civil or political rights for the individual. Not all citizens are equal. In recent decades members of former landlord, capitalist or bourgeois families have been denied equal treatment, and even today, in some instances and in some areas, they remain objects of suspicion. Persons considered hostile to the Communist Party's objectives are frequently denied justice.[16]

There are as yet very few voluntary organizations within China to monitor citizens' rights. Apart from the most general statements in the Constitution, there is no official effort to inform citizens of any rights they may have, nor any education in their use.

Refugees or immigrants, relatively few in number, and usually ethnic Chinese, have generally been obliged to integrate rapidly into the broader community, enjoying no more rights than anyone else.

The final group of indices is concerned with the nature of "civil society" — those associations through which people independently manage their own affairs. Seven sets of questions are proposed to address this dimension of the democratic culture:

24. How far is there agreement on nationhood within the established state boundaries, and to what extent does support for political parties cross regional, linguistic, religious or ethnic lines?
25. How tolerant are people of divergent beliefs, cultures, ethnicities, life-styles, etc., and how free are the latter from discrimination or disadvantage?
26. How strong and independent of government control are the associations of civil liberty, and how accountable are they to their own members?
27. How publicly accountable are economic institutions for their activities, and how effective is their legal regulation in the public interest?
28. How pluralistic are the media of communication in terms of ownership and accessibility to different opinions and sections of society, and how effectively do they operate as a balanced forum for political debate?
29. How extensive are literacy and education for citizenship, and how equal are the chances for future citizens to participate in economic, social and political life?

30. To what extent do people have confidence in the ability of the political system to solve the main problems confronting society, and in their own ability to influence it?

In China there has historically been a strong consensus on nationhood based largely on Chinese ethnicity and civilization.[17] This has been projected onto other territories with ethnic and historic ties to China, such as Taiwan, Hong Kong and Macao, and to areas historically acknowledging Chinese suzerainty, such as Tibet.

The only fully functioning political party in China, the Communist Party, is a Leninist party with restricted access and functioning largely in secret.

In the years since 1949, there have been extended periods of extreme intolerance of divergent beliefs and cultures, and especially of foreign influence.

All significant associations in civil society in mainland China have been controlled by and accountable only to the Communist Party. Economic institutions, though they report to the appropriate Ministries, are not publicly accountable; the degree of legal regulation varies, and may or may not be geared to the public interest.

Xinhua News Agency for many years originated *all* news, for distribution to other organs of the media. Although this is no longer the case, Xinhua remains the main source of all important news reports, especially about policy matters. Journalists in China operate under guidance from the Communist Party both to report the news and to disseminate Party propaganda.[18] Access to the media is therefore restricted, and only limited debate of the issues is tolerated.

Citizens are under constant pressure through education and propaganda campaigns to show patriotism and support for the policies of the Communist Party. For those who do not, opportunities to participate fully in the country's economic, social and political life are severely proscribed.

It is impossible to assess the degree of genuine support for and confidence in the political system, as research of this kind is effectively impossible to conduct in China. Anecdotal evidence suggests that, following Tiananmen especially, citizens feel they have very little ability to influence political outcomes, and have turned to economic activity instead.

Democracy and modernization

And so, in the final analysis, is modernization likely to bring democracy in any form to China? The eminent political economist and China specialist Jack Gray observed towards the end of his career that there are a number of preconditions for sustainable democracy:

These include national unity; the destruction of inherited parasitic or counter-productive property structures; the reconciliation or assimilation of minorities, so that the nation becomes one moral community; the replacement of hierarchy by more egalitarian forms of association, probably including markets; the emergence of a civil society replacing or supplementing ascriptive ties; a government whose writ runs everywhere; opportunities for participation in social affairs; education, at least to the level of widespread literacy; economic developments which serve the majority of citizens; a standard of living which allows real choices and promotes self-esteem; the creation of a general consensus on basic issues to the extent that hostility to the consensus is marginal; a society able to operate on the assumption of limited government; traditions which include values and habits which encourage moderation and self-restraint in the solution of problems; exposure to democratic ideas. Traditions of secular government may also play a part.[19]

There is clearly some overlap here with the requirements envisaged in Beetham's schema above, but to reinforce the argument, it may be useful to simply note again where China stands with regard to these conditions.

China, as observed, exhibits a strong sense of national unity. The parasitic or counter-productive property structures of the traditional regime were largely swept away in the revolution of 1949, though it could be maintained that in certain respects the mechanisms of state ownership subsequently introduced were also counter-productive. These too have now been very substantially reformed, and state ownership as a whole much reduced.

As noted, minorities have largely been reconciled or assimilated, an achievement made possible by their relatively small scale within the broad mass of China's population, which is 97 per cent Han Chinese. The principal remaining issues concern Tibet and Taiwan, and China's significant Muslim population in Xinjiang and elsewhere.

The replacement of hierarchy in the economic sphere, and the introduction of markets, have certainly been achieved to a considerable degree since the early 1980s, and indeed have been critical to the rapid pace of modernization. In the political sphere, a tighter grip is maintained, with the state reserving the right to dictate to the population, and the Party directing the state. Egalitarian forms of association have not been encouraged, and in some cases not permitted.

For the reasons given in the discussion of the Beetham schema above, it would be implausible to suggest that civil society has yet evolved in China to the point of replacing ascriptive ties. The network of ascriptive ties binding China's citizens to the state and the Party since 1949 has been at times all-encompassing, and has included organizations that have been hierarchically tasked and led from the centre, membership in which has been to all intents and purposes compulsory for those chosen to take part. These have included those discussed in Chapter 6 above, such as the trade unions, the Women's Federation, the Youth League and the Party itself, among others. Citizens have also been expected to take part in various rectification campaigns, political study classes, and routine and *ad hoc* committees and small groups of all kinds intended to guide them, resolve day-to-day problems, and generally monitor their behaviour. The transition from this set of requirements to a situation in which citizens may form and join their own associations, is ongoing, but will take time. This issue is discussed further below.

The Beijing government's writ does run everywhere within China's borders, though there are centrifugal tendencies evident in certain provinces and regions of China.

The opportunities for participation in social affairs are greater than previously, provided the activity does not contravene the Party's objectives.

Literacy overall in China among adults is now claimed to stand at over 90 per cent,[20] a notable achievement given the size of the population. Secondary education is now the norm, while increasing numbers attend university, with a good proportion of those able to study abroad.

Economic development has been rapid in China over the past two decades, and increasing levels of prosperity have benefited almost all citizens. However, as noted in Chapter 10, marked disparities exist in the extent to which people have benefited — as between east and west China, between city and countryside, and between social groups within cities.

In consequence of this, real choices are still available only to a relative minority of the population, while the self-esteem of some may have been diminished by their own relative failure to prosper in a society that now seems to value material goods above all else.

The general consensus on basic issues on which the Party has in the past both insisted and prided itself appears to have been substantially eroded. Even on the matter of increasing growth and prosperity, which the Party sees as underpinning its popular support, there may be little agreement that the Party has contributed in a positive way to this, and little gratitude to the Party for it in actual fact — rather, a widely held view that the Party should have removed the obstacles to growth much sooner. As a general rule, it is difficult to know how much consensus exists in Chinese society, as opinion sampling remains highly problematic and subject to official control and hidden agendas.

China has clearly not, since 1949, been a society able to operate on the assumption of limited government. On the contrary, government has until recently intervened comprehensively in the lives of citizens. As government now gradually withdraws from some spheres of activity, these sectors may experience unstructured or even chaotic movement, with some criminal involvement, before institutions and patterns of behaviour will emerge that will offer stability without the threat of government intervention.

In terms of values and habits that encourage moderation and self-restraint in the solution of problems, it can be argued that China's record is mixed. On the one hand, the Confucian morality and emphasis on family life of traditional China, and the strong moral code of Communist China, might suggest that moderation and decorum would be apparent in the resolution of disputes. Yet this has often not been the case, with extreme measures and horrifying punishments all too often inflicted upon people challenging the state especially, in both traditional and post-1949 China. The record here is not good, and although the evidence of recent years has been mildly encouraging, the situation has been marred by the emblematic Tiananmen massacre of 1989.

Exposure to democratic ideas is a process which is hard to measure, and about which it is difficult to generalize. As this chapter has tried to show, a relative few people have been involved in the various democratic experiments, or perhaps brushes with democracy might be a better description, in China over the past hundred years. Different people among them have understood and interpreted democracy differently. In the new century, while more and more educated Chinese are travelling abroad for periods of study or for other reasons, and have the opportunity to observe at first hand democracy as it is practised overseas, there is for the time being almost a conspiracy of silence among them over its possible application to China. This may be in part, as the Party hopes, because they are more interested in business, and in opportunities for material gain. It may in part also be because of the memories of Tiananmen. There can be little doubt, however, that the issue will not go away, and will remain to challenge, and menace, the Party at some future point.

Finally, the traditions of secular government to which Gray refers are not an issue in the case of China; for most of its traditional history, and all of its recent past, China has been a secular state.

In terms of Gray's preconditions for sustainable democracy, therefore, China in the new century appears to satisfy some, but on other counts there is little evidence that the preconditions exist. In certain cases a trend may be apparent that may or may not continue, or whose outcome if it does continue may be difficult to predict. Problematic areas, using Gray's schema, seem most notably to be the persistence of hierarchical and authoritarian political institutions, the undeveloped nature of civil society, economic disparities, uncertain consensus on major issues, the chaos that might accompany a withdrawal of government intervention in certain areas of activity, and a mixed record of problem-solving without resort to violence.

Perhaps the key to this puzzle is civil society, the evolution of which may in turn be a consequence of modernization. While there may be no teleological process in operation here, nothing inevitable about the sequence of events, the balance of probabilities may nonetheless suggest movement through the exigencies of modernization towards an enhanced civil society and ultimately towards greater prospects for democracy. In this sense, some form of democracy may well turn out after all to be the "fifth modernization."

The evolution of a form of civil society containing some of those elements described by Beetham, Gray and others may well be under way. The presumption here is that the rising level of economic activity in China, and of prosperity overall, is generating a new middle class which, if the pattern found elsewhere is replicated, will bring about an increasingly self-governing civil society and ultimately a demand for meaningful participation in central and local government. Yet the outstanding question must surely be, if this does happen what will be the reaction of the Communist Party? Could the Party have a role in a China whose political institutions had been transformed? What would that role be?

Perhaps the first point to bear in mind is that the Party itself encompasses a wide variety of private views on this question. There are those, often now quite elderly, who still struggle with the trauma of the changes of the past thirty years, and who would still defend the actions of the Party during the Tiananmen incident. They would tend to the firm belief that China must be strictly controlled if chaos is to be avoided, and that the only way of achieving this is through a strong authoritarian central government, closely monitored by a vigilant Party.

At the other extreme is the view expressed to the author by a very senior government official and Party member, that China is no longer really a 'communist country', and that in a few years time "...China's political life will be as pluralistic and diverse as its economic life is now."[21]

In between stands the great rank and file of Party members, for whom Party membership may mean anything from a vaguely defined expression of patriotism to a way of achieving power and wealth as rapidly as possible. The Party, perhaps fearful of the outcome, has not sought to harvest the great variety of opinions within itself, to let a hundred flowers bloom, a hundred schools of thought contend.

Already, the Party's control over the economic life of China — its original raison d'être — has materially diminished. Through the process of engagement with the international economy, both private and foreign ownership have been introduced, the profit motive has replaced social production, material incentives have replaced moral ones, supply and demand are regulated increasingly by the market, both at home and overseas. The Party has unleashed these developments, but is so dependent on the prosperity they have brought that it is hardly in any position, except perhaps in the detail of implementation, to influence the consequences.

If the Party has a much reduced economic role, does it still have a future as a political arbiter or as a moral force? In the political sphere, it may be useful to recall that the Leninist-style political party, with its founding principle of democratic-centralism, was conceived primarily as an instrument through which to achieve political power by armed struggle — which it did in Russia in 1917, and in China finally in 1949. There was no "roadmap" for what would happen after power had been achieved. In the event, in both cases the Party eliminated all political opposition and dominated and led the process of economic construction in ensuing decades.

In Marx's view, if there was ever to be a transition to "communism," all parties would ultimately disappear, and the state itself would wither away. In the Soviet Union under Stalin, such an eventuality was never likely. China came closer with the more idealistic vision of Mao Zedong, but in the end China too chose a path to modernization that enhanced rather than diminished inequalities, and the state stayed put (perhaps, as Marx might have said, to defend them). Yet there are political implications to the type of economy that is evolving in China. The Chinese economy in the twenty-first century has come to encompass many different sectors, roles and interests, including those of the ordinary men and women who work in it. Such an economy requires not just a single political arbiter — indeed one that may not possess within itself the necessary skills to make informed judgements — but rather a variety of political choices able to represent the diversity of the new activity.

It has been suggested in Chapter 6 that the Party in some degree inherited the mantle of moral arbiter from the Confucian administrative elite of traditional times. That certainly appears to have been so for much of the period from its founding in 1920 down to the beginning of the opening up to foreign influence around 1980. Yet the Party had barely had time to reassert its authority at its Eleventh Congress in 1977 and begin to resume power and prestige usurped during the Cultural Revolution before engagement with the outside world began, causing its moral authority to be challenged by new ideas. In the event, it proved impossible to separate foreign technology from other aspects of overseas theory and practice, and the result was to undermine the Party's claim that on all things it knew best.

Today there is a much more sanguine view of the Party and its role. For most Chinese people, even those who are its members, it can claim the right to speak because it is there and has not yet been effectively challenged. Moreover it meddles in their personal affairs less than it did. Yet for most, the notion that the Party occupies the moral high ground, in traditional terms that it constitutes "rule by wise men," would in the new century seem laughable. For most people, the Party is no longer an institution to be respected, rather it is to be used where possible, or otherwise got around and ignored.

In sum, therefore, it is hard to see how in the longer term the continued existence of the Chinese Communist Party with its present form and function can be compatible with the new stresses and demands of China in transition. There is already nascent pressure for the further development of civil society, and with Chinese people keen and able progressively to take matters into their own hands, the political expression of this can only be a matter of time. Whether this takes the form of a demand for, or push towards, democracy on the Western model is, however, rather less clear.

CONCLUSION

For almost 200 years China has been striving to assert its sovereignty, not merely in the literal sense of a great traditional power seeking acceptance in the modern community of nations, but also in its attempt to come to terms with industrial technology, and provide its citizens with a life of greater dignity. For centuries prior to the First Opium War, the high degree of self-sufficiency of China's pre-industrial economic life meant that international trade, the pursuit of foreign relations, and the introduction of foreign ideas could be regarded as matters at the discretion of the Empire, but not essential to its survival. The Confucian orthodoxy, and Confucian administrative structures, ensured that China's economic and social system would endure, even while dynasties and individuals rose and fell. Some would say that the success of the existing structures discouraged the application of technology to the point at which an industrial revolution might have occurred in China, or China might have "opened up" the West.

The fact remains that the introduction of "modern" technology and "modern" ideas to China, beginning in the nineteenth century, was accompanied by aggression driven by the political and commercial expansion of the Western powers. The acquisition of Western technology for "self-strengthening" and for defence was attempted by China later in the century, but found wanting. From then on, the solutions that were tried involved new ideas as well as the application of practical technology — Guang Xu and his "one hundred days of reform" in 1898, the Guomindang and its programme of "nationalism, democracy and the people's livelihood" in the early twentieth century, and the Communists, with Marxism, Leninism Mao Zedong Thought, in later years.

Yet none of these approaches succeeded in addressing the complex set of difficulties facing China in transition. Guang Xu's reforms were forestalled by his arrest and imprisonment by the conservative Empress Dowager. The Nationalists under Chiang Kai-shek in practice later abandoned democracy and the people's livelihood. The Communist Party Sinicized Marxism, and once in power imposed an orthodoxy whose emphasis on the citizen's moral duty to the state owed far more to Confucius than to Marx or Lenin.

Moreover, it could be argued that throughout all the attempts to come to terms with the modern age, there has been some evidence of a persistent reluctance to accept both the "*ti*" and the "*yong*," the "essence" as well as the "practical application," of modernity. The self-strengtheners of the 1870s could not conceive China abandoning its traditional social usage and political arrangements, though they wanted some of the practical, and particularly the defence mechanisms of modernization. There was felt to be an irresolvable conflict between what was Chinese, or could be made Chinese, and what was fundamentally foreign.[1] Even quite recently, and well into the reform period of the past thirty years, some of China's more conservative leaders continued to feel that it was possible to acquire from the West and from Japan the technology to make China a great modern power, without importing the freedom of thought and enquiring habits of mind that make that technology work in practice. They continued to believe in "Chinese learning for the essence, Western (or Japanese) learning for the practical application" without the broader context of ideas from which that learning emanates.

In the light of these previous attempts at modernization, this book has sought to explain developments in China over the past thirty years especially. Of course, new external stimuli were presented to China as the processes of economic globalization began to take root, with their attendant social and political expectations; these are explored in the text. But another important set of causes for China's behaviour and path of development over this period lies in its previous political and cultural history, right up until the process of opening up began in 1979. It is contended here that China's behaviour over the past thirty years, and indeed since the 1949 revolution, can only be more fully understood if these practices, traumas, and habits of mind are taken into account. So how has this case been made?

Deng Xiaoping's call to his people to address the "Four Modernizations" summed the task up by referring to the need to modernize agriculture, industry, science and technology, and national defence. But as noted above, the theme of the whole period since the confrontation between China and the technologically superior West began in the nineteenth century has been modernization. Therefore the early discussion at the beginning of this book seeks to clarify what this term means, and how the sweeping changes it required could have posed an overarching dilemma for a civilization that has had trouble with the very concept of change.

The narrative in the three ensuing chapters seeks to establish some of the outstanding characteristics of pre-modern Chinese society, and then sets down a brief chronology of events from the First Opium War to the present day, focusing mainly on the period from the founding of the People's Republic in 1949.

Certain characteristics of traditional Chinese society were considered to be particularly important. The primacy of agriculture in traditional China, and its technical sophistication, supported the enormous (by the measure of the time) population which gave rise to this great civilization and its accomplishments. It also determined the ways in which Mao Zedong adapted Marxism to China, while agriculture was also the focus for much early policy in the People's Republic. The transition from agriculture to mechanized industry as a primary economic focus has in recent years become a benchmark for modernization, despite concerns about food security. Moreover the extensive bureaucracy in traditional China, which came about in large part because of the need to supervise water conservation, grain storage and other aspects of intensive agriculture, formed a significant precedent for the bureaucracy of present-day China.

Confucianism, the ideology of the scholar-gentry in traditional times, provided political themes which have endured down to the present: these included "rule by wise men" (or at least by those who claim superior knowledge and understanding), a preference for morality over law, mutual obligations between rulers and ruled, and (rediscovered in recent times) the need for harmony within society; this is not to say that the content of the morality and obligations was not perverted to serve particular policy objectives. Even the social mobility of the dynastic era has its counterpart in the willingness of the Party to accept the lowest in society into the ranks of the highest, although the campaigns mounted against people from a landlord, wealthy or educated background had no precedent.

The ethnocentrism of traditional China is being steadily eroded today by the greatly increased pattern of contact with the rest of the world, though the preference for innovations "with Chinese character-istics" may still be significant. The failure of traditional China to exploit its own technology and achieve its own industrial revolution has no direct counterpart in contemporary China, though interestingly the commercialization of technology may in reality owe more to the state (MOST) than to private initiative.

The chronology of the period from the mid-nineteenth century to the present day also flags up a series of issues that have conditioned China's responses in recent times. The experiences of the unequal treaty system, of foreign exploitation of Chinese resources and Chinese labour, of invasion by Japan, and of isolation by much of the world after the founding of the People's Republic have all taken their toll on China's ability to trust foreigners in the country's great project of reconstruction; these episodes reinforce the preference for a good per-sonal relationship, in business or scientific co-operation for example, over a legalistic contractual arrangement.

Life under the People's Republic for the first thirty years brought its own hard lessons: that personal rivalries and struggles for power are just as likely under the Communist Party as among the transitional warlords or in the Imperial courts of the dynastic era; that despite offers of aid from apparently friendly states, taken up for a while, China ultimately stands alone and must never abandon its quest for self-sufficiency in all things essential to its way of life; that ideology and political commitment cannot ultimately solve China's problems, and indeed can rapidly become a blight on the discussion of policy alternatives, and even worse, an excuse for acts of violence and great inhumanity. All Chinese carried this psychological "baggage" with them into the latest phase of modernization.

Particular consideration has been given to a number of broad themes in the remaining chapters of this book, which draw on the political and cultural context of China's past for their explanation. China's Confucian heritage has been examined in greater detail, well beyond its political dimensions, to explore Confucian ideas about virtue and moral behaviour, the importance of the family, its impact in historical writing and in capturing Chinese mythology, on poetry and, through prose literature, on attitudes to education, to commerce and to the centrality of Chinese culture (and by implication the lesser importance of the outside world). The ways in which Confucianism acted as a brake on change, and on modernization in particular, have been considered, as has — through its negation — Confucianism's role as a spur to the intellectual renaissance in China beginning in 1919, and the founding of the Communist Party.

The political strands of Confucian thought are taken up again in the discussion of orthodoxy, in which it is suggested that Confucianism constituted the "ideology" of traditional China. When Mao Zedong's own revision of Marxism-Leninism to suit China's circumstances is examined, many points of resonance with Confucius come to light: the mutual obligations of rulers and subjects, noted above, different roles ascribed to different groups in society, a strong sense of rule by divine right, and the widespread control of thought. These habits of mind on the part of the authorities did not cease suddenly with the death of Mao, or the opening up of China in 1979, but continue to resonate down to the present day.

The reaction to Mao and to the primacy of ideology, and especially to the Cultural Revolution, did produce a recognition that China could no longer be driven by ideology. Deng Xiaoping urged Chinese people to "seek truth from facts" rather than from political theory, ending the role of ideology as the primary determinant of perceived reality. This has affected everything from statistical methods used in China to the reporting of news. Among the realities to be recognized was that China desperately needed foreign technology; to have this through the involvement of foreign companies it needed commercial law; to have the stability needed to make rapid modernization work it also required law of every other kind. Thus the moral judgement of the Party began to give way to law as the arbiter of behaviour, a process still under way.

China's policy on science and technology has also been conditioned by historical factors. Among these have been the aggression to which China was subjected in the nineteenth and early twentieth centuries owing to the technical superiority of the foreign powers, and application of technology in China in the first half of the twentieth century principally to the military sphere, enabling and prolonging warlord strife and the civil war until the Communist victory of 1949.

Soviet domination of technology transfer in the 1950s, and the politicization of debates over technology policy in the 1960s and 1970s, along with the persecution of many scientists during the Cultural Revolution, all militated against the rational discussion of science and technology policy options. While inward technology transfer has been the agreed policy since 1979, this too has been subject to lingering issues from earlier times, notably the hybrid nature of the Chinese economy — part-command and part-market — differing skills and conflicting agendas among China's leaders, attitudes to research and development, and debates over the role central planning should play in scientific discovery and the commercialization of innovation.

Command structures inherited from the early period of Soviet influence continue to set the parameters of political life in China. The wasteful duality of Party and state, the heavy bureaucratization of policy-making and implementation, the problematic nature of "democratic centralism" with its democratic and centralized aspects — seemingly contradictory in practice — and the difficulties posed by the need to balance regional and sectoral interests, to counter nepotism and corruption within both the Party and state, to obtain and act upon accurate statistical information in a country as large as China: all these and many other issues stemming from the nature of China's political structures affect the quality of everyday life in China. Minor experiments in village democracy, in extending the role of the National People's Congress and in other fields, are yet to have any significant impact on a system essentially unchanged since the early 1950s.

China's enterprises continued for many years in the 1980s to exhibit the deficiencies that had characterized them in one form or another since they were first set up, usually in the 1950s. As management techniques gradually came under review changes were implemented, first through the Contract Management Responsibility System and then through the Modern Enterprise System. Yet while most adapted to the new part-market economy (and some were forced to close), issues with echoes from the past continued to plague many of them. Political and cultural factors played havoc with rational decision-making within enterprises, while new problems emerged which were made harder to resolve because practices from the past were so entrenched; these problems included the need to respect intellectual property rights, the need to adjust to new policies requiring fiscal responsibility, the need to upgrade (and pay for) technology, and the issue of how to handle the relationship between private and state control of enterprises through new mechanisms of governance such as Boards of Directors.

The question may be asked whether it is any easier for citizens in China to articulate (or realize) their private goals today than it was in

Mao's China, or even earlier on. Here any judgement must take account of the systemic context in which individuals live, a context much affected by all of the considerations noted above. China's past bears down on the individual, both the remote past and more recent events. While undoubtedly people have much greater access to new ideas (many from abroad) than ever before, they are still subject to many constraints.

Thus, mass organizations may now convey concerns in both directions between the individual and the authorities, but only within clear limits; students may access the internet and the man or woman in the street may read about events in the outside world through Chinese newspapers, or see them on television, but the Party's Propaganda Department remains active, and wary of anything that may challenge Party objectives. Ultimately, Party membership may remain the safest option for bright young people seeking to get on in China today.

Moreover it is not easy for citizens to complain about or take action on matters of serious concern in Chinese society. Such matters may include the unequal distribution of wealth, the widespread corruption in government, the growing environmental problems China faces, or the lack of institutional frameworks through which to resolve issues. The scope to address any of these matters, unless and until they become a focus of Party concern, is quite limited.

And so finally to the "fifth modernization" — democracy. Here it is appropriate to recall that China has had no real experience of democratic government at any point in its history. Its brushes with the concept of democracy — through the prorogued Parliament of 1913, as an element in the New Culture movement debates after 1919, by means of the "big character posters" of Wei Jingsheng on "Democracy Wall" in 1979, and in the course of the events leading up to the Tiananmen massacre of 1989 — have all been short-lived.

In this case, what conditions the possibilities may be the absence of any indigenous experience, rather than the weight of historical events. As young Chinese people born since Tiananmen increase in numbers, and focus their attention on their prospects for a good life in their newly prosperous country, it may be naïve to expect that the goal of some of their forebears of more than twenty years ago will be uppermost in their minds or among their aspirations. Almost certainly this is what the Party hopes.

Today, as it continues on its journey "from Mao to market," China stands at a crossroads. On the strength of its massive engagement with the globalized international economy, its sheer size, and its highly sophisticated civilization, it will without a doubt be one of the two or three principal players on the international stage in the present century. China's participation in world affairs will be without precedent. In this sense its ability to resolve the various pressing domestic issues referred to in this brief volume will be of the utmost consequence to us all. One cannot but wish China well.

NOTES

PREFACE

1. The meaning of the term "modernization" will be explored in Chapter 1.
2. See, for example, most recently, John Farndon (2008), *China Rises*, Bergsten; Freeman, Lardy and Mitchell (2009), *China's Rise: Challenges and Opportunities*, and Barry Naughton (2006), *The Chinese Economy: Transitions and Growth*, each of which emphasizes the progress China has made and problems encountered in achieving growth and meeting the economic and systemic goals which, in the West, are conventionally seen as desirable.
3. It is not the purpose here to select any particular cultural theory and test it against the Chinese reality. Rather, the author agrees with those observers who believe that there is no consensual definition of culture in the contemporary period, and tends to accept Williams' broader description of culture as "a whole way of life," in association with intellectual and artistic activity — a signifying system "through which necessarily...a social order is communicated, reproduced, experienced and explored." Culture in this view is a way of expressing a given social order.

   It is also appropriate to borrow from the earlier view that culture is linked to ideology. In the Chinese case it may be, as we shall see, that culture has served and supported ideology both in traditional and in more recent China, and may both influence and be determined by the economic base. The relationship is a complex one.

   The culture to be discussed here, and to which reference will be made throughout, is principally that determined by the set of values and institutions associated with Confucius. Chinese history, of course, contains within it many instances of rebellion against those values, and a few cases of alternative ways of thinking and acting being embraced; however, the centrality of Confucianism in times past, and the persistence of elements of it into the present day, make it the leading determinant of culture in China in the broadest sense. The principal elements of Confucian culture are the focus of Chapter 5.

239

The meaning of politics is perhaps more easily accessible and less contentious. The old definition of politics as "who gets what, when and how" is still valid, though of course political processes, institutions and political ideology vary widely from place to place. In China in traditional times Confucius' political views were the orthodoxy of the state, more recently those of Marx, Lenin and Mao Zedong have held that position. In contemporary China politics and orthodoxy may not be so obviously attached to one another, but politics is as much a part of daily life as it ever was. The political dimension is discussed especially in Chapters 2, 6 and 8 below.

1. MODERNIZATION, DEVELOPMENT AND CHANGE

1. Yet there is no logical necessity in the application of Darwin's theories of natural evolution to social phenomena. Marx himself was able to greatly admire the work of Darwin, while in his studies of society he focused on class struggle and the role of technology in propelling society forward. See correspondence between Marx and Darwin at Downe House, Kent.
2. The brief discussion that follows will not be new to scholars of the subject, but is rehearsed here for the benefit of the general reader, and to recall the context of the modernization process in China.
3. Prominent writers on the theory and the process of development over the past half century have included Simon Kuznets, who saw a growth in income inequality as an inevitable stage in the development journey; Michael Lipton, who has emphasized urban bias in development; Samuel Huntington, who has focused on the political dimension of development; and of course economists of the World Bank. The view that development theory and institutions have in fact sought to undermine the independence of emerging states and to stunt their growth has been put, among others by Charles Bettelheim, Immanuel Wallerstein, and more recently Mike Mason.
4. See John Passe-Smith (1993), "The Persistence of the Gap: Taking Stock of Economic Growth in the Post-World War II Era", in Mitchell Seligson and John Passe-Smith (eds), *Development and Underdevelopment*, pp. 15–30.
5. The concept of change may be approached from a number of disciplinary perspectives. In History, change is an outcome for which an explanation must be sought in a variety of factors. In Politics change is often an objective to be achieved through the manipulation of assets and individuals. In Business the management of change is seen today as a sub-discipline in itself.

2. HISTORICAL FACTORS AND OBJECTIVE CONSTRAINTS

1. On the impact of the West in Asia, standard texts from the mid-twentieth century onward tended to take the essentially "common" nature of the

Western impact as the basis for their analytical framework. Some see it as broadly benevolent, modernizing and "civilizing"; in the case of China, see especially, for example Kenneth Scott Latourette (1934–64), *The Chinese: Their History and Culture*; Fairbank, Reischauer and Craig (1965) *East Asia: the Modern Transformation*; and even Immanuel Hsu (1975), *The Rise of Modern China*. Other authors are less sanguine about the use of force in achieving domination, and more inclined to see the rise of nationalism in Asia as a legitimate response to aggression. See, for example, Jack Gray (1990), *Rebellions and Revolutions: China from the 1800s to the 1980s*.

2. For an example of this disenchantment with development see Lawrence Harrison, "Underdevelopment is a State of Mind", in M. Seligson and J. Passe Smith (1993), *Development and Underdevelopment*, pp. 173–81.

3. It is estimated that the population of China supported by early Chinese agriculture, focused in the valley of the Wei River, reached almost sixty million by the end of the first Han dynasty in 8 AD. This figure is based on a census undertaken in 2 AD, and was an enormous number by the standards of the time. See Jacques Gernet (1968) *Ancient China from the Beginnings to the Empire*, p. 89.

4. Other orthodoxies challenged Confucianism from time to time, notably Buddhism whose rituals and ceremonies "became an integral part of state and imperial observances" (Arthur Wright) during the Tang Dynasty (618 to 906 AD) prior to the great persecution of 841–5, and the *potpourri* of beliefs which held sway at the court of the Yuan (Mongol) Dynasty (1279 to 1368). However, as a political philosophy and a system for governing China down to the twentieth century, Confucianism proved in the long run to be unrivalled.

5. See below.

6. For a detailed account of how this delicate balance worked, see, for example, Ho Ping-ti (1962), *Ladder of Success in Imperial China: Aspects of Social Mobility, 1368–1911*, still perhaps the best work in this area. While such nepotism could be taken to unsustainable lengths, in most cases these practices lent a degree of flexibility to the political structure, encouraging loyalty to the Throne that sanctioned them.

7. Ibid.

8. See especially Joseph Needham's multi-volume work, *Science and Civilization in China*, begun following his term as the first British Science Counsellor to China during the Second World War.

9. Mark Elvin (1973), *Pattern of the Chinese Past*.

10. See, for example, Jonathan Spence (1990), *The Search for Modern China*; Jack Gray (1990), *Rebellions and Revolutions: China from the 1800s to the 1980s*; and on the Twentieth Century especially, Rana Mitter (2004), *A Bitter Revolution: China's Struggle with the Modern World*.

11. The two treaties that were the cornerstones of the "Treaty Port system" were the Treaty of Nanjing of 1842, and the Treaty of Tianjin of 1858

and 1860. Under the former, the "Co-hong" monopoly of foreign trade through Canton (Guangzhou) was abolished, a "fair and regular tariff" for trade was agreed in principle, five ports were to be open to foreign trade — Canton, Amoy, Fuzhou, Ningbo and Shanghai — Hong Kong Island was ceded to Britain in perpetuity, and China was obliged to pay an indemnity to Britain of 21 million Mexican dollars. Under the latter, first agreed in 1858 but finally ratified with additional provisions in 1860, Britain and France obtained the right to have permanent diplomatic legations in the capital Beijing, diplomatic relations on a footing of equality, and further indemnities, and Britain acquired Kowloon, opposite Hong Kong Island, in perpetuity. Ten more ports were opened up to trade. The opium trade was made legal, and Christian missionary activity permitted. Other nations gained similar rights in the 1840s and 1850s through the "most favoured nation" principle, enshrined in treaties from 1843. The principle of extraterritoriality, the application of foreign law to foreign nationals on Chinese soil, also began to be applied from 1843.

12. Albert Feuerwerker, "Economic Trends in the Late Ch'ing Empire, 1870–1911", in J.K. Fairbank and Kwang-ching Liu (eds) (1980) *The Cambridge History of China*, vol. 11, part 2, p. 29. This could also be said to be true of the arsenals and shipyards set up in this period. For the conflict between Chinese culture and foreign technology see Rudi Volti (1982), *Technology, Politics and Society in China*, Chapter 2.

13. Robin Porter (1994), *Industrial Reformers in Republican China*, pp. 4–7.

14. Thomas G. Rawski (1989), *Economic Growth in Prewar China*, offers a revisionist view of the Chinese economy under the Guomindang, based on the projection of such figures as are available from the 1920s and 1930s. There remains a degree of uncertainty over how accurate and how internally consistent these figures actually were.

15. See, for example, Sherman Cochran (1980), *Big Business in China: Sino-Foreign Rivalry in the Cigarette Industry 1890–1930*.

16. Though some would argue that even the commercial interests became progressively alienated from the Nationalist cause by the incessant demands the government made of them for money. See Parks M. Coble Jr. (1980), *The Shanghai Capitalists and the Nationalist Government, 1927–1937*, also Lloyd Eastman (1974), *The Abortive Revolution: China under Nationalist Rule 1927–1937*.

3. CHINA UNDER THE PEOPLE'S REPUBLIC

1. Of the considerable volume of material now published on the events of the past sixty years, relatively few texts cover this period comprehensively. Among these are Julia Strauss (ed.) (2007), *The History of the People's Republic of China, 1949–1976* for thought-provoking essays on the early

years and the Cultural Revolution; Maurice Meisner (1999), *Mao's China and After: a History of the People's Republic* for the first fifty years; and Bill Brugger and Stephen Reglar (1994), *Politics and Society in Contemporary China* for the period up to the mid-1990s. More commonly, studies may be found of particular aspects of China's recent development, such as the collectivization and Commune programme of the 1950s, the Cultural Revolution of the 1960s, the reforms of the 1980s, the market economy of the 1990s, and China's political engagement with the world in the new century.

2. The Plan was first announced in 1953, but its contents were not made public until 1955. See Gray (1990), p. 296.

3. Succinct summaries of the First Five Year Plan and its problems are contained in Brugger and Reglar (1994), pp. 16–19, and Gray (1990), pp. 295–300. Critical factors in the decision to follow the Soviet model were the belief that there were some similarities in the objective conditions of China in 1950 and Russia after its revolution; the natural inclination to follow the lead of a fraternal Communist party; and the lack of choice following the outbreak of the Korean war and the implementation by the US of the policy of isolation and containment of China.

4. These figures are from O. Edmund Clubb's (1964) early study *Twentieth Century China*, p. 331. Clubb was the last American Consul-General in Beijing before the US Government withdrew diplomatic recognition.

5. Ibid.

6. Publication of "The High Tide of Socialism" at this time in 1955 was motivated by a desire to forestall the loss of momentum in achieving revolutionary change in the countryside.

7. See James Wang (1999), *Contemporary Chinese Politics: An Introduction*, p. 290. For a more detailed discussion of educational reforms see, for example, Suzanne Pepper (2000), *Radicalism and Education Reform in Twentieth Century China: The Search for an Ideal Development Model*.

8. This estimate, derived from official sources, appears in retrospect to have been optimistic. The 1982 census revealed that 28.2 per cent of "the work force" were still "illiterate or semi-illiterate", while only recently does that figure appear to have come down to 15 per cent of the "adult population." See Spence (1990), p. 690, and Robert Benewick and Stephanie Donald (2009), *The State of China Atlas*, p. 83.

9. China and the Soviet Union did not see eye to eye on everything in this period; from as early as 1955 a succession of issues arose between the erstwhile allies, which would lead ultimately to the Sino-Soviet split of 1960. Among the causes of tension were China's decision to play a leading role at the conference of Non-Aligned states in Bandung in 1955, the progressive failure of China's grain deliveries to the Soviet Union as payment on account for technical assistance received, and the disagreement dating from the Eighth Congress of the Communist Party of the Soviet Union in 1956

at which the Soviet Communist Party renounced the "inevitability" of war with the capitalist West; China still adhered to this principle. See below.

10. The issue of what would now be called "food security" has deep roots in China's dynastic past, and continues to this day to be a matter of prime concern, made more so by the threat to grain production from the impacts of climate change.

11. For a concise discussion of the issues at stake at this time see Wang (1999), pp. 24–6, and Gray (1990), pp. 326–35.

12. Jack Gray takes the view that Mao was happy to allow a relaxation of central control, principally because he felt that local peasant initiative, albeit subject to certain guidelines, would be best able to address rural needs.

13. See Jack Gray, "The Cultural Revolution: The Development of Two Lines in Economic Policy" in Stuart Schram (ed.) (1973), *Authority, Participation and Cultural Change in China*; see also Gray (1990), pp. 307–10.

14. Ibid. This approach was first put forward by "social missionaries" in the 1930s, and was incorporated into the wartime Industrial Co-operative Movement of the 1940s. See Robin Porter (1994), *Industrial Reformers in Republican China*.

15. Wang (1999), p. 26.

16. Gray (1990), p. 335. For further references, see also below, Chapter 6, note 37.

17. Chinese Communist Party, Foreign Language Press Beijing (1966), *Decision of the Central Committee of the Chinese Communist Party Concerning the Great Proletarian Cultural Revolution*.

4. FROM MARXISM TO MARKETISM

1. Spence (1990), p. 649, citing official sources. The author of the present work sub-edited the New China News Agency news story that finally put out this information to the outside world while he was working at Xinhua in Beijing in 1979.

2. Quoted in Spence (1990), p. 738.

3. David Goodman (1994), *Deng Xiaoping and the Chinese Revolution*, p. 95.

4. Spence (1990), p. 45, quoting from a report in the *New York Times* of 30 June 1989.

5. See Robin Porter (1993), "The Impact of Recent Political Events on China's Trade and Development", *Melbourne Journal of Politics*, vol. 21, pp. 117–34.

6. Richard Robison and David Goodman (1996), *The New Rich in Asia*, p. 227. See also Orville Schell (1985), *To Get Rich is Glorious: China in the '80s*.

7. The 7 per cent figure was put forward because of concerns over overheating of the economy. If anything, however, the rate of growth has since increased further.

8. See Porter (1993).

9. This resurgence may in part be attributable to renewed competition for investment by multinational corporations. This rate of growth was considered unsustainable, however.

10. Benewick and Donald (2009), p. 37.

11. Since the turn of the twenty-first century inflation has been broadly been kept under control, reaching no higher than 4.8 per cent, this in the year 2007. See ibid.

12. This reflected not only China's increasing marketing expertise and awareness of the tastes of its customers, but also the much higher value-added in the products it was able to make, a consequence of the higher technology now incorporated in them — notably in electronic goods, for example.

13. Benewick and Donald (2009), p. 15.

14. Ibid., p. 98.

15. Ibid., p. 100.

16. For example, at a meeting in Melbourne in 2001 Mike Moore, former New Zealand Prime Minister and then Head of the World Trade Organization was asked what would happen if China, once it became a member of the WTO, failed to abide by the rules of that body. "Well," he said, after a moment's thought, "it would probably collapse."

5. THE CONFUCIAN HERITAGE IN THEORY AND PRACTICE

1. See, for example, the latest edition of William Soothill's (1995) classic translation of *The Analects*. A more recent translation and commentary may be found in Raymond Dawson (ed.) (2000) *Confucius The Analects*. It should be noted that in this chapter reference is deliberately made to some sources from the early part of the twentieth century — perhaps the period of greatest debate among Western scholars of the Chinese classical tradition.

2. Donald Munro (1969), *The Concept of Man in Early China*, p. ix.

3. Charles Moore, in Charles A. Moore (ed.) (1967), *The Chinese Mind*, p. 5.

4. Arthur Wright, in Arthur Wright and Denis Twitchett (eds) (1962), *Confucian Personalities*, p. 8.

5. Arthur Wright, in Wright and Twitchett (eds) (1962), p. 7.

6. W.T. de Bary, Wing-tsit Chan and Burton Watson eds (1964), *Sources of Chinese Tradition, Vol. 1*, p. 18.

7. Arthur Wright, ibid., p. 7.

8. Burton Watson in John Meskill (ed.) (1973), *An Introduction to Chinese Civilization*, pp. 619–20.

9. See *The Spring and Autumn Annals (Chun Qiu)* on the history of the early Chinese state of Lu (722 BC-481 BC), possibly compiled by Confucius but drawing heavily on the work of other chroniclers of the period; Sima Qian,

(tr.) Burton Watson (1996), *Records of the Grand Historian: Han Dynasty*; and Pan Ku, with Homer Dubs (tr.) (1938), *History of the Former Han Dynasty (Han Shu)*.

10. See L. Cranmer-Byng (tr. and ed.) (1908), *The Book of Odes*.

11. The *Songs of the South (Chu Zi)* were the work of a number of poets of the time from the southern Chinese state of Chu, notably Ju Yuan, a scholar and former statesman who had been banished as a result of political intrigue.

12. Burton Watson in Meskill (1973), p. 623.

13. See especially Arthur Cooper (tr. and ed.) (1973) *Li Po and Tu Fu*, and Eva Shan Chou and Fu Du (1995), *Reconsidering Tu Fu: Literary Greatness and Cultural Context*.

14. See C.H. Brewitt-Taylor (tr.) (2002), *Romance of the Three Kingdoms*, or Moss Roberts (tr. and ed.) (1999), *Three Kingdoms*. The novel is attributed to Luo Guanzhong.

15. Shi Naian (attributed) and J.H. Jackson ed. (1963), *Water Margin: The Outlaws of the marsh*, or Shi Naian and Sidney Shapiro translators (1980), *Outlaws of the Marsh: The Water Margin*. It is often suggested that Luo Guanzhong may have written the final chapters of this book, as he had earlier been a student of Shi Naian.

16. Wu Chengen, Arthur Waley (tr.) (1961), *Monkey*.

17. Clement Egerton (tr.) (1979), *The Golden Lotus*.

18. Hsueh-Chin Tsao (Xueqin Cao) (1996), *Dream of the Red Chamber*. This novel is also known as *The Story of the Stone*, and some translations are published using this title. The writer, Gao E, is credited with having completed the final chapters of the book.

19. Jonathan Spence (1990), *In Search of Modern China*, pp. 108–9.

20. Burton Watson in Meskill (1973), p. 639.

21. Yu-kuang Chu in Meskill (1973), p. 592.

22. Burton Watson in Meskill (1973), p. 619.

23. The rapid expansion in China's engagement with the outside world since the Four Modernizations were announced, at the end of the 1970s, has reduced this problem to some extent. Many opinion formers and senior scientific and technical people have learned foreign languages, most frequently English, and have been able to study abroad. The widely-felt enthusiasm for change has given added impetus to the acquisition of knowledge, despite linguistic barriers.

24. W.T. de Bary *et al.* (eds) (1964), vol. 1, p. 23.

25. At times Confucian scholars did question the wisdom of monopolies that might seem oppressive towards the general population — see John Meskill (1973), pp. 46–7 — but their reservations were more about the manner of implementation rather than the principle involved.

26. Hsueh-Chin Tsao (Xueqin Cao) (1996).

27. W.T. de Bary *et al.* (eds) (1964), vol. 1, p. 29.

28. For an account of the origins and tenets of Daoism see Yie Wang, Adam Chanzit and Zeng Chuanhui (2006), *Daoism in China: an Introduction*.
29. One of the best accounts of Buddhism in China from the historical point of view remains Kenneth Ch'en's (1972) *Buddhism in China: A Historical Survey*.
30. C.P. Fitzgerald (1951, 1964 etc.), *Birth of Communist China*, see especially the chapter on "Revolution and Orthodoxy."

6. ORTHODOXY, IDEOLOGY AND LAW

1. The concept of the Mandate of Heaven appears to have first been enunciated by the Kings of the early Zhou period, around 1100 BC, to legitimize their rule. A concise discussion of the concept, based on text from the *Book of History* and the *Book of Rites*, is contained in de Bary *et al.* (eds) (1960), pp. 6–7 and 174–82.
2. See notably in *The Analects* (11/11 and 6/20).
3. See *The Analects*, for example (12/17, 2/3 and 12/19).
4. Franz Schurmann (1968), *Ideology and Organization in Communist China*, p. 15.
5. Schurmann (1968), p. 18.
6. Mary Wright (1967), *The Last Stand of Chinese Conservatism: the T'ung-Chih Restoration, 1862–1874*.
7. For a nuanced consideration of the complexities of this period see the essays in F. Gilbert Chan and Thomas Etzold (1976), *China in the 1920s: Nationalism and Revolution*.
8. See Jerome Grieder (1970), *Hu Shih and the Chinese Renaissance: Liberalism in the Chinese Revolution*.
9. See, for example, Charles Hayford (1990), *To the People: James Yen and Village China*, on James Yen and the rural reconstruction movement of the 1920s and 1930s, and Robin Porter (1994), *Industrial Reformers in Republican China*, on the movement to reform conditions of industry in the same period.
10. These two events were deeply significant in the influence they had on young Chinese intellectuals. The October 1917 revolution in Russia suggested that even the most recalcitrant and repressive of governments could be overthrown, while the massacre of several hundred peaceful demonstrators by British troops at Amritsar in India on 13 April 1919, just three weeks before the May 4th incident in China, advanced the cause of Indian nationalism and Asian anti-imperialism very considerably.
11. See *The Analects* (12/7) cited in de Bary *et al.* (eds) (1964), p. 33.
12. See *The Mencius* (4 A 9 and 5 A 5), cited in de Bary *et al.* (eds) (1964), pp. 93 and 96.
13. Mao Zedong (1937), *On Guerilla Warfare*.
14. As above, Chapter 2, see Parks M. Coble Jr. (1980) *The Shanghai Capitalists and the Nationalist Government, 1927–1937*, also Lloyd Eastman

(1974), *The Abortive Revolution: China under Nationalist Rule 1927–1937*. Thomas Rawski (1989), *Economic Growth in Prewar China*, takes a more positive view of the role of government in stimulating the economy.

15. See above, Chapter 3.
16. *The Analects* (4/16).
17. In 1723, for example, 6 million taels of silver, out of the total tax revenue of 35 million taels, was from taxation of commercial activity. The remainder was from the "land and head tax." Spence (1990), pp. 75–76. Returns for this year are likely to have been relatively accurate, as they formed part of the argument for the fiscal reform programme of the new Emperor, Yongzheng.
18. As indicated in an earlier chapter, the ties between the landlord class, the scholars, and the Confucian officialdom were very close, and a single individual could perform all three roles in the course of one lifetime. The natural inclination of propertied classes in all societies to be conservative was reinforced in China's case by the desire of the official for social stability and the instinct of the scholar to look back to an idealized ethical past in which each group did its job and knew its place.
19. In government (as opposed to the Party), the same problem exists. In the new century the issue of a mechanism for succession accepted by all is still unresolved, despite the fact that power passed from Premier Zhu Rongji to Premier Wen Jiabao in 2003, and from President Jiang Zemin to President Hu Jintao, also in 2003, apparently without incident.
20. A succinct summary of the mechanisms of mobilization in China may be found in Chapter 6, "Political Processes: Mobilization and Participation", in Flemming Christiansen and Shirin Rai (1996), *Chinese Politics and Society: An Introduction*. For a contemporary view of the means of propaganda employed in the PRC over the years see Anne-Marie Brady (2008), *Marketing Dictatorship: Propaganda and Thought Work in Contemporary China*. Particularly good on the early years is James R. Townsend (1969), *Political Participation in Communist China*. On the functioning of the Chinese media, see Robin Porter (ed.) (1992), *Reporting the News from China*.
21. See Townsend (1969).
22. Townsend (1969), see especially Chapter 4.
23. For a discussion of the ongoing relevance of the *Bao jia* concept of collective responsibility in China from the Qin Dynasty to the Qing Dynasty and to the present day see Joanna Waley-Cohen in Karen Turner, James Feinerman and R. Kent Guy (2000), *The Limits of the Rule of Law in China*, Chapter 5.
24. John K. Fairbank and Edwin O. Reischauer (1960), *East Asia: The Great Tradition*, p. 374.
25. On the maintenance of order in traditional China see, for example, Brian McKnight (1992) *Law and Order in Sung China*.

26. *Cha Guar*, or "Teahouse" in the Beijing dialect, is set in a Beijing teahouse at different times in the early twentieth century. The characters gather over tea to philosophize and speculate about life and the politics of the day. Interestingly, this was one of the first of the modern classics to be revived after the Cultural Revolution, playing to packed houses in Beijing in 1979.

27. "On New Democracy", *Selected Works of Mao Tse-tung*, Vol. 2, pp. 339–40.

28. See Robin Porter, "Shaping China's News: Xinhua's Duiwaibu on the Threshold of Change", in Porter (ed.) (1992), *Reporting the News from China*, pp. 1–18.

29. Yunnan University Journalism Department, translated by Jennifer Grant, Australian National University (1979), *Xinwen Xiezuo (Newswriting)*. Guidelines prepared for students of journalism. Cited in Porter (ed.) (1992).

30. Snow and Smedley were perhaps the most prominent among half a dozen foreigners to write sympathetically about the revolutionary process in China during the 1930s and 1940s. See Edgar Snow (1938, 1961), *Red Star over China*, and Agnes Smedley (1956), *The Great Road: The Life and Times of Chu Teh*. Snow and Smedley were both American journalists; each lived and travelled extensively in China.

31. "On Practice", *Selected Works of Mao Tse-tung*, Vol. 1, p. 297.

32. "On Practice", p. 308.

33. "On Practice", p. 304.

34. See above, Chapter 3. For a detailed account of the origins and course of the Hundred Flowers movement see Spence (1990), pp. 563–73.

35. See John Fairbank, Edwin Reischauer and Albert Craig (1965), *East Asia: The Modern Transformation*, p. 876, for an early evocation of this point. The distinction has subsequently been taken up in discussion in various journal articles about opposition in the Chinese political system.

36. "On the Correct Handling of Contradictions Among the People", *Selected Works of Mao Tse-tung*, Vol. 5.

37. Recent work on the Cultural Revolution period has included Paul Clark (2008), *The Chinese Cultural Revolution: A History*; Joseph Esherick, Paul Pickowicz and Andrew Walder (eds) (2006), *The Chinese Cultural Revolution as History*; and Kam-yee Law (ed.) (2003), *The Chinese Cultural Revolution Reconsidered: Beyond Purge and Holocaust*. In addition Jung Chang's *Wild Swans* (1991), and Chang and Halliday (2005) *Mao: The Unknown Story*, while not wholly focused on this period, provide an exile's account which has been influential in forming Western views of the Cultural Revolution. Earlier work which has stood the test of time includes the articles by C.K. Yang, "Cultural Revolution and Revisionism", and Franz Schurmann, "The Attack of the Cultural Revolution on Ideology and Organization", both in Ho Ping-ti and Tsou Tang (eds) (1968), *China in Crisis*, pp. 501–24 and 525–78 respectively; Jack Gray and Patrick Caven-

dish (1968), *Chinese Communism in Crisis: Maoism and the Cultural Revolution*; and the collection of original materials by K.H. Fan (ed.) (1968), *The Chinese Cultural Revolution: Selected Documents*.

38. James Wang (6th ed.,1999), *Contemporary Chinese Politics: An Introduction*, p. 26.

39. "Decision of the Party Central Committee Concerning the Great Proletarian Cultural Revolution", also the "Communique of the Eleventh Plenary Session of the Eighth Central Committee of the Communist Party of China", in Fan (ed.) (1968), pp. 161–73 and 173–82 respectively.

40. "Decision of the Party Central Committee....", point 1, in Fan (ed.) (1968).

41. "Decision of the Party Central Committee....", point 5, in Fan (ed.) (1968).

42. Deng, adapting an old Chinese proverb, is quoted as saying this first on the occasion of a discussion of rural policy as long ago as 1962, but as the circumstances seemed to fit he used the metaphor again early on in the modernization process.

43. The new body of law progressively passed and put into force in China began with work on a Code of Civil Procedure in 1979 (completed in 1986), and went on to include a revised Marriage Law in 1980, Economic Contract Law in 1981, Trademark Law in 1982, Patent Law in 1984, and Inheritance Law in 1985. This process of enactment of new laws was accompanied by the setting up of a Justice Ministry, the complete overhaul of the court system, and the establishment of new Law Schools in the universities, enabling the mass training of lawyers. See Spence (1990), pp. 704–11.

7. TECHNOLOGY AND POLITICAL POWER

1. Technology is taken here to mean "a process or activity...involving the systematic application of organized knowledge, tools and materials for the extension of human faculties, the purposes being problem-solving and the control or manipulation of the environment." See Yeu-farn Wang (1993), *China's Science and Technology Policy, 1949-1989*, p. 11, also Denis Goulet (1977), *The Uncertain Promise: Value Conflicts in Technology Transfer*. A diagrammatic representation of the formal structures controlling implementation of China's science and technology policy for the period up to 1998 may be found in Tony Saich, "Reform of China's Science and Technology Organizational System", in D.F. Simon and M. Goldman (1989), *Science and Technology in Post Mao China*, p. 74. For much of the period since the late 1970s the key body has been the State Science and Technology Commission, responsible to the Science and Technology Leading Group under the State Council. The SSTC has ostensibly exercised a supervisory role over all matters of science and technology in the production Ministries, the Ministerial Research Institutes, and the Chinese Academy of Sciences and its Research Institutes. It has not, however, been responsible for tech-

nology for national defence, which since 1985 has been the preserve of the Commission of Science Technology and Industry for National Defence. The Commission's functions were taken over by the new Ministry of Science and Technology in 1998.

This chapter draws from a paper by Paul Forrester and Robin Porter, "Technology and Politics in China: Influences upon the Process of Innovation in China", presented at the University of Montreal in 2000, and published in Tarik M. Khalil, Louis Lefebvre, and Robert Mason (2001), *Management of Technology: The Key to Prosperity in the Third Millennium*.

2. Richard Suttmeier, "Science, Technology and China's Political Future - a Framework for Analysis", in D.F. Simon and M. Goldman (1989), Conclusion.

3. Yeu-farn Wang (1993), p. 147 etc.

4. Tony Saich, "Reform of China's Science and Technology Organizational System", in Simon and Goldman (1989), Chapter 3.

5. Quan Li (1991), "Technology Policy and Technological Innovation in the People's Republic of China", unpublished PhD thesis.

6. Fred Steward and Quan Li, "Changing Patterns of Collaboration between Research Organizations and Business Enterprises in Technological Innovation in China", in D.H. Brown and R. Porter (1996), *Management Issues in China: Volume 1, Domestic Enterprises*, Chapter 8.

7. Denis Fred Simon and Merle Goldman, "The Onset of China's New Technological Revolution", introduction to Simon and Goldman (1989).

8. See Richard Conroy (1992), *Technological Change in China*, p. 11.

9. Robin Porter and Paul Forrester, "The Politics of Management in People's China: From the Contract Management Responsibility System to the Modern Enterprise System and Beyond", *Asia Pacific Business Review*, special issue edited by Malcolm Warner, Spring/Summer 1999, pp. 47–72.

10. Conroy (1992), p. 15.

11. See especially Jiang Xiaojuan, "Chinese Government Policy Towards Science and Technology and its Influence on Technical Development of Industrial Enterprises", in Charles Feinstein and Christopher Howe (1997), *Chinese Technology Transfer in the 1990s: Current Experience, Historical Problems, and International Perspectives*.

12. Q.Y. Yu (1999), *The Implementation of China's Science and Technology Policy*, pp. 71–3.

13. See Suttmeier, in Simon and Goldman (1989), pp. 376–77 etc., for observations typical of those made by Western business practitioners in China. A concise introduction to technology transfer to China from a practitioner's point of view, written by one with twenty years' experience, is Bernard Stokes' "Technology Transfer", in R. Porter and M. Robinson (1994) *The China Business Guide*, Chapter 5.

14. See Mark Elvin (1973), *The Pattern of the Chinese Past: A Social and Economic Interpretation*, p. 314.

15. Ho Ping-ti (1962), in his classic *Ladder of Success in Imperial China*, shows how even the poorest family in traditional China might reasonably hope to educate its bright male offspring to the point at which they could gain access to a career in the elite civil service. In such circumstances there would be little incentive to pursue a lower status and less remunerative alternative. See also the discussion of attitudes to technology in Rudi Volti (1982), *Technology, Politics and Society in China*, Chapter 2.

16. For example, the voyages of General Cheng Ho in the early fifteenth century under the Ming dynasty were said to have been motivated by Emperor Ming Yung-lo's desire to hunt down the designated heir of his predecessor. See John Meskill (1973), *An Introduction to Chinese Civilization*, p. 162.

17. A comprehensive and sympathetic treatment of the Chinese response to this dilemma is contained in Mary Wright (1967), *The Last Stand of Chinese Conservatism: The T'ung-Chih Restoration, 1862-1874*.

18. See for example Frederic Wakeman (1975), in *The Fall of Imperial China*, chapter 9.

19. Thomas Rawski (1989), *Economic Growth in Pre-War China*, pp. 195-6.

20. See Richard C. Bush (1982), *The Politics of Cotton Textiles in Kuomintang China, 1927-1937;* see also Sherman Cochran (1980), *Big Business in China: SinoForeign Rivalry in the Cigarette Industry, 1890-1930*.

21. This policy of "leaning to one side", problematic from the beginning, was nonetheless an attempt to give practical recognition to the leading role of the Soviet Union as the first revolutionary Marxist state. See Wang Gungwu (1977), *China and the World since 1949*, pp. 33-35.

22. The Soviet approach to the management of industry remained Stalinist and authoritarian. Only later, following the departure of the Russian experts, would experiments be undertaken in allowing employees a greater measure of participation in the day to day running of their factories.

23. See Robin Porter (1994), *Industrial Reformers in Republican China*, pp. 91-6 and 133-44.

24. Jack Gray (1990), *Rebellions and Revolutions: China from the 1800s to the 1980s*, pp. 307-9.

25. Social reformers had spent the decade of the 1920s trying unsuccessfully to bring some resolution to the human problems created by large-scale industry in the cities. Their failure in this task led some to consider the social and economic possibilities that might be opened up by the adoption of small-scale rural industry to meet part of the need for manufactured goods. See Robin Porter (1994).

26. A useful contemporary summary of this approach is contained in E.L. Wheelwright and Bruce McFarlane (1970), *The Chinese Road to Socialism*, Chapter 9.

27. In essence, this generally meant testing any project or point of view against the orthodoxy and objectives of the Communist Party, as the representative of the interests of the great mass of Chinese people. At times during

the Cultural Revolution, it could also mean the prevalence of the views of those individuals laying claim to the most radical opinions and/or the most proletarian pedigree. For a selection of readings on this aspect of Mao's thought see, for example, Stuart Schram (1969), *The Political Thought of Mao Tse-tung*, Chapter VI.

28. It should be noted that where national security so required, exceptions were made, as with work on China's atomic and space programmes, both of which began at this time. For an early assertion of the need to balance heavy industry on one hand, and light industry and agriculture on the other, the cities on one hand, and the countryside on the other, see especially Mao Tse-tung's essay "On the Ten Major Relationships", published in 1956, in Mao Tse-tung (1977 edition), *Selected Works* of *Mao Tse-tung: Volume 5*, pp. 284–307.

29. For a Chinese account of the new approach see Zhang Peiji "China's Strategy and Policy on Utilizing Foreign Capital" in Richard D. Robinson (ed.) (1987), *Foreign Capital and Technology in China*, pp. 9-16 especially.

30. Recently, an Equity or Contractual Joint Venture, or licence agreeement, for any project involving a total investment (debt and equity) of more than US$30 million has required approval from the Ministry of Foreign Trade and Economic Co-operation (MOFTEC; the name later changed to the Ministry of Commerce). In fact, however, policy has evolved over time on this matter of central approval for major projects, reflecting the state of the centralization debate and the structures, needs and influence of the particular industry concerned. Moreover, for contractual purposes, separate approval must be obtained from the tax authorities, foreign exchange authorities and customs administration, while local approval must be obtained for everything from use of the utilities to compliance with environmental regulations. See Philip Rapp, "The Legal Framework", in R. Porter and M. Robinson (1994), Chapter 8.

31. The writer had occasion in 1993 to visit a major brewery in Hangzhou which admitted that it had constructed a joint venture with a Hong Kong company purely for tax reasons. Their partner had contributed no technology or knowhow to the enterprise, a state of affairs which, the brewery enterprise indicated, was far from uncommon. Interview at Westlake Brewery, Hangzhou, July 1993.

32. Here the drawback is usually that staff of the FTC have little technical knowledge, while the difficulty of liaising with the Ministry concerned may cause delay and make agreement on the precise technology to be acquired harder to achieve.

33. Feinstein and Howe (1997), p. 8.

34. Q.Y. Yu (1999), p. 70.

35. See Robin Porter, "Centralization, De-centralization and Development in China: The Automobile Industry", in N. Campbell and J. Henley (eds) (1990), *Joint Ventures and Industrial Change in China*.

36. One account in the mid-1990s suggested that as much as half of China's industrial output was then generated by 100,000 state-owned firms. These employed 108 million, and supported a total, including dependents, of over 250 million people. See Lincoln Kaye, "The Withering State", *Far Eastern Economic Review,* 23 Feb. 1995, p. 50.

37. See Robin Porter, "Politics, Culture and Decision-Making in China" in D.H. Brown and R. Porter (eds) (1996), Chapter 4.

38. Joseph Needham (1954 etc.), *Science and Civilization in China.* See also Needham (1967), *The Grand Titration: Science East and West.* Wen-yuan Qian (1985), *The Great Inertia: Scientific Stagnation in traditional China* presents an alternative view of the achievements of science in China before the modern era.

39. Typical is the example of the Beijing Energy Training Centre, a research unit originally attached to Tsinghua University, which was obliged to set up a factory to enable its "surplus" staff to earn a living making semi-conductors, reactor equipment, and luminous powder with which to decorate watches. Interview at the Beijing Energy Training Centre, September 1995.

40. The State Science and Technology Commission, originally founded as a unit under the State Council in 1958, was disbanded during the Cultural Revolution when its leading members were criticized for alleged "elitism." The Commission was reinstated by the Fifth National People's Congress in 1978, and superseded by the Ministry of Science and Technology in 1998.

8. COMMAND STRUCTURES

1. James Wang (1999), *Contemporary Chinese Politics: An Introduction,* p. 161.

2. The official figure given for 2007 was seventy-three million. Cited in Robert Benewick and Stepanie Hemelryk Donald (2009), *The State of China Atlas: Mapping the World's Fastest-growing Economy,* p. 66.

3. For a detailed account of the 17th Party Congress see the *China Daily* coverage on the website www.english.people.com.cn, or the Xinhua News Agency coverage on www.chinaview.cn

4. For an indication of the place of this organ in the Party hierarchy see Benewick and Donald (2009), pp. 64–5. It is claimed that 510,000 Party members were punished by the Commission and its subsidiary bodies in the five years from 2002 to 2007. See Xinhua News Agency, www.news.xinhuanet.com/english/2007–10–26

5. For example, the Central Party School in Beijing, the Party's own university for top cadres, has completely revitalized its curriculum in recent years, and was in 2005 in discussion with British higher education institutions and with the British Embassy on international collaboration in management development education.

6. People's Daily Online, www.english.people.com.cn, 6 Aug. 2007.
7. These provincial, regional, and municipal Party structures help to ensure that the Communist Party's writ runs throughout all levels of administration. An account of how the Party is supposed to function at these lower levels is contained in the Party's Constitution, Chapter IV. The Constitution may be consulted in English online at www.news.xinhuanet.com/english/2007/10.
8. For an account of specified Party activity at the primary level, see the Party Constitution, above, Chapter V.
9. See James Wang (1999), p. 101.
10. The functions and responsibilities of the State Council are described in detail on the *People's Daily* website, www.english.people.com.cn/data/organs/statecouncil The use of China's main daily newspaper website to provide information about the role of different organs of state is an illustration of the dual "news" and "propaganda" remit of the media in China.
11. Wang (1999), p. 160.
12. The section in Benewick and Donald (2009), entitled "Who Runs China", pp. 64–5, provides a graphic illustration both of the overlap of responsibilities between Party and state, and of the very small number of people who actually control the levers of power in China.
13. This happened in the period immediately prior to the Cultural Revolution, when factionalism and indiscipline within the Party were widespread. See above, Chapter 3.
14. See the next section.
15. See Robin Porter, "Politics, Culture and Decision-making in China", in D.H. Brown and R. Porter (eds) (1996), *Management Issues in China: Volume 1, Domestic Enterprises*, pp. 85–105.
16. Sean Breslin, "Centre and Province in China", in Robert Benewick and Paul Wingrove (eds) (1995), *China in the 1990s*, pp. 65–7.
17. An excellent volume which explores the many dimensions of the flexing of regional power is David S.G. Goodman and Gerald Segal (eds) (1994), *China Deconstructs: Politics, Trade and Regionalism*. While the prophecy of some that China might split apart under regional pressures has not come to pass, many of the tensions identified in this book continue to play out in Chinese political life.
18. See in particular J. Bruce Jacobs and Lijian Hong, "Shanghai and the Lower Yangzi Valley" in Goodman and Segal eds. (1994), pp. 224–53 on the change in fortunes for Shanghai which resulted from Jiang Zemin's appointment, as seen from the perspective of 1994.
19. Attention to these issues, the Party hopes, will help to deflect criticism by China's trading partners, and especially the US, which might otherwise lead to protective measures being instituted in those markets. Recent health and safety concerns over Chinese-made toys are a case in point, providing ammunition for the protection lobby in the United States.

20. Roughly translated "Once there is chaos, then comes the crackdown." See also Chapters 9 and 10.
21. See Tony Saich, "China's Political Structure", in Benewick and Wingrove (eds) (1995), p. 38.
22. See John Dearlove, "Village Politics", in Benewick and Wingrove (eds) (1995), p. 129.
23. See below, Chapter 11.

9. POLITICS, CULTURE AND THE MANAGEMENT OF CHINA'S ENTERPRISES

1. See Paul Forrester, "The Challenges Facing Manufacturing Managers in Chinese Factories", in D. Brown and R. Porter (eds) (1996), *Management Issues in China: Volume 1, Domestic Enterprises*, pp. 143–66.
2. See D. Morris, "The Reform of State-owned Enterprises in China: The Art of the Possible", *Oxford Review of Economic Policy*, vol. 2, no. 4, 1995, pp. 54–69.
3. See Paul Forrester and Robin Porter, "The Politics of Management in People's China: From CMRS to Modern Enterprise System and Beyond", in Malcolm Warner (ed.) (1999), *China's Managerial Revolution*, pp. 47–72. See also W.C. Wedley (ed.) (1992), *Changes in the Iron Rice Bowl: The Reformation of Chinese Management*.
4. J. Wu in "The Reference for the Economist" vol. 59, 1, 1989, cited in Chen Derong (1995), *Chinese Firms between Hierarchy and Market: The Contract Management Responsibility System in China*.
5. See P.K. Lee (1988), *Industrial Management and Economic Reform in China, 1949–1984*. See also Victor Nee, "Organizational Dynamics of Market Transition: Hybrid Forms, Property Rights and Mixed Economy in China", *Administrative Science Quarterly*, vol. 37, no. 1, 1992, pp. 1–27.
6. See Zheng Guangliang, "The Leadership System" in Gene Tidrick and Chen Jiyuan (eds) (1987), *China's Industrial Reform*, pp. 306–12 especially. See also A.G. Walder, "Factory and Manager in an Era of Reform", *China Quarterly*, vol. 118, no. 2, 1989, pp. 242–64.
7. See W.A. Byrd, "Contractual Responsibility Systems in Chinese State-owned Industry: A Preliminary Assessment", in N. Campbell, S. Plaschaert and D. Brown (eds) (1991), *The Changing Nature of Management in China*; D.A. Hay, D.J. Morris, G. Liu and Yao Shujie (1994), *Economic Reform and State-owned Enterprises in China, 1979–1987*; and Peter Nolan (1993), *State and Market in the Chinese Economy: Essays on Controversial Issues*.
8. See N. Campbell and J. Henley (eds) (1990), *Joint Ventures and Industrial Change in China*; see also John Child (1994), *Management in China in the Age of Reform*.
9. John Child and Lu Yuan, "Industrial Decision-making under China's Reform, 1985–1988", *Organization Studies*, vol. 11, no. 3, 1990, pp. 321–51.

10. Chen (1995).

11. See Forrester and Porter, in Warner (ed.) (1999), p. 59 especially.

12. Chen (1995). See also Forrester and Porter in Warner (1999).

13. See Robin Porter, "Centralization, Decentralization and Development in China: the Automobile Industry", in Campbell and Henley (eds.) (1990).

14. See Forrester and Porter in Warner (ed.) (1999).

15. Ibid.

16. K. Lee, "An Assessment of the State Sector Reform in China: Viability of 'Legal Person Socialism'", *Journal of the Asia Pacific Economy*, vol. 1, no. 1, 1996, pp. 105–21.

17. Professor X, Centre for Management Studies, Central Party University, Beijing, speaking in 1996 when interviewed by the author and his colleague. Cited in Forrester and Porter, in Warner (ed.) (1999), p. 69.

18. Professor Z, China Enterprise Management Association, Chinese Academy of Management Science, Beijing, interviewed in 1996. Cited in Forrester and Porter, in Warner (ed.) (1999).

19. The account given above of management systems in China is drawn from Paul Forrester and Robin Porter, "The Politics of Management in People's China: From CMRS to Modern Enterprise System and Beyond", in Malcolm Warner (ed.) (1999), *China's Managerial Revolution*, pp. 47–72.

20. M. Blecher, "State Administration and Economic Reform", in D. Goodman and G. Segal (eds) (1989), *China at Forty: Mid-Life Crisis?*

21. See Robin Porter, "The Impact of Recent Political Events on China's Trade and Development: a View from Europe", in the *Melbourne Journal of Politics*, 21, 1993, pp. 117–34.

22. The section which follows on the impact of politics and culture on decision-making is based on earlier work by Robin Porter, published as "Politics, Culture and Decision-making in China", in D. Brown and R. Porter (eds) (1996), pp. 85–105.

23. For the origins of these imperatives see, for example, selections from the *Analects* of Confucius: "Do not do unto others what you would not want others to do to you." (15/23); on the "five virtues" — courtesy, magnanimity, good faith, diligence, and kindness — "He who is courteous is not humiliated..." (17/6); "Courtesy without decorum becomes tiresome. Cautiousness without decorum becomes timidity, daring becomes insubordination, frankness becomes effrontery." (8/2). See also S.M. Lee-Wong (2000), *Politeness and Face in Chinese Culture*, New York: P. Lang. Another source, though hard to obtain, is K.K. Hwang (1983), "Face and Favour: Chinese Power Games", unpublished manuscript, University of Taiwan. Much of what Confucius had to say about "humanity", and many of his prescriptions for behaviour in social situations, have to do with integrity, with acting honourably. Where conflict occurs, dignity is lost.

24. See Yang Lien-sheng, "The Concept of "Pao" as a Basis for Social Relations in China", in J.K. Fairbank (ed.) (1967), *Chinese Thought and Institutions*.

257

25. See Hwang, "Face and Favour: Chinese Power Games", in Fairbank (1967). See also Nigel Campbell and Peter Adlington (1988), *Chinese Business Strategies: A Survey of Foreign Business Activity in the PRC*.

26. See in particular accounts in the Book of History, *Shu Ching*.

27. Highly readable accounts that offer greater detail than is provided in the present volume are to be found in Spence (1990), *The Search for Modern China*, and Gray (1990), *Rebellions and Revolutions: China from the 1800s to 2000*.

28. Three composite case studies are presented in Porter, "Politics, Culture and Decision-making in China", in D. Brown and R. Porter (eds) (1996), pp. 85–105. The model used in this piece for analysis of the process of strategic decision-making is that of Henry Mintzberg, as expressed in H. Mintzberg, D. Raisinghani and A. Theoret, "The Structure of Un-structured Decision Processes", *Administrative Science Quarterly*, 21, June 1976, pp. 246–75.

10. PUBLIC POLICIES, PRIVATE GOALS

1. For a thoughtful account of this ethos in the new China see Richard Robison and David Goodman, "The New Rich in Asia: Economic Development, Social Status and Political Consciousness", and David Goodman, "The People's Republic of China: The Party-state, Capitalist Revolution and New Entrepreneurs", both in Richard Robison and David S.G. Goodman (eds) (1996), *The New Rich in Asia: Mobile Phones, McDonald's and Middle-class Revolution*, pp. 1–18 and 225–42 respectively.

2. This somewhat speculative list is based on the writer's frequent interaction with Chinese people through periods of residence and prolonged visits since 1972.

3. See Chapter 6.

4. The author personally sub-edited this news story at Xinhua headquarters in Beijing in 1979.

5. This figure of seventy-three million was given for total membership of the Party at the time of the 17th Party Congress in October 2007.

6. Figures for GDP growth are from the China National Bureau of Statistics, reproduced on the website www.chinability.com/GDP, "GDP growth in China 1952–2009."

7. Corruption was highlighted by President Hu Jintao at the 17th Party Congress in October 2007 as one of the most pressing issues facing China, along with environmental degradation and income inequality between coastal cities and the interior.

8. As the environment has moved up the agenda in the deliberations of the Party Central Committee, some of the ecological and societal drawbacks to the Yangzi scheme, which at the time of writing is close to being completed, have begun to be better appreciated.

9. This warning was given in a paper presented by a senior member of the State Environmental Protection Agency at a conference attended by the writer in Beijing in 2004.

11. THE FIFTH MODERNIZATION

1. In the next section, China's early exposure to democracy is explored in order to establish how limited has been its experience of democratic thought and institutions. It will be contended that while democracy may be regarded as the "fifth modernization" by some, both inside and outside China, its achievement in a society with such strong contrary traditions will take time and extraordinary commitment. This chapter draws on material prepared for a paper in which the author sought to examine the political cultures of China and Hong Kong. See Robin Porter, "Towards a Democratic Audit in Hong Kong: Some Issues and Problems", in Robert Ash, Peter Ferdinand, Brian Hook and Robin Porter (eds) (2000), *Hong Kong in Transition: The Handover Years*.

2. Chen Duxiu, "Call to Youth", 1915, cited in Ssu-yu Teng and John Fairbank (1973), *China's Response to the West*, p. 245.

3. Mao Zedong, "On New Democracy", 1940, and "On the People's Democratic Dictatorship", 1949, *Selected Works of Mao Tse-tung*, volume 2 and volume 4 respectively.

4. It remains to be seen whether the tendency elsewhere for a progressively more numerous and affluent middle class to demand the right to political participation will be repeated in China.

5. See R. Dahl (1971), *Polyarchy: Participation and Opposition*; A. Inkeles (ed.) (1991), *On Measuring Democracy: Its Consequences and Concomitants*; S.P. Huntington (1991), *The Third Wave: Democratization in the Late Twentieth Century*; D. Beetham (1993), *Auditing Democracy in Britain*, Democratic Audit Paper no. 1, 1993, University of Essex, Human Rights Centre.

6. T. Vanhannen (1990), *The Process of Democratization: A Comparative Study of 147 States, 1980–1988*.

7. B. Parekh, 'The Cultural Particularity of Liberal Democracy', in D. Held (ed.) (1993), *Prospects for Democracy*.

8. A. Hadenius (1992), *Democracy and Development*.

9. See Beetham (1993); see also David Beetham (1995), *The Democratic Audit of the UK*.

10. David Beetham's ideas for a democratic audit have developed over a period of years (cf. recent formulations in Beetham 1993 and 1995 listed in the bibliography to this book). The precise questions used here were taken with permission from David Beetham (1997), "Conducting a Democratic Audit", unpublished paper, 1997. Beetham's framework, while not expressly designed to be applied to China, offers a useful lens through which to understand the prospects for democracy there.

11. Although at the time of writing it is more than ten years since village democracy was first tried experimentally in China, there is broad agreement among analysts that pressure from the Party in support of favoured candidates remains widespread.

12. See above, Chapter 3. The exclusion of these "class enemies" from any opportunity for power or influence was an overarching concern of policymakers in the first three decades of the People's Republic.

13. For the structure and function of the Xinhua News Agency see R. Porter, "Shaping China's News", in R. Porter (ed.) (1992), *Reporting the News from China*.

14. There can occasionally be exceptions to this general rule. One early example of an NPC challenge came in 1995 when it sent back the then draft Energy Conservation Law to the State Council for amendment because it considered the level of detail in the law to be inadequate. Observers, including many in China itself, live in the hope that the NPC will assert itself more, but this is by no means a discernible trend at the time of writing.

15. The writer attended a murder trial in 1979 at which an account was given by the Prosecutor and the police of the evidence against the accused, the verdict and sentence were then pronounced by the judge, and the death sentence scheduled to be carried out the following day. Several foreign residents were invited to this trial, as the Party believed it would show how due process was being followed in China's courts. Although much progress has since been made in establishing the rule of law in China, the continuing absence of any effective human rights for those accused of a crime, or of any clear separation between the Judiciary and the will of the state, remains a very serious problem.

16. See Carlos Wing-hung Lo, "Criminal Justice Reform in Post-Crisis China: A Human Rights Perspective", *Hong Kong Law Journal*, 27, 1997, part 1, pp. 90–107. Perhaps one of the best-known cases is that of Wei Jingsheng, in prison from 1979 to 1992 for advocating democracy as the "fifth modernization", and again from 1995 for a further fourteen years for continuing to speak out against the Chinese government. Wei was finally released in 1998 and took refuge in the United States. More recently, treatment of so-called "petitioners" in Beijing, especially those who have come to the capital with their grievances from other parts of the country, and those who have been displaced by preparations for the Olympics has been particularly harsh.

17. The survival of the Chinese state over more than 2000 years, despite occasional occupations and temporary break-ups, is often attributed to the strength and unifying force of Chinese civilization and culture. One consequence of this is that even in the modern period, all ethnic Chinese are regarded as potential citizens of China, no matter where they may have been born.

18. See *Xinwenxiezuo* (Newswriting), an official guide to the reporting of news in China for trainee journalists published by Yunnan University, translated by Jennifer Grant, Australian National University, unpublished paper, 1979.

19. Jack Gray, unpublished paper, 2004. An abridged version of this paper appeared in the *China Quarterly* as "Mao in Perspective", vol. 187, Sept. 2006, pp. 659–79.

20. The *China Statistical Yearbook, 2007*, claims that the percentage of people fifteen or over who were "illiterate or semi-literate" in that year was only 9 per cent, however this figure may be optimistic, and it is clear that in certain parts of rural China the illiteracy level is likely to be much higher. See Benewick and Wingrove (2009), *The State of China Atlas: Mapping the World's Fastest-growing Economy*, p. 97.

21. The official in question was a Vice Minister. That some very senior Chinese officials should be willing to express such an opinion to a foreigner is an indication both of the presence of differing views at the very top of the Party as to what China's political future might hold, and that some at least feel sufficiently confident that there is a wind of change blowing to be willing to speak their minds.

CONCLUSION

1. See the closing passages in R. Porter, "The Impact of Recent Political Events on China's Trade and Development: A View from Europe", *Melbourne Journal of Politics*, vol. 21, 1993, pp. 117–34, for an early summation of the writer's views in this respect.

BIBLIOGRAPHY

Ash, R., P. Ferdinand, B. Hook and R. Porter (eds) (2000), *Hong Kong in Transition: The Handover Years*, Basingstoke: Macmillan.

Becker, J. (1996) *Hungry Ghosts: Mao's Secret Famine*, New York: Free Press.

—— (2002) *The Chinese*, Oxford University Press.

Beetham, D. (1993) *Auditing Democracy in Britain*, Democratic Audit Paper no. 1, 1993, University of Essex, Human Rights Centre.

—— (1995) *The Democratic Audit of the UK*, London: Routledge.

—— (1997) "Conducting a Democratic Audit", unpublished paper.

Benewick, R. and S.H. Donald (2005) *The State of China Atlas*, Berkeley: University of California Press.

Benewick, R. and S.D. Hemelryk (2009) *The State of China Atlas: Mapping the World's Fastest-growing Economy*, Berkeley: University of California Press.

Benewick, R. and P. Wingrove (eds) (1995) *China in the 1990s*, Basingstoke: Macmillan.

Benton, G. (ed.) (2008) *Mao Zedong and the Chinese Revolution* (4 volumes), Abingdon, Oxon.: Routledge.

Bergsten, F., C. Freeman, N. Lardy and D. Mitchell (2008) *China's Rise: Challenges and Opportunities*, Washington: Centre for Strategic and International Studies and the Peterson Institute for International Economics.

Bettelheim, C. (1968) *The Transition to Socialist Economy*, New York: Humanities Press.

Blecher, M. (1989) "State Administration and Economic Reform", in D. Goodman and G. Segal (eds) *China at Forty: Mid-life Crisis?* Oxford: Clarendon Press.

Brady, A.M. (2008) *Marketing Dictatorship: Propaganda and Thought Work in Contemporary China*, Lanham, Maryland: Rowman and Littlefield.

Breslin, S. (1995) "Centre and Province in China", in R. Benewick and P. Wingrove (eds) *China in the 1990s*, Basingstoke: Macmillan.

Brewitt-Taylor, C.H. (tr.) (2002) *Romance of the Three Kingdoms*, Vermont: Charles Tuttle.

Brown, D.H. and R. Porter (eds) (1996) *Management Issues in China: Volume 1, Domestic Enterprises*, London: Routledge.

Brugger W. and S. Reglar (1994) *Politics and Society in Contemporary China*, Stanford University Press.

Bush, R.C. (1982) *The Politics of Cotton Textiles in Kuomintang China, 1927-1937*, New York: Garland.

Byrd, W.A. (1991) "Contractual Responsibility Systems in Chinese State-Owned Industry: A Preliminary Assessment", in N. Campbell, S. Plasschaert and D. Brown (eds) *The Changing Nature of Management in China*, Greenwich, Conn.: JAI Press.

Campbell, N. and P. Adlington (1988) *Chinese Business Strategies: A Survey of Foreign Business Activity in the PRC*. Oxford: Pergamon.

Campbell, N. and J. Henley (eds) (1990), *Joint Ventures and Industrial Change in China*, London and Greenwich, Conn.: JAI Press.

Campbell, N., S. Plaschaert and D. Brown (eds) (1991) *The Changing Nature of Management in China*, Greenwich, Conn.: JAI Press.

Cao X. and Gao E (attributed), John Minford and Edwin Lowe (tr.) (2010) *Dream of the Red Chamber*, Hong Kong: Periplus Editions.

Chan, F.G. and T. Etzold (1976) *China in the 1920s: Nationalism and Revolution*, New York: New Viewpoints Press.

Chen, D. (1995) *Chinese Firms between Hierarchy and Market: The Contract Management Responsibility System in China*, New York: St. Martin's Press.

Chen Duxiu (1915) "Call to Youth", cited in S. Teng and J.K. Fairbank (1970) *China's Response to the West*, New York: Atheneum.

Ch'en', K. (1972) *Buddhism in China: A Historical Survey*, Princeton University Press.

Child, J. and Y. Lu (1990) "Industrial Decision-making under China's Reform, 1985–1988", *Organization Studies*, 11 (3), pp. 321–51.

Child, J. (1994) *Management in China in the Age of Reform*, Cambridge University Press.

Chinese Communist Party (1966) *Decision of the Central Committee of the Chinese Communist Party Concerning the Great Proletarian Cultural Revolution*, Beijing: Foreign Language Press.

Christiansen, F. and S. Rai (1996) *Chinese Politics and Society: An Introduction*, London: Prentice-Hall.

Chu, Y.K. (1973) "The Chinese Language", in J. Meskill (ed.) *An Introduction to Chinese Civilization*, Boston: D.C. Heath and Co.

Clark, P. (2008) *The Chinese Cultural Revolution: A History*, Cambridge: Cambridge University Press.

Clubb, O.E. (1965) *Twentieth Century China*, New York: Columbia University Press.

Coble, P.M. Jr. (1980) *The Shanghai Capitalists and the Nationalist Government, 1927–1937*, Cambridge, Mass.: Harvard University Press.

Cochran, S. (1980) *Big Business in China: Sino-foreign Rivalry in the Cigarette Industry, 1890-1930*, Cambridge, Mass.: Harvard University Press.

Confucius, (tr. and ed.) R. Dawson (2000) *The Analects*, Oxford: Oxford University Press.

Conroy, R. (1992) *Technological Change in China*, Paris: OECD.

Cooper, A. (tr. and ed.) (1973) *Li Po and Tu Fu*, Harmondsworth: Penguin.

Cranmer-Byng, L. (tr. and ed.) (1908) *The Book of Odes*, London: John Murray.

Dahl, R. (1971) *Polyarchy: Participation and Opposition*, New Haven: Yale University Press.

De Bary, W.T., W. Chan and B. Watson (eds) (1964) *Sources of Chinese Tradition, Volume 1*, New York: Columbia University Press.

Dearlove, J. (1995) "Village Politics", in R. Benewick and P. Wingrove (eds) *China in the 1990s*, Basingstoke: Macmillan.

Eastman, L. (1974) *The Abortive Revolution: China under Nationalist Rule 1927–1937*, Cambridge, Mass.: Harvard University Press.

Egerton, C. (tr.) (1979) *The Golden Lotus*, Torrance, Cal.: Heian International Publishers.

Elvin, M. (1973) *The Pattern of the Chinese Past: A Social and Economic Interpretation*, Palo Alto, CA: Stanford University Press.

Esherick, J., P. Pickowicz and A. Walder (eds) (2006) *The Chinese Cultural Revolution as History*, Palo Alto, CA: Stanford University Press.

Fairbank, J. and M. Goldman (2006) *China: a New History*, Cambridge, Mass.: Harvard University Press.

Fairbank, J. and E. Reischauer (1960) *East Asia: The Great Tradition*, Boston: Houghton Mifflin.

Fairbank, J., E. Reischauer, and A. Craig (1965) *East Asia: The Modern Transformation*, Boston: Houghton Mifflin.

Fairbank, J. (ed.) (1967) *Chinese Thought and Institutions*, Chicago: University of Chicago Press.

Fan, K.H. (ed.) (1968) *The Chinese Cultural Revolution: Selected Documents*, New York: Monthly Review Press/Grove Press.

Farndon, J. (2007) *China Rises*, London: Virgin Books.

Feinstein, C. and C. Howe (1997) *Chinese Technology Transfer in the 1990s: Current Experience, Historical Problems, and International Perspectives*, Cheltenham: Edward Elgar.

Feuerwerker, A. (1980) "Economic Trends in the Late Ch'ing Empire, 1870–1911", in J.K. Fairbank and K.C. Liu (eds), *Cambridge History of China*, Cambridge: Cambridge University Press.

Fitzgerald, C.P. (1951, 1964) *The Birth of Communist China*, Harmondsworth: Penguin.

Forrester, P. (1996) "The Challenges Facing Manufacturing Managers in Chinese Factories", in D. Brown and R. Porter (eds), *Management Issues in China: Volume 1, Domestic Enterprises*, London: Routledge.

Forrester, P. and Porter, R. (1999) "The Politics of Management in People's China: From the Contract Responsibility System to the Modern Enterprise System and Beyond," in M. Warner (ed.) *Asia Pacific Business Review*, special issue Spring/Summer 1999, pp. 47–72.

Gernet, J. (1968) *Ancient China from the Beginnings to the Empire*, Berkeley: University of California Press.

Gittings, J. (2006) *The Changing Face of China: From Mao to Market*, Oxford: Oxford University Press.

Goodman, D. (1994) *Deng Xiaoping and the Chinese Revolution*, London: Routledge.

——— (1996) "The People's Republic of China: The Party-state, Capitalist Revolution, and New Entrepreneurs", in R. Robison and D. Goodman (eds) *The New Rich in Asia: Mobile Phones, McDonald's and Middle-class Revolution*, London: Routledge.

Goodman, D. (ed.) (2008) *The New Rich in China: Future Rulers, Present Lives*, Abingdon, Oxon.: Routledge.

Goodman, D. and G. Segal (eds) (1989) *China at Forty: Mid-life Crisis?*, London: Routledge.

——— (1994) *China Deconstructs: Politics, Trade and Regionalism*, London: Routledge.

Goulet, D. (1977) *The Uncertain Promise: Value Conflicts in Technology Transfer*, New York: IDOC/North America.

Grant, J. (tr.) (1979) "*Xinwenxiezuo* (Newswriting)", unpublished paper, Canberra: Australian National University/Yunnan University.

Gray, J. (1973) "The Cultural Revolution: The Development of Two Lines in Economic Policy" in S. Schram (ed.), *Authority, Participation and Cultural Change in China*, Cambridge: Cambridge University Press.

——— (1990) *Rebellions and Revolutions: China from the 1800s to the 1980s*, Oxford University Press.

——— (2004), "Mao in Perspective", unpublished paper written shortly before Jack Gray's death, accessible in full on freewebs.com/jack-gray. An abridged version of this paper appeared in the *China Quarterly* with the same title in 2006 (vol. 187, Sept., pp. 659–79), and may also be found in the four volume set, cited above, edited by Gregor Benton (2008).

Gray, J. and P. Cavendish (1969) *Chinese Communism in Crisis: Maoism and the Cultural Revolution*, New York: Praeger.

Grieder, J. (1970) *Hu Shih and the Chinese Renaissance: Liberalism in the Chinese Revolution*, Cambridge, Mass.: Harvard University Press.

Hadenius, A. (1992) *Democracy and Development*, Cambridge: Cambridge University Press.

Harrison, L. (1993) 'Underdevelopment is a State of Mind', in M.A. Seligson and J. Passe-Smith (eds) *Development and Underdevelopment*, Boulder, Colorado: Lynne Rienner.

Hay, D.A., D.J. Morris, G. Liu and S. Yao (1994), *Economic Reform and State-owned Enterprises in China, 1979–1987*, Oxford: Oxford University Press.

Hayford, C. (1990) *To the People: James Yen and village China*, New York: Columbia University Press.

Held, D. (ed.) (1993) *Prospects for Democracy*, Cambridge: Polity Press.

Ho, P. (1962) *Ladder of Success in Imperial China*, New York: Columbia University Press.

—— and Tsou T. (eds) (1968) *China in Crisis*, Chicago University Press.

Hsu, I.C.Y. (1975, 2000) *The Rise of Modern China*, Oxford: Oxford University Press.

Huntington, S.P. (1991) *The Third Wave: Democratization in the Late Twentieth Century*, Norman, Oklahoma: University of Oklahoma Press.

Hwang, K.K. (1983) "Face and Favour: Chinese Power Games", unpublished manuscript, Taibei: University of Taiwan.

Inkeles, A. (ed.) (1991) *On Measuring Democracy: Its Consequences and Concomitants*, New Brunswick, NJ, and London: Transaction Publishers.

Jacobs, J.B. and L. Hong (1994) "Shanghai and the Lower Yangzi Valley", in D. Goodman and G. Segal (eds) *China Deconstructs: Politics, Trade and Regionalism*, London: Routledge.

Jiang, X. (1997) "Chinese Government Policy towards Science and Technology and its Influence on Technical Development of Industrial Enterprises", in C. Feinstein and C. Howe (eds) *Chinese Technology Transfer in the 1990s: Current Experience, Historical Problems, and International Perspectives*, Westport, Conn.: Quorum Books.

Kaye, L. (1995) "The Withering State", *Far Eastern Economic Review*, 23 Feb.

Khalil, T.M., L. Lefebvre, and R. Mason (eds) (2001) *Management of Technology: The Key to Prosperity in the Third Millennium*, Amsterdam and London: Pergamon.

Kuznets, S. (1989) *Economic Development, the Family, and Income Distribution: Selected Essays*, Cambridge: Cambridge University Press.

Latourette, K.S. (1964) *The Chinese: their History and Culture*, New York and London: Macmillan.

Law, K. (ed.) (2003) *The Chinese Cultural Revolution Reconsidered: Beyond Purge and Holocaust*, Basingstoke: Palgrave Macmillan.

Lee, K. (1996) "An Assessment of the State Sector Reform in China: Viability of Legal Person Socialism", *Journal of the Asia Pacific Economy* 1 (1), pp. 105–21.

Lee, P.K. (1988) *Industrial Management and Economic Reform in China, 1949–1984*, Oxford: Oxford University Press.

Lee-Wong, S.M. (2000), *Politeness and Face in Chinese Culture*, New York: P. Lang.

Lipton, M., (1977) *Why Poor People Stay Poor*, Cambridge, Mass.: Harvard University Press.

Lo, C.W.H. (1997) "Criminal Justice Reform in Post-Crisis China: A Human Rights Perspective", *Hong Kong Law Journal* 27 (1), pp. 90–107.

Luo Ganzhong (attributed) *Romance of the Three Kingdoms:* see C.H. Brewitt-Taylor (tr.) (2002) or M. Roberts (tr.) (1999).

Mao Tse-tung (1966) *Quotations from Chairman Mao Tse-tung*, Peking: Foreign Languages Press.

———— (various editions) *Selected Works of Chairman Mao Tse-tung*, Peking: Foreign Languages Press.

Mason, M. (1997) *Development and Disorder: a history of the Third World since 1945*, Toronto: Between the Lines Press.

McKnight, B. (1992) *Law and Order in Sung China*, Cambridge: Cambridge University Press.

Meisner, M. (1999) *Mao's China and After: A History of the People's Republic*, New York: Free Press.

Meskill, J. (1973) *An Introduction to Chinese Civilization*, Lexington, Mass.: D.C. Heath and Co.

Mintzberg, H., D. Raisinghani and A. Theoret (1976) "The Structure of Unstructured Decision Processes", *Administrative Science Quarterly*, 21 June, 1976, pp. 246–75.

Mitter, R. (2005) *A Bitter Revolution: China's Struggle with the Modern World*, Oxford: Oxford University Press.

Moore, C. (ed.) (1967) *The Chinese Mind*, Honolulu: University of Hawaii Press.

Morris, D. (1995) "The Reform of State-Owned Enterprises in China: the Art of the Possible", *Oxford Review of Economic Policy* 2 (4), pp. 54–69.

Munro, D. (1969) *The Concept of Man in Early China*, Stanford University Press.

Naughton, B. (2007) *The Chinese Economy: Transitions and Growth*, Cambridge, Mass.: MIT Press.

Nee, V. (1992) "Organizational Dynamics of Market Transition: Hybrid Forms, Property Rights and Mixed Economy in China", *Administrative Science Quarterly*, 37 (1), pp. 1–27.

Needham, J. (1954 onward) *Science and Civilization in China*, Cambridge: Cambridge University Press.

———— (1967) *The Grand Titration: Science East and West*, London: Allen and Unwin.

Nolan, P. (1993) *State and Market in the Chinese Economy: Essays on Controversial Issues*, Basingstoke: Macmillan.

Pan Ku, (tr.) by Homer Dubs (1938) *History of the Former Han Dynasty (Han Shu)*, London: Kegan Paul.

Parekh, B. (1993) "The Cultural Particularity of Liberal Democracy", in D. Held (ed.) *Prospects for Democracy*, Cambridge: Polity Press.

Passe-Smith, J. (1993) "The Persistence of the Gap: Taking Stock of Economic Growth in the Post-World War Two Era", in M.A. Seligson and J. Passe-Smith (eds) *Development and Underdevelopment*, Boulder, Colorado: Lynne Rienner Publishers.

Pepper, S. (2000) *Radicalism and Education Reform in Twentieth Century China: The Search for an Ideal Development Model*, Cambridge University Press.

Porter, R. (1990) "Centralization, Decentralization and Development in China: The Automobile Industry", in N. Campbell and J. Henley (eds) *Joint Ventures and Industrial Change in China*, Greenwich, Conn. and London: JAI Press.

—— (1992) "Shaping China's News: Xinhua's Duiwaibu on the Threshold of Change", in R. Porter (ed.), *Reporting the News from China*, London: Chatham House.

—— (1993) "The Impact of Recent Political Developments on China's Trade and Development", *Melbourne Journal of Politics* 21, pp. 117–34.

—— (1994) *Industrial Reformers in Republican China*, Armonk, NY: M.E. Sharpe.

—— (1996) "Politics, Culture and Decision-Making in China", in D. Brown and R. Porter (eds) *Management Issues in China: Volume 1, Domestic Enterprises*, London: Routledge.

Porter, R. (ed.) (1992) *Reporting the News from China*, London: Chatham House/Royal Institute of International Affairs.

Porter, R. and M. Robinson (1994) *The China Business Guide*, Keele, Staffs.: Ryburn.

Qian, Sima, (tr.) by Burton Watson (1996) *Records of the Grand Historian: Han Dynasty*, New York: Columbia University Press.

Qian, W. (1985) *The Great Inertia: Scientific Stagnation in Traditional China*, Beckenham, Kent: Croom Helm.

Quan, L. (1991) "Technology Policy and Technological Innovation in the People's Republic of China", unpublished PhD thesis, Birmingham: University of Aston in Birmingham.

Rapp, P. (1994) "The Legal Framework", in R. Porter and M. Robinson (eds) *The China Business Guide*, Keele, Staffs.: CBBC/Ryburn.

Rawski, T.G. (1989) *Economic Growth in Pre-War China*, Berkeley: University of California Press.

Roberts, M. (tr. and ed.) (1999) *Three Kingdoms*, Berkeley: University of California Press.

Robinson, R.D. (ed.) (1987) *Foreign Capital and Technology in China*, New York: Praeger.

Robison, R. and D. Goodman (1996) "The New Rich in Asia: Economic Development, Social Status and Political Consciousness", in R. Robison and D. Goodman (eds) *The New Rich in Asia: Mobile Phones, McDonald's and Middle-class Revolution*, London: Routledge.

Saich, T. (1989) "Reform of China's Science and Technology Organizational System", in D. Simon and M. Goldman (eds) *Science and Technology in Post-Mao China*, Cambridge, Mass.: Harvard University Press.

Schell, O. (1984) *To Get Rich is Glorious: China in the Eighties*, New York: Pantheon Books.

Schram, S. (1969) *The Political Thought of Mao Tse-tung*, Harmondsworth: Penguin.

Schram, S. (ed.) (1973) *Authority, Participation and Cultural Change in China*, Cambridge: Cambridge University Press.

Schurmann, F. (1968) *Ideology and Organization in Communist China*, Berkeley: University of California Press.

—— (1969) "The Attack of the Cultural Revolution on Ideology and Organization", in Ho Ping-ti and Tsou Tang (eds), *China in Crisis*, Chicago: Chicago University Press.

Seeberg, V. (2000) *The Rhetoric and Reality of Mass Education in Mao's China*, Lewiston, NY: Edwin Mellen Press.

Seligson, M.A. and Passe-Smith, J.T. (eds) (1993) *Development and Underdevelopment*, Boulder, CO: Lynne Rienner Publishers.

Shan Chou, Eva and Fu Du (1995) *Reconsidering Tu Fu: Literary Greatness and Cultural Context*, Cambridge: Cambridge University Press.

Shi Naian (attributed) ed. by J.H. Jackson (1963) *Water Margin: The Outlaws of the Marsh*, Hong Kong: Commercial Press.

Shi Naian (attributed) (tr.) by Sidney Shapiro (1980) *Outlaws of the Marsh: The Water Margin*, Beijing: Foreign Language Press.

Simon, D. and M. Goldman (1989) "The Onset of China's New Technological Revolution", in D. Simon and M. Goldman (eds *Science and Technology in Post-Mao China*, Cambridge, Mass.: Harvard University Press.

Simon D. and M. Goldman (eds) *Science and Technology in Post-Mao China*, Cambridge, Mass.: Harvard University Press.

Smedley, A. (1956) *The Great Road: the Life and Times of Chu Teh*, New York: Monthly Review Press.

Snow, E. (1938, 1961) *Red Star over China*, New York: Grove Press.Soothill, W. (ed.) (1910, 1995) *Confucius: The Analects*, Mineola, NY: Dover Publications.

Spence, J. (1990) *The Search for Modern China*, New York: W.W. Norton.

Steward, F. and Quan Li (1996) "Changing Patterns of Collaboration between Research Organizations and Business Enterprises in Technological Innovation in China", in D.H. Brown and R. Porter (eds) *Management Issues in China: Volume 1, Domestic Enterprises*, London: Routledge.

Stokes, B. (1994) "Technology Transfer", in R. Porter and M. Robinson (eds) *The China Business Guide*, Keele, Staffs.: CBBC/Ryburn.

Strauss, J. (ed.) (2007) *The History of the PRC 1949–1976*, Cambridge: Cambridge University Press.

Suttmeier, R (1989) "Science, Technology and China's Political Future—a Framework for Analysis", in D. Simon and M. Goldman (eds) *Science and Technology in Post-Mao China*, Cambridge, Mass.: Harvard University Press.

Teng, S.Y. and J. Fairbank (1973) *China's Response to the West*, New York: Atheneum.

Tidrick, G. and J. Chen (eds) (1987) *China's Industrial Reform*, Oxford University Press/World Bank.

Townsend, J.R. (1969) *Political Participation in Communist China*, Berkeley: University of California Press.

Tsao, H.C. (Xueqin Cao) (1996) *Dream of the Red Chamber*, Torrance, Cal.: Heian International Publishers.

Turner, K., J. Feinerman and R.K. Guy (2000) *The Limits of the Rule of Law in China*, Washington: University of Washington Press.

Vanhannen, T. (1990) *The Process of Democratization: A Comparative Study of 147 States, 1980–1988*, New York: Taylor and Francis.

Volti, R. (1982) *Technology, Politics and Society in China*, Boulder, CO: Westview Press.

Wakeman, F. (1975) *The Fall of Imperial China*, New York: the Free Press.

―――― and R. Edmonds (eds) (2000) *Reappraising Republican China*, Oxford: Oxford University Press.

Walder, A.G. (1989) "Factory and Manager in an Era of Reform", *China Quarterly*, 118 (2), pp. 242–64.

Waley-Cohen, J. (2000) "Collective Responsibility in Qing Criminal Law", in K. Turner, J. Feinerman and R.K. Guy (eds) *The Limits of the Rule of Law in China*, Washington DC: University of Washington Press.

Wallerstein, I. (1984) *The Politics of the World Economy: The States, the Movements and the Civilizations*, Cambridge: Cambridge University Press.

Wang, G. (1977) *China and the World since 1949*, London and Basingstoke, Macmillan.

―――― (1999) *Contemporary Chinese Politics: An Introduction*, New Jersey: Prentice-Hall.

Wang, Y. (1993) *China's Science and Technology Policy, 1949-1989*, Aldershot, Hants.: Avebury.

Wang Yie, A. Chanzit and C. Zeng (2006) *Daoism in China: An Introduction*, Warren, Conn.: Floating World Editions.

Warner, M. (ed.) (1999) *China's Managerial Revolution*, London: Frank Cass.

Watson, B. (1973) "Chinese Literature", in *An Introduction to Chinese Civilization*, Boston: D.C. Heath and Co.

Wedley, W.C. (ed.) (1992) *Changes in the Iron Rice Bowl: The Reformation of Chinese Management*, Greenwich, Conn.: JAI Press.

Wei, G.C.X., and X. Liu (eds) (2001) *Chinese Nationalism in Perspective*, Westport, Conn.: Greenwood Press.

Wheelwright, E.L. and B. McFarlane (1970) *The Chinese Road to Socialism*, New York and London: Monthly Review Press.

Wright, Arthur F. (1959,1971) *Buddhism in Chinese History*, Palo Alto, CA: Stanford University Press.

Wright, A. (1962) "Values, Roles and Personalities", in A. Wright and D. Twitchett (eds) *Confucian Personalities*, Palo Alto, CA: Stanford University Press.

Wright, A. and D. Twitchett (eds) (1962) *Confucian Personalities*, Palo Alto, CA: Stanford University Press.

Wright, M. (1967) *The Last Stand of Chinese Conservatism: The T'ung-Chih Restoration, 1862–1874*, New York: Atheneum.

Wu, J. (1989) Commentary in *The Reference for the Economist*, 59 (1).

Wu Chengen, (tr.) by Arthur Waley (1961) *Monkey*, Harmondsworth: Penguin.

Yang, C.K. (1969) "Cultural Revolution and Revisionism", in P. Ho and T. Tsou (eds) *China in Crisis*, Chicago: Chicago University Press.

Yang, L.S. (1967) "The Concept of "Pao" as a Basis for Social Relations in China", in J.K. Fairbank (ed.) *Chinese Thought and Institutions*, Chicago: Chicago University Press.

Yu, Q.Y. (1999) *The Implementation of China's Science and Technology Policy*, Westport, Conn.: Quorum Books.

Zhang, L., P. Link and A. Nathan (eds) (2001) *The Tiananmen Papers*, Washington: Public Affairs Press.

Zhang, P. (1987) "China's Strategy and Policy on Utilizing Foreign Capital", in R.D. Robinson (ed.) *Foreign Capital and Technology in China*, New York: Praeger.

Zheng, G., (1987) "The Leadership System", in G. Tidrick and J. Chen (eds) *China's Industrial Reform*, Oxford University Press/World Bank.

Zhong, Y. (2003) *Local Government and Politics in China: Challenges from Below*, Armonk, NY: M.E. Sharpe.

INDEX